the book of
REVELATION
& THE BIBLE

AS NEVER EXPLAINED BEFORE

Ryan & Amanda

I hope this book is as much of
a blessing for you to read as it
was for me to write.

May God bless you both in
this venture.

the book of
REVELATION
& THE BIBLE

AS NEVER EXPLAINED BEFORE

PETER J. DAVIS

TATE PUBLISHING *& Enterprises*

The Book of Revelation and The Bible As Never Explained Before
Copyright © 2010 by Peter J. Davis. All rights reserved.

No part of this publication may be reproduced, stored in a retrieval system or transmitted in any way by any means, electronic, mechanical, photocopy, recording or otherwise without the prior permission of the author except as provided by USA copyright law.

Scripture quotations marked (TNEB) are taken from *The New English Bible©*, Copyright © 1961, 1970. Used by permission of Oxford University Press and Cambridge University Press.

All scriptures noted KJV were compared first to the King James Version, copyright © 1984, 1977 by Thomas Nelson Inc. Publishers out of Nashville.

All scriptures noted NKJV were compared second to the New King James Version, copyright © 1979, 1982, and 1980 by Thomas Nelson Inc.

All scriptures noted TNJB were compared fourth to The New Jerusalem Bible, copyright © 1999 by Doubleday, a division of Random House, Inc., and Darton, Longman & Todd Ltd.

Biblical text copyright © 1985 by Darton, Longman & Todd Ltd. and Doubleday, a division of Random House, Inc.

The opinions expressed by the author are not necessarily those of Tate Publishing, LLC.

Published by Tate Publishing & Enterprises, LLC
127 E. Trade Center Terrace | Mustang, Oklahoma 73064 USA
1.888.361.9473 | www.tatepublishing.com

Tate Publishing is committed to excellence in the publishing industry. The company reflects the philosophy established by the founders, based on Psalm 68:11,
"The Lord gave the word and great was the company of those who published it."

Book design copyright © 2010 by Tate Publishing, LLC. All rights reserved.
Cover design by Amber Gulilat
Interior design by Stefanie Rane

Published in the United States of America

ISBN: 978-1-61663-172-7
1. Religion, Christian Theology, Eschatology
2. Religion, Christian Theology, General
10.11.04

DEDICATION

In loving memory of my only son, Adrian K. Davis, who was taken from me on October 18, 2007, by an assassin's bullet, another victim of the out-of-control plague of gang violence running rampant throughout the inner cities of America. Otherwise, this book is for the whole world to read, but especially for all those who have ever pondered over the meaning of this, perhaps the greatest puzzle God has ever handed mankind to solve—the Book of Revelation.

TABLE OF CONTENTS

9   Introduction

13   Preface to the Message of the Seven Churches

15   The historic Record of the Seven Churches
(and Other Important Biblical
Misunderstandings Explained)

67   Deciphering the Hidden Message of the Seven Churches

99   The Scroll with the Seven Seals
(Revelation Chapter Four)

117   The Kingdom of God

139   The Seven Seals
(Revelation Chapter Six)

153   The Seven Trumpets
(Revelation Chapter Eight)

163   The Seven Thunders

175   The Great Red Dragon
(Revelation Chapter Twelve)

181   The Beast and the False Prophet
(Revelation Chapter Thirteen)

221   The Occult history of the Third Reich
(a challenge to the reader)

225   The Seven Plagues of the Seven Bowls
(Revelation Chapter Fifteen)

231   The Great Whore of Babylon
        (Revelation Chapter Seventeen through Eighteen)

247   The Record of the Kings of Israel

257   The Record of Bible Quotes

265   Biblical References and Sources Noted

269   Historical References and Research Sources Noted

INTRODUCTION

For nearly two thousand years, the book of Revelation has remained a book full of some of the most intriguing mysteries of the ages. Even as many renowned Christian authors and doctors of theology of our own time have tried repeatedly to solve the many riddles contained within this book, none have gotten them completely right; for it was for God to decide who the author of that book would be and when the time would be right for its understanding to be made known to the world. That time is now as the world in which we are all living has finally come to be viewed through the pages of the book of Revelation. Yes, for the wise it can be said that the signs of the times are suddenly upon us and blessed are those who wait on the Lord while dutifully doing his will. But for the unbelievers this will be a time when the truth shall be a very rude awakening as their worst nightmares will be brought before them.

Some will wonder why I was chosen to bring this understanding to the world at such a time as this. Perhaps it was because I was in the first instance willing to take up this seemingly impossible mission as God offered it to me. Otherwise, it may very well be that it was a mission that I was born to fulfill. As I have been shown a great many things by the Holy Spirit, one of those things has been that we are all born to fulfill a specific purpose in life, whether it is to serve the greater good or the greater evil; mine has been to write this book. It has been a burning desire that I have always had but also one that has taken me nearly my entire life to prepare for.

To know the truth as God would have it to be known is but to achieve the unachievable dream or to reach the unreachable star and then to behold its glory in awe of the power that has caused it to happen. Such has been my journey, and what an

9

incredible journey it has been. I began not knowing what I was to write but only knew that the truth would be forthcoming as the Spirit granted each understanding to me one section and sometimes even one verse at a time. And so this process went on section by section and chapter by chapter. But always I had to first become obedient to his will and instruction to study each section of the Bible, sometimes gathering every verse on a particular subject first and then later researching the historical record. Only then while in silent prayer and meditation would each understanding come. And when it would come, it would be like a great flood of knowledge, at times almost overwhelming for my ability to comprehend it, but my instruction was to write it all down, as it was too much to remember or even to speak about at one sitting. The following book is the product of that venture and journey into the unknown world of the book of Revelation. A world that now stands looming before us as we live out its verses and watch as the prophecies of Revelation become fulfilled one by one before our very eyes.

I have heard some ask the question: but why do I need to know about the meaning of the book of Revelation anyway when I have my faith in God and I am living a good and blessed life already? To all of you who might also be thinking this same thought, I can only tell you this: that to finally know the true meaning of the book of Revelation and the true meaning of the Bible itself as it was originally written and intended to be understood, right down to the deepest levels of understanding and of the very mysteries contained within it, is to know the very heart and mind of God. But it is also to know the very place in his kingdom where you shall reside when it is finally brought down to earth to bring peace to all those chosen to live within it for a thousand years. All will not live equally within the kingdom of God as it is first of all a sovereign system of government, having at its head a presiding king, a King of kings and Lord of lords, if you will. And beneath him there shall be all his subordinate kings and lords whom shall also be his holy royal priests and judges. These shall in turn have their royal subjects who shall serve them and who shall also live within the inner kingdom. But beyond the walls of this royal kingdom there will also be those who reside at the lowest level of his kingdom. If you want to know of which you shall be, then you need to read this book.

I originally thought that this book would be for only God's people to read, but as time has gone along, the Spirit of God has made it known to me that because this book is, in essence, a gift from God; it is, as such, for the whole world to read. This book is also designed to take the reader on their own journey through the pages of *history* and the inspired *word of God* and will allow them a rare opportunity to retrace the steps that have taken me years to prepare for. It will also challenge the reader to retrace all the actual research that I have done on both the historic record and the inspired word of God that together have cost me over six years of exhaustive work under the direction of the *Holy Spirit*. It will be on the basis of these three witnesses: the historic record, the inspired word of God, and the Holy Spirit by way of these very explanations that the truth as it is contained within this book will be made known to all those who seek it with an open heart; for now is the time for the book of Revelation to be understood.

May the peace and grace of God be upon all those who will come to take up this venture and take to heart all these things that have been written, as I can only attest with all the humility and grace that has been bestowed on me that these things are from God.

PREFACE TO THE MESSAGE OF THE SEVEN CHURCHES

There are actually seven levels of understanding to this very powerful message to the seven churches. But before I begin to decipher them, I need to first present the historic record behind the seven churches and as well to the rest of the book of Revelation, which is also referred to as "the Revelation of John" in the Bible. This account is necessary so that I can draw upon the historic facts that in and of themselves will lend a great deal of support to this first series of deciphered explanations. Later I will present those historic accounts regarding the rest of the book of Revelation. Then, along with these accounts, I will also be presenting all the scriptural affirmations that support them. These are all the scriptures that I have found all throughout the Bible that give their own proof that this deciphered explanation is in fact from God. As another part of this chapter, I will also be presenting some very profound and spiritually inspired scriptural explanation regarding those scriptures that for too long have been misunderstood.

THE HISTORIC RECORD OF THE SEVEN CHURCHES
(AND OTHER IMPORTANT BIBLICAL MISUNDERSTANDINGS EXPLAINED)

We begin with a message from Jesus Christ himself given through the Apostle John to the seven churches of Ephesus, Smyrna, Pergamum, Thyatira, Sardis, Philadelphia, and Laodicea. First, it should be noted that these seven churches are real archeological locations whose ruins still exist today in the eastern Mediterranean country of Turkey. It is also possible to visit these seven archeological sites and view their ruins on a tour bus, as it has become one of Turkey's main tourist attractions. However, if it is not within your means to make such a trip, then you can also purchase the video called *The Seven Churches of Revelation Rediscovered,* directed and presented by David Nunn. This video is beautifully done from an archeological as well as biblically historical standpoint, and I highly recommend its viewing to go in conjunction with the reading of this section of my book.

Regarding the historic record: It appears after a close review of the book of Acts, or as it is also referred to as in the Bible, the Acts of the Apostles, that these seven churches were the result of years of work coming from a widespread concerted effort that, in part, were from the outreach ministries of the Apostles Peter, John, and most notably Paul, whose first three missionary journeys took him all throughout multiple regions of the Mediterranean, including the region of these seven churches. On the other hand, these seven churches were also the result of many followers coming from each of their ministries, including some from John the Baptist's ministry, whose followers, after fleeing the intense persecutions of Palestine, were found as far north as Asia. Paul discovered some of these followers of John on his second trip to Ephesus and immediately began to explain the good news about Jesus to them; afterward he baptized them and they were filled with the Holy Spirit (reference Acts 19:1–8).

However, as the evidence shows, these seven churches are still primarily the handiwork of the Apostles Peter, John, and Paul. This would account for how John, as well as Peter, had come to be so acquainted with the people in this region of Asia as we can see for ourselves by the different letters that they had each written to them. It may also be that John had actually visited each of these seven churches at some point before his exile to the island of Patmos. Although there is no historic record to prove this, it seems very likely because of the way in which he greets them in the beginning of the book of Revelation in his message to these seven churches. But the one thing that is not disputed is that the people of all seven churches knew and respected the greatness of all three of these apostles and especially the sacrifice that they would each make in the end.

THE RECORD OF PETER

Historically, the Apostle Peter is accredited with having first brought the Christian faith to the Gentiles when he baptized Cornelius, the Roman centurion, after receiving the vision from God of the unclean things (reference Acts 10:34–38). After that, the Apostle Peter spent the next seven years preaching in various cities of Palestine, where he made many converts. During that time, he was met with some opposition from the Jewish supreme council but was not seriously persecuted until about AD 42 during the time of the Jewish Passover when King Herod Agrippa, by the popular demand of the Jewish people, decided to have James, the brother of John, beheaded for preaching the gospel. Then, because of the great ovation of the people at the execution of James, King Agrippa also decided to have Peter arrested and thrown into prison as well. However, he decided to hold off on Peter's execution until after the eight-day celebration of the Passover was complete so as to gain for himself an even greater popularity from the Jewish people. But an angel of the Lord helped Peter escape from prison where he was then forced to flee the city.

We last hear of the Apostle Peter in the book of Acts 15:6–11 as he is presiding over a meeting of the apostles and elders of the church in Jerusalem, which included Paul, Barnabas, and the Apostle John, when they were trying to decide the issue about whether or not the law of circumcision should be a determining factor before the baptism of the Holy Spirit could be administered to the Gentiles as it was with the Jews. It was finally decided after a long and heated debate led by Paul that the Jewish law of circumcision was not necessary for the Gentiles. But in keeping with the everlasting covenant brought forth through Abraham and the ensuing law that followed it, circumcision would remain in effect for all the Jews. Where it follows, that if circumcision remained in effect for all the Jews, then it would also remain in effect for "all Israel" (reference Acts 21:18–25), regarding Paul's out-of-step position from the church on the Mosaic Law and the law of circumcision. I will be speaking more on the importance of this meeting and its outcome later when I get to that section of my book called "The Law of Circumcision."

It was at the conclusion of this same meeting that the apostles and the elders, with agreement of the whole congregation, sent their two representatives of Judas and Silas to join the company of Paul and Barnabas as they went back to fulfill their commission of preaching the gospel to all the Gentiles that Jesus had personally given Paul to do (reference Acts 15:22–25, Galatians 1:15–17). After this, it was also decided that Peter, James, and John, who had also become known as the three pillars of the church, would keep their focus on the conversion of the Jewish people.

After this, the works of the Apostle Peter are not known to us except by speculation until he returned to Rome somewhere around AD 64. It is here that history records his final labors in the church for having laid himself down as the authoritative foundation of what would eventually become known as the legal establishment of the Roman Catholic Church in 313 by Constantine. He would be crucified upside down in AD 67 in fulfillment of the prophecy Jesus spoke to him in John 21: 18–19 during the great persecutions of Emperor Nero.

In the years leading up to this time, evidence shows that Peter traveled widely throughout the Middle East and ranged as far north as the Asian Minor, preaching the gospel, healing the sick, raising the dead, or otherwise shepherding his sheep as Jesus had commanded him. This is the area spoken of in the first letter of Peter, where he addresses his fellow brethren in Christ who had been scattered there from Jerusalem and were now living in the regions of Pontus, Galatia, Cappadocia, Asia, and Bithynia. Where Pontus and Bithynia were divided regions situated along the southern coastal area of the Black Sea and Galatia, Cappadocia and Asia were situated in the inner most regions of what is today known as Turkey. The seven churches are found to be from this same region of what was then known as Asia. So as we can see, Peter also had some affiliation with these seven churches.

There are some scholars who also believe that Peter then went on to Greece and founded the church in Corinth. But as I have studied the facts given within the accounts by Luke, who is the author of the book of Acts, it appears that it was actually Paul who founded this church and Peter, who came later, that consecrated its establishment. Also tradition teaches that Peter founded the church of Antioch as well, but once again the accounts given by Luke in Acts 11:19–23 dispute this claim. Here, in this account, we see that it was actually Jews, as well as some native converts from Cyprus and Cyrene, fleeing from the persecutions in Jerusalem that started this church. But what is important to realize here is that up until the time before Stephen was stoned in Jerusalem, Jerusalem was the location of God's first centralized church headed by Peter, who was also being assisted by the other apostles. So in effect, it was his church members who laid the groundwork for this church's beginning in Antioch, where it should be safe to say that Peter was not far behind them. It also follows that Peter probably spent a great deal of unaccounted time there after he too had to flee from Jerusalem.

GOD'S AUTHORITY RECENTERED

It was also at this particular moment that Jerusalem, God's former holy city and center on earth, had become officially cutoff by God, and Rome, the symbolic center of the pagan Gentile world, suddenly came into focus as God's new authoritative center for his up and coming universal church of God. For it is clear to see that God the Father meant this as both a poetic as well as a symbolic gesture to his former people who had rejected his Son as being their Messiah and finally murdered him, just as they had murdered and stoned so many of the hundreds of other prophets and messengers his Father had sent before him. Now, finally they were even casting his newly established church out of his holy city. Because of this and all the rest of the things that they had done, God was now cutting this generation of Israel completely out of their inheritance and grafting into his kingdom a new chosen people from the pagan Gentile world who had never known him but who would be willing to believe in him by faith. Where henceforth, Paul, in quoting the prophet Isaiah, told the Romans that, "Though the people of Israel are like the sand of the sea, only a remnant will be saved" (Romans 9:27, TNJB; also read Romans 10:11–14).

As a further punishment, God was now even vowing to hold this generation of Israel accountable for the blood of every prophet killed since the foundation of the world, from the blood of Abel to the blood of Zechariah, who perished between the altar and the sanctuary. It is written that this generation will have to answer for it all (reference Luke 11:47–51; also read Luke 13:34–35).

THE REMNANT OF ISRAEL

But in saying, "only a remnant of Israel will be saved," the Apostle Paul was not just speaking about those from among the Jews who had come to believe in the gospel of Jesus Christ. He was also speaking about those in the past from either the house of Israel or the house of Judah who had remained loyal to the God of hosts by their obedience to the holy Law that was handed down to them through Moses, as well as those Israelites in the future who, against all the odds, would also remain faithful to this gospel even up through the time of the beast's great reign of terror described in chapter 13 of the book of Revelation. This is also the time that we as most Christians refer to as the great tribulation period, which marks the end of the age of man as we know it and ushers in the beginning of the one-thousand-year reign of Christ here on earth.

But there is yet another group whom Ezekiel, in chapter 36, speaks about, who are also considered by God to be a part of this group called "the remnant of Israel who will be saved," and they are the survivors of all Israel who are still left on earth when Christ comes to put an end to the beast's great reign of terror, spoken of at the end of chapter 19 in the book of Revelation. It is this group that I will be primarily focusing on throughout the remainder of this book, as there is a great distinction that must be made between these survivors and the rest of the Israelites who shall be saved and those who will not. These are the descendants from both the house of Israel and the house of Judah, who were each scattered across the face of the earth at different times in history. The house of Israel, which was also referred to as the northern kingdom of Israel, whose capital was Samaria, eventually became known to us as the "Ten Lost Tribes of Israel." They were last heard of in 721 BC after they were conquered by the Assyrians, led by King Shalmaneser, and then taken off into exile as a punishment by God for all their rebellious sins and abominations committed against him. It appears from there they were taken into the northern most regions of Mesopotamia and Medes, today known as modern Syria and Iraq. Then in 612 BC, after Nineveh, the capital city of the Assyrian empire, was completely destroyed by the Babylonians, they simply disappeared according to the historic account.

The house of Judah's historic record, on the other hand, lies before us in rich context. This house consists primarily of the two remaining tribes of Judah and Benjamin but also has in their company some of the Levites who chose to cross over to the house of Judah at the time of King Solomon's death. These then are all those who we more affectionately refer to as the Jews, and they would be taken off into exile by the Babylonians in 598 BC under

King Nebuchadnezzar. The exile of Judah is also orchestrated by God through the warnings of the prophet Jeremiah because of her great sins of infidelity committed against him and the lack of compassion shown toward the poor, the widowed, the orphaned, and the downtrodden. She is also likened by God as being just like her sister Israel who also played the harlot by turning their faces away from the One who had delivered them out of Egypt and worshiping the worthless gods of men. At that time, they were regarded as the southern kingdom of Judah, whose capital was Jerusalem. The city of Jerusalem and the first Jewish temple would then be completely destroyed during the second conquest of the city by the Babylonians. Then in 536 BC, King Cyrus of Persia conquered Babylon, and two years later, by royal decree, he allowed all those Jews who wished to return home to rebuild Jerusalem to do so. Upon their return home, under the leadership of a congregation of both priests and Levites, they very quickly took upon themselves the very arduous task of rebuilding the city's walls and, most importantly, the temple, which was finally completed in 516 BC.

From then on, Jerusalem continued to be the capital of Judah as a province under the Persian, Greek, and Roman Empires. It was during the time of Herod the Great that it experienced a short period of independence and that the temple complex received its last upgrade before it was finally destroyed under Titus in AD 70. This was the result of Jewish civil war and a revolt against Rome that left the second temple burnt and the rest of the city repeatedly sacked and in ruins.

Then in 135, after crushing the Bar Kokhba's revolt, the Roman Emperor Hadrian resettled the city as a pagan province of Palestine, and the Jews were henceforth forbidden to enter the city except for one day out of the year when they would be allowed to come to the one remaining wall of the second temple and wail over its loss and destruction. The name Palestine appears to be a derivative from the name of Philistine or, as the region right next to Israel was also known, Philistia. It may also be that the Emperor Hadrian chose this name as the ultimate insult to the Jews for all the trouble that they had caused him and his empire. Before this time, the province had been known as Judea. The city itself was renamed Aelia Capitolina and would keep this name until 313 when Emperor Constantine I changed its name back to Jerusalem. This was also around the same time that he officially stopped the persecutions of all Christians and made Christianity the legal and universal faith of the Roman Empire.

It seems that from AD 70 through about the next 1,878 years that the Jewish people would remain in this seemingly permanent state of exile as they now joined their sister Israel in being dispersed across the face of the earth. It is also throughout this time that the Jewish people would continue to suffer great persecution across many of the nations ranging throughout the north Asian and European continents. It would not be until 1948 after the great holocaust committed by Hitler in the Second World War that Jerusalem and the land of Israel would once again be established as a Jewish state by the United Nations.

With regard to the city of Jerusalem: Though Jerusalem's origin by way of the historic record appears to be uncertain, its first inhabitants were clearly heathens, or more specifically, the Amorites under king Adoni-Zedek, which inhabitants were later completely annihilated by Joshua's Army under the command of God. Some years later the city of Jerusalem eventually became inhabited by the Jebusites as noted in the first chapter of the book of Judges. Otherwise the first mention of this city being called Jerusalem in the Bible is found in the book of Joshua at the beginning of chapter 10 and is not a name given by the Amorites, but is clearly a name given and ordained to Joshua by God. It appears that the site of Jerusalem, the predestined holy city of God, was established secretly by God during the time when the everlasting covenant between himself and Abraham was being created in Genesis 17:7–8.

It is in the book of Joshua that Joshua is given strict orders by God to kill and annihilate every king, every people, and every living thing that is found within the boundaries of this holy land that God had promised to Israel. It takes Joshua the rest of his lifetime to rid and purge the greater portion of this land from all the people and their possessions that have defiled it before Israel can be allowed to inhabit it as her patrimony and assigned possession. In the end, Joshua completely annihilates, burns, and destroys some thirty cities and towns along with all their kings. After his death only the few remaining Jebusites found within the holy city of Jerusalem are spared by the sons of Benjamin and allowed to coexist with the Israelites, even unto the time of King David, where once again Jerusalem, because of the many sins of the nation, is lost and will have to be retaken from under heathen control.

The delays put upon the Israelites by God from taking possession of this promised land and his holy city are all well documented throughout the records of the different books written by Moses in the Bible, especially from the book of Exodus. As to the reason why these surviving Jebusites were allowed to live when so many others were completely annihilated seems, in part, due to the difficulty in the mountainous terrain surrounding Jerusalem's location and also the willingness of the Jebusites to surrender and make peace with the Israelites as the Hivites had also done from the cities of Gibeon, Kephirah, Beeroth, and Kiriath-jearim (reference Joshua 9:1–18). The other reason why God may have allowed this cohabitation to exist with the Jebusites in Jerusalem is perhaps due to the very meaning of the name Jerusalem itself, which means "city of peace."

With regard to the exile of all Israel: History has shown in the 1,878 years leading up to her reestablishment that Jerusalem has been perhaps one of the most hotly disputed cities in the civilized world as it continues to be to this very day. It is presently divided between three religious faiths: the Jews, the Christians, and the Muslims, each claiming to have their own

THE BOOK OF REVELATION AND THE BIBLE
AS NEVER EXPLAINED BEFORE

legal right to this city. It appears that Jerusalem will remain in this hopeless state of deadlock until Christ comes again to restore this city to its original place as his undisputed holy city chosen and ordained by God to rule the world, whereby Rome shall remain in her stead until such time as Christ comes for his bride, which is symbolic of the church.

The other fact that must be remembered in all of this is this: it was by God's hand that all Israel was banished from the land of Israel, and it will not be until God has commanded it that all Israel shall return. In the meantime, God, through the prophets, has made it known that at the time of his Son's second coming "only a remnant of all Israel will be saved." What these Jews and the other Israelites both share in common at this particular time of the end is this: they will each still reject Jesus as their Messiah and will continue with this rejection until they have both come to either see the one to whom they had pierced, in the case of the Jews (reference Revelation 1:7, and Zechariah 12:10), or in the case of the ten lost tribes, see the one to whom they had refused to worship and believe in. Only then will they all fall on their faces and repent of all the abominations that they had committed against their God and beg his forgiveness. At which time, God will reconcile himself back with his firstborn people, but it will not be for anything good that they may perceive to have done for God because all their deeds were wicked in his eyes. Rather, it will be as God tells us through the prophet Ezekiel in Chapter 36 that it is for the sake of his own holy name that he forgives and reconciles himself back to these who are the descendants of his firstborn people (Ezekiel 36:16–29).

Then after all the nations armies assembled around God's holy mountain have been destroyed, along with the beast and the false prophet, the returning King of kings and Lord of lords, will gather these who are the only survivors left on earth from all Israel back to Zion, where they will finally be allowed to inherit the land promised to them by God through their forefathers. All the rest of the dead, who are called the whole house of

Israel, will not be allowed to enter what will then be called "the millennial kingdom" but will only be allowed to enter what will later be called "the eternal kingdom" after the one-thousand-year reign of Christ on earth has come to pass away.

JUDAH AND ISRAEL: A HOUSE DIVIDED

Two questions that have often aroused my curiosity during my research of the twelve tribes of Israel have been: First, why were the twelve tribes of Israel separated into these two different houses in the first place? And second, when did this separation first occur in the Bible?

Before I get into to this, I would like to clarify this one thing. The Bible does make a mention of a number of different houses and their various different contexts besides these two dividing Israel. For instance, there's the house of David, the house of Joshua, the house of God, the house of bondage, and the house of sin, to name a few. Jesus said, "In my Father's house are many mansions: if it were not so I would have told you" (John 14:2, NKJV). Paul tells us, "But Christ as a son over his own house; who's house we are, if we hold fast the confidence and the rejoicing of hope firm to the end" (Hebrews 3:6, NKJV). Solomon tells us when speaking through his proverbs about the unfaithful harlot, "Her house is the way to hell" (Proverbs 7:27, NKJV). When the jailer asked Paul and Silas what he must do to be saved after the earthquake, they replied: "Believe on the Lord Jesus Christ, and you will be saved, you and your household" (Acts 16:31, NKJV). Joshua said, "But as for me and my house, we will serve the Lord" (Joshua 24:15, NKJV).

We can see from all this that every man has his own house and even some women. However, some houses are perpetual and others are not. Also, salvation is still contingent upon everyone in a particular house being subservient to God through the house patriarch. Of those houses that are perpetual, we see that the house of God is first and foremost, followed by the house of David, the house of Judah, and finally the house of Israel. Of

THE BOOK OF REVELATION AND THE BIBLE
AS NEVER EXPLAINED BEFORE

those that are not perpetual, we see the house of bondage and the house of sin, as is the case with the harlot's house, and all these houses lead to hell and damnation. But of the two houses of Judah and Israel, there is something even more significant here that needs to be mentioned.

God, in his infinite wisdom, saw the need to separate and to distinguish one of the twelve sons of Jacob at the beginning for the purpose of carrying the king's line that would come through him and ultimately be traced from Jesus Christ all the way back to David. That son's name was Judah. The reason Judah was selected over Reuben, who was the firstborn son of Jacob and who, under normal circumstances, would have received this blessing by birthright, is because Ruben committed incest with his father's concubine Bilhah and as such disgraced his father and thereby forfeited his birthright. The reason Simeon and Levi were skipped over being the next two eldest sons after Reuben was because the two of them had plotted and carried out the murder of Hamor and his son Shechem, along with all the other males of the city of Shecham, for the dishonor Shecham had done to their full-blooded sister Dinah. In doing this thing, they also had disgraced their father and as such had also forfeited their chance at receiving the rank and blessings of the firstborn. Consequently, this high honor was granted to Judah even though Judah, along with all his other brothers except for Reuben and Benjamin, had each plotted Joseph's murder. Yet it was Judah who finally convinced the other brothers in the absence of Reuben to sell Joseph into slavery instead of killing him. Now, because Judah had been a participant in the plotting and selling of Joseph into slavery, only a part of the patriarchal blessing of the firstborn would remain with him. But that part was none other than receiving the high honor of having the king's scepter traced back through his lineage in the house of Judah through the line of David. Otherwise, the only thing that would be traced through the lineage of the house of Israel throughout the next approximate 3,600 years would be disobedience and wickedness. Reference Genesis 37:11–36 regarding the plotting and selling of Joseph into slavery; also read Genesis 48:1–22 regarding the blessings of Ephraim and Manasseh. Then read Genesis 49:1–27 regarding the blessings that Jacob (also called Israel) gave to each of his twelve sons near the time of his death. Pay particular attention to the blessings given to both Judah and Joseph. Also reference 1 Chronicles 5:1–2 for another perspective on why the patriarchal blessings of the firstborn were divided between Judah and Joseph and not given to Reuben.

THE RECORD OF PETER CONTINUED

Another critical fact to remember about Peter is that his authority came directly from God the Father, through his Son, Jesus Christ. So as I begin to explain the deeper meaning within this message to the seven churches, I will be drawing upon just how important the understanding of this one fact truly is. Whereas it is written, after Peter affirmed his faith in Jesus as being the Messiah and Son of the living God, Jesus replied to Peter, saying, "Blessed are you, Simon Bar- Jonah, for flesh and blood has not reveal this to you, but My Father who is in heaven. And I also say to you that you are Peter, (the rock) and on this rock I will build My church" (NKJV) "and the gates of hell shall not prevail against it. I give you the keys of the Kingdom of Heaven, that whatever you bind on earth shall be bound in heaven and whatever you loose on earth shall be loosed in heaven" (Matthew 16:17–19, NKJV-KJV).

What most Christians do not realize about these scriptures in particular is that they are loaded with hidden meaning. First of all, the words *bind* and *loose* are words that were understood by the twelve apostles as being legal terms that were then being used by the Jewish supreme council, which granted them God's ultimate authority on earth to pass judgment on anyone who would be brought before them. They used this same authority to pass the death sentence on Jesus and all the rest of the prophets that they had killed in the years gone by before he was brought before them and accused of blasphemy and sedition. This authority was understood to be both summary and final and was also understood by all the Jews as being granted to them by God. On the other hand, it was also understood by all the Jewish people that having this authority did not give them the power or the right to change even the very least part of the holy Law. For the Law that was handed down to them by God through Moses was also summary and final until such time as the Messiah should come and then only he had the right to make any such changes.

So when Jesus granted this authority to Peter, it was also understood, at least in part, by the others what all Jesus was meaning by this as stated above. They understood then that Peter was basically being given the same legal authority as that of the presiding high priest of the Jewish supreme council, whose Levitical priesthood order could be traced through the succession of men to Aaron, all of whom had become bound by the Law of the old covenant between God and Moses and who likewise had failed miserably in the eyes of God in perfecting the inward love and holiness of God's chosen people. But what I'm sure they didn't understand until later was that this old priesthood order was being made obsolete by Christ who was now bringing to them a new holy royal priesthood order. It was being established by his Father through himself as the newly appointed high priest by his sacrifice that was soon to come in the succession of Melchizedek, the immortal King of Salem, and everlasting priest of the God Most High. But the office of high priest had to first be taken from its present location on earth to its newly appointed place in high heaven and this could only be done by the sacrificial death and ascension of Christ.

With regard to Melchizedek: The name Melchizedek, in the first place, means king of righteousness; next, he is the king of Salem, which means king of peace, and is also where the city of Jerusalem derives its name, for Jerusalem means city of peace. Melchizedek also has no father and no mother, no lineage; his years have no beginning, his life no end. He is like the Son of God: he remains a priest forever (Hebrews 7:1–3). But in the old covenant, where a high priest was needed on earth to perform the animal sacrifices and to act as man's holy representative before God through Melchizedek, his appointed and immortal priest in heaven, now in the new covenant, Jesus has come in the succession of Melchizedek as the Father's newly appointed and everlasting high priest in heaven. With this succession the office of high priest on earth and also Melchizedek's office as God's official go-between was there and then made obsolete. But Melchizedek's priesthood continues on, even though his former position in office had now come to its end by the vested virtue of the Lamb's own sacrifice and sprinkled blood. It is by this same sacrifice that Jesus has entered the real sanctuary once and for all and secured the eternal deliverance for anyone who would just believe in him. In effect, Jesus has now become our all in all. He is our Lord and Savior, the Lamb of God, our King of kings and Lord of lords, our one and only true living prophet whom we follow and try to emulate; he is our deliverer and judge, he is the Son of God and the Word of God, but he is especially our newly appointed and everlasting high priest whom from this point on shall be the only one in all heaven who is worthy enough to cleanse us by his own shed blood and present us to his Father on the day of our deliverance when we enter his kingdom. For the complete context of this understanding (reference Hebrews 7:1–28.)

THE KEYS OF THE KINGDOM OF HEAVEN

And Jesus said this to Peter: "*And I will give unto thee the keys of the Kingdom of Heaven;* and whatsoever thou shalt bind on earth shall be bound in Heaven: and whatsoever thou shalt loose on

THE BOOK OF REVELATION AND THE BIBLE
AS NEVER EXPLAINED BEFORE

earth shall be loosed in Heaven" (Matthew 16:19, KJV). With regard to the keys of the kingdom of heaven: the keys that Jesus gave Peter then pretty much gave him full authority over the church that was later to be founded upon each of the twelve apostles. In effect, this made Peter the newly appointed presiding chief priest of the church on earth, and these keys also granted him, as well as the other apostles, special powers to heal the sick, to raise the dead, and even to bless or curse anyone who would be so deserving. All this went above and beyond the authority of the high priest of the Jewish supreme council. They could never have imagined commanding such power and authority in the old covenant as the Apostle Peter was now commanding in the new as he kept a careful watch over the many lambs and sheep entrusted to him within the different fellowships of God's church.

All through the book of Acts we see just how Peter exercised this authority with sometimes deadly accuracy. An example of this is shown in the case when Ananias and his wife, Sapphira, were caught lying to God over the price at which they had sold their land to give to the church. It was by this same authority invested in Peter that they each dropped dead when he called them to account for their actions in Acts 5:1–10. Again, as Peter was on his way to visit the people of Lydda, he met a man named Aeneas who had been bed ridden with paralysis for eight years. Whereby Peter said to him: "Aeneas, Jesus the Christ heals you. Arise and make your bed.' Then he arose immediately" (Acts 9:34, NKJV). Then while in Lydda, word was sent to Peter from Joppa that Tabitha, a kind and very generous woman of God, had just passed away, and they had faith that he could do something for her. Peter, upon hearing their request immediately went to them and after hearing all their heartwarming reports about her went into her room and raised Tabitha back up from the dead (reference Acts 9:36–41). But these are only a sample of the many accounts given about Peter in the book of Acts showing that his authority was indeed a head above all the rest.

But perhaps the most telling example of this comes from Jesus himself where he asks Peter three times, one for each of the times that he had denied him:

> "Simon son of Jonah, do you love Me more than these?" He said to Him, "Yes, Lord; you know that I love You." He said to him, "Feed my lambs," He said to him again a second time, "Simon son of Jonah, do you love Me?" He said to Him, "Yes, Lord, you know that I love You." He said to him, "Tend My sheep." He said to him the third time, "Simon son of Jonah, do you love Me?" Peter was grieved because He said to him the third time, "Do you love Me?" And he said to Him, "Lord, You know all things; You know that I love You." Jesus said to him, "Feed my sheep" John 21:15–17, (NKJV).

It was after this third time that I believe Peter finally realized why it was Jesus was doing this and also how necessary it was that he be atoned for his three denials of him earlier. Then on the basis of this atonement, Jesus then gave Peter, and only Peter these three commands: to feed his lambs, to tend his sheep, and to feed his sheep.

There can be no doubt from this that Peter was the one chosen by God to head the church in Jesus' absence. After which, Jesus would be ascending back up to heaven to take his seat at the right hand of his Father as the newly glorified Lamb of God, but most importantly the new High Priest of his soon-to-be-established, blood-bought church. Later, it would be this same church that would span the face of the globe and be built upon each of his twelve apostles who are regarded in the book of Revelation as the twelve foundation stones of the church. Here their names can be seen written on the twelve foundation stones lying beneath the city wall of the new Jerusalem as it comes down out of heaven in Revelation 21:14. But the centralized church destined to hold the keys of the kingdom and all God's authority on earth would later be built upon the rock of Peter in 325 by Constantine. It is here that the tomb of Peter lies in state to this day, buried beneath the foundation of the Saint Peter's Basilica, just as Jesus said it would be! There is no other church, temple, or mosque in the world that can make this claim, and it did not happen by chance or coincidence. In fact, it happened in just the same way that God said it would happen—by the power of his word.

With regard to the other disciples, what they probably didn't completely understand until later about all this was that they too had each been given a share of this same authority as Peter had but to a lesser degree. They were now appointed by Jesus as the other, lesser bench members, or holy royal priests, if you will, of this newly adopted Jewish supreme council of the church, but their mandate was totally changed by the gospel of Jesus Christ.

It is this concept of the *holy royal priesthood* that Peter spoke about in 1 Peter 2:5–6, 9–10 that has become completely lost to all the scattered churches that profess to be of God, the only exceptions being that of the Roman Catholic Church and its close counterpart, the Eastern Orthodox Church. However, since the first split of the Eastern Orthodox Church in 1054, leading all the way up to the Protestant Reformation in the 1500s, the church as a whole has ceased to be as one as Satan and his army of fallen angels began to infiltrate, divide, and then finally to conquer God's churches with his perversions of the truth. Until today, as you look out across the face of the earth, you can now see the great damage that Satan has done and continues to do to all God's scattered flocks that have allowed themselves to become severed from its one, true, authoritative center in Rome. Now, instead of the Holy Spirit being net-worked out from the Father's one true center on earth, we see that the evil spirit of corruption, self-righteous arrogance, and manmade doctrine has long since taken charge of nearly all of God's churches instead of the one to whom the Lord had appointed in his absence with the special command to feed his lambs, to tend his sheep, and to feed his sheep in his absence!

33

To be clearer, when Jesus gave Peter these three commands he was not being redundant. Neither was his message meant for Peter alone, but in a broader sense, it was also meant for all the future church leaders as well.

With regard to the lambs: His message here was not just for the children of Peter's future fellowships but it was also meant for the children of those fellowships beyond Peter's who would, during the next approximate two thousand years, become entrusted to the care of this one church through its many different schools, hospitals, and other institutions that it would build; and for the less fortunate, through the many different orphanages that would be built for their care as well. For here Jesus sets the priority for all the future leaders of this church whose duties he likens unto those of a good shepherd, whereby they are being commanded here in this scripture to keep a vigilant watch over his flocks as they become entrusted to them; and to always be ready to ensure their safety and to provide them with security as they feed them from his word according to the capacity of their age, which must be different from the adults. But he is also telling them to be ever on their guard against all the ravenous wolves that will always be lurking about trying to get at them. Paul makes his own reference to this scripture with his remarks to the fellowship in Miletus about how they, as shepherds of the Lord, should not only keep a careful watch over their sheepfold, but also themselves, as savage wolves would certainly come in after his departure, and he further warned that they would not spare the flock (reference Acts 20; 28–31).

Today this message has largely fallen on deaf ears as the church leaders from within the Catholic Church have forsaken the many helpless children entrusted to its care over a greater regard for the church's personal reputation. In doing this thing these church leaders have not just allowed these ravenous wolves access to their entrusted sheepfolds but they have also protected them and kept them safe from any harm. And by their continual cover-ups, spanning three or perhaps even

THE BOOK OF REVELATION AND THE BIBLE
AS NEVER EXPLAINED BEFORE

four decades, they have allowed these ravenous wolves the freedom to move and to devour God's helpless little lambs at their
leisure, almost as if these wolves were the precious little ones
that God had entrusted them with and the lambs were there
only for their sadistic dining pleasure. And now the ugly truth
about this whole evil thing has come to light and one of those
responsible has become pope. God's message now to the pope
and to all those who may have otherwise played their own part
in this great tragedy is for each of them to take upon themselves
the personal responsibility to make all things right by the victims and to further see to it that all the perpetrators of these
heinous crimes are brought before a court of law and punished
severely. And if they cannot find it within themselves to do this
because their own guilt in this matter is just too much for them
then they need to step down from whatever position they hold
within this church and allow someone else to take their place
who can. Only then will Satan's onslaught against this church
be brought to an end and the time for reconciliation and healing
begin. And only then will the credibility and reputation of this
once great church truly be restored.

But even in the midst of all this evil and corruption that
has been allowed to enter into God's one true church, there
is still a very special priesthood order of men that can only be
found within it that has survived Satan's onslaught and who
remain to be called one of the chosen *holy royal priests* of God,
or otherwise *God's elect.* I will reveal who these specially chosen,
perfected, and holy ones are later when I decipher the hidden
meaning behind the "Seven Thunders."

As for the keys of the kingdom that Jesus specifically gave
to Peter, they were intended to remain on earth as part of the
temporal authority he had granted to his church and be passed
on from chief priest to chief priest or, as it has become known
today within the Catholic Church, from pope to pope. It, however, was not an authority meant for everyone to lay hold of, as
so many Protestant Christians would like to mistakenly believe.

With regard to the proclamation that Jesus made to Peter in Matthew 16; 17–19, which states how God's church would be built upon his rock and also how the gates of hell would not be allowed to prevail against it: To this and to all the Christian churches that have twisted this holy scripture into meaning something that it was never intended to mean, I have this revelation of the truth to present to you. In the Greek, it reads, "You are Cephas." Literally translated, it means Peter or the rock. In the Aramaic, it reads Kephas; literally translated, it means the rock or Kipha, rock. In the Latin, it reads Petrus, or Peter, the rock. Also, Paul refers to Peter as Cephas in Galatians 1:18, 2:9–14.

Therefore, the rock as it was used by Jesus in this context was intended to mean Peter and was not meant as a reference to himself, as millions of Protestant Christians and Mormons alike have so vehemently chosen to believe in a feeble attempt to justify their separation from the *one, true, church of God* that the *gates of hell* as told by Jesus would not be allowed to prevail against. Having said all this, I must also say that the Catholic Church may indeed have its problems, but Saint Peter's Basilica is still Christ's center of authority on earth.

To support this claim, I give you this historic record. For centuries after the crucifixion of Peter, the whereabouts of his entombed remains had become lost to the world. Then in the holy year of 1950, the tomb of the Apostle Peter, who is now regarded as Saint Peter by the Catholic Church, was discovered beneath Saint Peter's Basilica in Rome and was announced to the world by Pope Pius XII, thus showing to the world once and for all that God's church had literally been built upon the rock of Peter, just as Jesus said it would be.

To give further emphasis to this critical point, Jesus, in the year 312, almost three hundred years after the death of Peter, gave Constantine a vision during his battle with Maxentius, who was at that time his rival over the rule of the western empire. This is where Jesus appeared to Constantine in the form of the flaming cross and promised him victory over Maxentius if he would put the sign of the cross with the first two letters of his name on all his soldiers' shields. After the victory, Constantine immediately became converted and a strong believer in Christianity. In the following year, Constantine, after convening a meeting with Licinius, the emperor of the eastern empire, would be responsible for converting the entire eastern and western empires over to Christianity through a statement of policy he enacted which was then agreed upon by both emperors called the Edict of Milan. And it was with this agreement that Constantine gave the world the greatest proof that Rome was to be the location of God's official church that the gates of hell would not be allowed to prevail against as was told to Peter.

As history has shown, Satan has brought the gates of hell along with everything else against this church, but he has not been able to bring this church down. More importantly, Satan has not been able to sever the papal line that was started with Peter. For God's authority rests on this church as this church rests upon the tomb of Peter, and every pope stemming from Peter remains on record in one unbroken line to this day, a line that remains with each pope having served his term of representing the temporal authority of God over his one true church here on earth, even though some of the popes were embroiled in corruption throughout the centuries. This is no different to God than the king's scepter, now in the hands of his Son, Jesus Christ, being traced back through all the good as well as the corrupt kings from the house of Judah, which succession of kings ended with Zedekiah by way of King Nebuchadnezzar of Babylon. However, what is interesting to note here, is how the lineage of Christ is not traced back through Zedekiah or his other two brothers, Jehoahaz, and Jehoakim, but rather it is traced back by God through King Josiah's youngest son, Jeconiah, because all Zedekiah's sons were slain before him for his betrayal to King Nebuchadnezzar and his other two brothers and one nephew, Jehoahchin, were each changed into eunuchs. As such, the king's scepter would be traced back from Jesus through the linage of Joseph, through Jeconiah to Josiah, all the way back to King David just as the temporal authority of God's one true church will also be traced back from the last legitimate pope to sit in Rome to Peter just before Christ comes for his bride. And just as God omitted the one illegitimate queen Athaliah from the king's succession he will likewise omit all the illegitimate popes from its line of succession as well. Of the twenty-two kings and one illegitimate queen (Athaliah), only ten were found to be righteous in the eyes of God. There were no righteous kings to be found from within the house of Israel. The complete record of kings from both the house of Judah and the house of Israel may be found in 1st and 2nd Kings in the Old Testament and may also be viewed in the end pages of this book. Notice, how there are eighteen kings in all documented from Josiah back to King David. Otherwise the complete record of popes from Benedict XVI all the way back to the apostle Peter, may be viewed on the internet under: Lists of popes-Wikipedia, the free encyclopedia, or from within the pages of the World Book Encyclopedia under Pope.

THE LAW AND THE PROPHETS

On the other side of this equation is the fact that as the other disciples were each being given this very special authority on earth, it was also being taken away from the other, formerly known chief priests of the Jewish supreme council. No longer would anything that they decided be recognized by God. They were now officially cut off and dead to God, just as the old covenant had now also become dead to him. But having said that, this did not mean that the Law and the prophets had been done away with. On the contrary, the old covenant was dead to only those things that the new covenant did not carry over unto itself. The Law and the prophets did carry over, but they carried over into the new covenant in their completion and not as they were in their incompletion. However, this does not mean that the foundation of the Law is any less important to God than those things that brought the Law to its completion. For this is what Jesus meant when he said, "Do not imagine that I have come to abolish the Law or the prophets; I have come not to abolish, but to complete them. In truth I tell you, till heaven and earth disappear, not one dot, not one little stroke, is to disappear from the Law until all its purpose is achieved." (Matthew 5:17–19, TNJB). Jesus then goes on to give a complete contextual rendition of just what he means by this and also tells of the consequences that will be paid by anyone who teaches otherwise in Matthew 5:19–20.

But what exactly is the "Law and the prophets?" Jesus tells us in two different places in the Gospel of Matthew just what he means by the Law and the prophets. First, he states, "Whatever you want men to do to you, do also to them, for this is the Law and the prophets" (Matthew 7:12, NKJV). Jesus then goes on to break this down to us by teaching us that the completion of the Law basically encompasses his entire gospel message, and that message is all about becoming perfected in God's love, as I will be explaining later in much greater detail. Then Jesus puts it another way a little later on in his teaching to the people when asked this trick question by the Pharisees:

> 'Master which is the greatest commandment of the Law?' Jesus said to him, 'You must love the Lord your God with all your heart, with all your soul, and with all your mind. That is the greatest and the first commandment. The second resembles it: 'You must love your neighbor as yourself. On these two commandments hang the whole Law, and the prophets too' (Matthew 22:36–40, TNJB).

These two excerpts taken out of the teachings of Jesus in the Gospel of Matthew may seem, on the surface, quite simple. However, in actuality they encompass quite a lot. First of all, if you study everything that the prophets of old have said, you will see that there is this one prevailing message that they were all trying to get across to the Israelites then had they only listened.

That message was and still is all about love, the love of their God and the love of their fellow man. For God has always made it known to us, since the time of King Saul, that he would much rather have our love and obedience than animal sacrifice. Also, that in conjunction with the circumcision of the flesh, the Lord has always wanted the circumcision of the heart as well; a circumcised heart is a heart circumcised in love. It is because of the Israelites' failure to achieve this one simple desire of the Lord that the consequences for their actions had to be written and finally carried out by God through the prophets of old. But it is also because of their failure that God has now opened up his coming kingdom to the rest of the Gentile world if they too would only just believe and abide in his commandments. However, it is still very disheartening to see that just as the Israelites then had refused to listen to the Lord's simple message of love, even now in this great country we call the United States so many Americans are doing the same thing, as they have blinded themselves to this truth. Now, just as the consequences written for the Israelites' failure to believe and trust in the Lord fell upon them, so shall these same consequences written by the prophets of old fall upon us as well and, in fact, on any nation that refuses to accept this final offer made by the Lord for its salvation.

To love the Lord your God with all your heart, with all your soul, and with all your mind means that we must be obedient to all his commandments. It must also be stated that to be obedient to all his commandments is not just about having a comprehensive understanding of the entire gospel message itself, but it is also about having a comprehensive understanding of the entire Bible; hence, the Law and the prophets, all of which entails becoming perfected in the love of God, which is really what it means to be a Christian or Christlike.

In conjunction to our being obedient to God's Ten Commandments, which are, in fact, the foundation of the Mosaic Law, it is important to understand that these are not complete without God's rendition from the book of Leviticus of what it also means to be in keeping with his laws of holiness. These may be found and studied all throughout the book of Leviticus but especially in chapters 17 through 27, keeping in mind that some of these laws mentioned are no longer in effect because of the new covenant that was brought through Jesus Christ's own self-sacrifice and the completion of the Law, which came through his Father's own new gospel message. Especially done away with are those things having to do with animal sacrifice, whole offerings, and grain offerings that are either offered up for the atonement of sins or, in the case of the grain offerings, as a food offering of soothing odor given to the Lord.

With regard to land and animal tithes, Moses tells the Israelites that the Lord commands that the first 10 percent of all grain and fruit tree harvests belongs to him. Moses also tells the Israelites that 10 percent of all animal increase, whether it is of cattle or of sheep, also belongs to the Lord. It is based on these commandments from the book of Leviticus that we as Christians have substituted our own personal tithes and gift offerings to go in place of them. This may be an offering of either tithe or a gift taken out of our paychecks or may even be taken as time, energy, and resources spent helping our neighbor or the poor in need to go in place of these kinds of offerings presented unto the Lord. Regarding tithes on land and animals (reference Leviticus 27:30–34).

There are a number of other things that are also still in effect as stated in the book of Leviticus. Especially pay attention to those things regarding sexual immorality, sexual perversion, and justice. It appears that the Lord has a special regard for the ill treatment of the poor, the widowed, the orphaned, and especially the downtrodden. Also still in effect is anything that has to do with the Ten Commandments, read Leviticus chapters 17–20, 25, and 26.

Then there are those things having to do with ritual cleanliness and community cleanliness as mentioned in chapters 21 through 22. It is interesting to note how remarkably similar these ancient community standards of cleanliness are to our modern-day laws and community standards set forth by our nation's many different state departments of health. However, most of these things with regards to ritual cleanliness have been superseded by the completion of the Law as well. But the Lord in the new covenant is still interested in clean and healthy bodies as well as clean living places. However, with this completion of the Law, the Lord is just as interested in us having as clean and pure a heart and mind as he is in the outward appearance of our bodies and community dwelling places, hence the circumcision of the heart.

Unfortunately, the loud and boisterous temptations and perverted ways of this world have long since drowned this simple message out as pornography, sex outside of marriage, homosexuality, along with all the other various forms of sexual perversion, body piercing, tattooing, violent crime, abortion, partial birth abortion, punk rock, heavy metal, gangster rap, satanic worship, drugs, spring break, and girls gone wild, to mention only a few of the things out there, appear to be taking over the hearts, bodies, and minds of so many of our young people. All these things, according to the Lord, desecrate both body and soul, as our hearts and bodies under the new covenant are supposed to be God's new holy temple and dwelling place. Reference 1 Corinthians 6:19–20 and also 1 Corinthians 3:6–17 regarding his new holy temple. Also reference Leviticus 19:28 regarding body gashing and tattooing.

Then there are the food and drink offerings, the holy seasons, the sacred assemblies, and days of atonement that are mentioned in chapter 23. These things, for the most part, have also been superseded by the new covenant. But the holy seasons, the sacred assemblies, and the making of atonement for our sins have each still carried over in their modified forms through the completion of the Law. For example, we now make atonement for our sins by confession, repentance, and the taking of the sacraments as opposed to animal sacrifice. The sacred assemblies have now become our church services that we attend on Sundays where we give thanks and praise to God for all his blessings. Otherwise, the holy seasons, for the most part, have become superseded by those days and seasons coming forth out of the new covenant, such as Palm Sunday, the week of Lent, Good Friday, Easter, Ash Wednesday, the week of Advent and Christmas. All these are still very much regarded within the Catholic Church and also in its close counterpart, the Eastern Orthodox Church as being holy days with respect to their seasons. The Protestant churches, on the other hand, only consider as being holy the seasons of Easter and Christmas. Unfortunately, the Sabbath day, which is also supposed to be kept holy, has, to a great number of Christians in all the churches, become just another optional day of rest.

Also pay attention to those things that God says through Moses to the Israelites shall remain forever or until the end of time, such as the annual celebration of the Lord's pilgrim Feast of Tabernacles (which is the same pilgrim feast as that of the Passover celebrated by the Jews). This feast is to be celebrated for seven days out of each year. Then in chapters 23 and 24, listen as Moses tells the Israelites how they are to keep the Sabbath day holy, as it is a covenant made between God and man for all time. In chapters 25 and 26, the Lord makes it very clear that living our lives in obedience to his commandments and being especially kind to the widow, the orphan, the poor, or any brother or sister in his or her time of need, is well worth his blessings. He also makes it known in chapter 26 of the terrible judgments that will await any nation, state, city, or person who wantonly chooses to disregard these commandments and go his own way. Today, the United States has become so lost in the doctrines of political correctness and the woes of global warming that they have forgotten these promises that were made to us by God in the book of Leviticus.

But the most important message in all of this is what Jesus told us in Matthew chapter 5 from the outset that the completion of the Law is not complete without the foundation from which that Law was built. This then brings me to the next important subject regarding the Law and the prophets that became such a hotly disputed issue when the Apostle Paul met with the rest of the remaining apostles and elders of the church to argue its validity.

THE LAW OF CIRCUMCISION

As I stated earlier, when the dispute arose within the church as to whether or not the Gentiles should be circumcised before being baptized, it was finally decided that because they were not bound by the everlasting covenant of Abraham as the Jews themselves, this was not necessary for them. Then the apostles and the elders of the church finally told Paul, as he was about to leave the assembly and return to his mission field, that if his Gentile converts would just abstain from meat that had been offered to idols, from blood, from anything that had been strangled, and from sexual immorality, that they would be doing right as Christians (reference Acts 15:23–29). But Paul would soon become greatly out of step with the church's deep regard for the Law and the prophets and especially the law of circumcision as he began to teach both Jew and Gentile alike that salvation in Christ had nothing to do with either. He went on to teach that salvation was based entirely upon faith and the grace of God. This view taken by Paul soon created a lot of animosity between himself and the authoritative church center, as well as the rest of the Jewish community at that time (reference Acts 21:18–26). Even today this view has become the norm that is widely accepted in most every Christian church. Where it is now that Christians the world over have become very comfortable in dismissing everything the other eleven apostles and Jesus had to say about this matter, as they have quite blindly taken Paul's side.

Which then begs the question: who was right between them in their two opposing views concerning salvation? Was Paul, in saying that the Mosaic Law was now rendered obsolete along with the law of circumcision, as he believed and taught that it is only by faith and the circumcision of the heart that we are all saved by the grace of God, or were the other apostles and elders of the authoritative church right in saying that the Mosaic Law and the everlasting law of circumcision were both necessary and had to come first before salvation through baptism could be administered to the Jews? Furthermore, why didn't Jesus intervene to settle this matter?

I must admit that I was also a little troubled by this apparent conflict that arose between the church and the Apostle Paul at that time. So I decided to take this matter to God myself in the manner of prayer and quiet meditation in the hope of finding the answer to my questions. But as always, the Spirit directed me to the very Scriptures themselves and caused me to understand that through them shall the answer be made known. Then, after researching all the scriptures that I could find on this matter from within the Old and the New Testament, I lay down in quiet meditation and waited on the Lord to explain this mystery to me. The following is the answer that I received through the power of the Holy Spirit.

The reason why Jesus did not intervene is because they were both right in what they were teaching with respect to salvation, for they were each given two distinctly different commissions to fulfill. Paul was given a commission to preach the gospel to the Gentiles, and Peter, James, and John and all the rest of the apostles were given the commission to preach the gospel to the Jews. As such, Paul was right in saying that to God it didn't matter anymore whether we are Jew or Gentile, as salvation was now open to the whole world because of the crucifixion and resurrection of our Lord and Savior Jesus Christ. This meant that for the Gentiles, salvation was not contingent upon the Mosaic Law or the law of circumcision, for they had never known Abraham or Moses or, for that matter, the God of Abraham, Isaac, and Jacob, and as such, they were not bound by either covenant.

But Paul appeared to go one step too far when he began to teach the idea that now not even the Jews or, for that matter, any Israelite was bound by the old Mosaic Law or the everlasting law of circumcision as long as they had each put their faith in Jesus Christ and went to the next highest level of perfection and received the circumcision of the heart, and that is true. But here is the catch that will explain the mystery of God's purpose in all this, as the Holy Spirit has explained it to me.

What Paul was not telling us then was that there would be a consequence later for any Jew or Israelite who would be so bold as to relinquish the Mosaic Law and break the everlasting covenant that would come whether or not they had put their faith in Jesus Christ, and that consequence was, and still is, that they themselves will become Christian converts, but their children will no longer be Israelites. Rather, upon their own choice of action, their children will become Gentiles and, as a result, forfeit the rights of their lineage. This is not that much of a problem unless they are in the last two surviving groups to be divided by God at his second coming; whereas, if you have the fleshly seal of circumcision and have not taken the mark of the beast, you will be called home to the land of Zion and be a part of that group called: "the remnant of Israel who will be saved." But if you are not circumcised and have instead taken the mark of the beast, you will be either destroyed or banished from the inner kingdom where all the survivors of Israel who will be saved, as well as all the rest of those called the remnant of Israel will also be, and made to live in the outer kingdom along with all those who will be called the survivors of Gog and Magog.

This consequence also remains for all those people who thought they were Christians but who were instead deceived by Satan in believing that they were saved when, in fact, they were not. They too will reside with Gog and Magog in the outer most regions of God's kingdom, which is the lowest level, and the place where all those left alive who have taken the mark of the beast and yet called upon the name of the Lord will also be

THE BOOK OF REVELATION AND THE BIBLE
AS NEVER EXPLAINED BEFORE

placed. Also, because only those who are circumcised can be called Israelites, only those priests from within God's one true church who have perfected themselves in his love and have this fleshly seal of circumcision will be chosen from among all the other ordained priests and called one of God's elect. These are the hundred and forty-four thousand who will be the only ones to receive the seal of God and will each be chosen, twelve thousand from the twelve tribes of Israel. There will be no Gentiles or women in their number. This, therefore, is the consequence for every Christian and church that chooses or teaches its people not to circumcise their male babies at birth.

THE TWELFTH APOSTLE

In speaking about the twelve apostles as often as I have, there has always been one question that always seems to linger on and that is who exactly was the twelfth apostle? In the book of Acts, Peter stands before the assembled brotherhood and quotes the Psalms by King David regarding Judas, where it describes his end and how another should be allowed to take his place from among their company. So as two names came up, Matthias was chosen by the casting of lots over Joseph Barsabbas (reference Acts 1:15–26). But is he the twelfth apostle spoken of in the book of Revelation? I tell you now that no, he is not. It has been revealed to me that the twelfth apostle is none other than the Apostle Paul. The scriptural context of this revelation comes from the words of Christ himself where Jesus asked his disciples after the multitude of former followers left him in the sixth chapter of John:

> "Do you also want to go away?" But Simon Peter answered Him, "Lord, to whom shall we go? You have the words of eternal life. Also we have come to believe and know that You are the Christ, the Son of the living God." Jesus answered them, "Did I not choose you, the twelve, and one of you is a devil" John 6:67–70, (NKJV).

47

He was speaking, of course, as we all know, of Judas Iscariot. But what we all failed to pick up on was the terminology that Jesus had used here. "Have I not chosen you, all twelve?" In saying this, Jesus was telling us that just as he had personally chosen one of the twelve to be a devil, he was also going to be personally choosing his replacement and granting him the same commission to come and follow him as he had with the other original twelve and that chosen apostle was Paul.

All the rest that followed after these twelve apostles would be chosen by men by the casting of lots and laying on of hands, which, although recognized by God for their temporal commissions on earth, would not be included in the honorary number of those first twelve chosen by God to reign with him for a thousand years as the judges of Israel. As such, God was actually giving each of them to whom he had personally chosen a very special honor within this commission, which will not be instituted until after his millennial reign on earth begins. There they will not only be the last twelve members of that very elite group known in the book of Revelation as the twenty-four elders whose thrones surround the throne of God, but they will also be known as they come to serve with the other twelve elders as the twenty-four judges of Israel. During and even after the millennium, the twelve apostles will be remembered for all eternity as the twelve foundation stones of his church that had been built upon their own self-sacrifice. The other twelve elders will also be remembered for all eternity.

To commemorate this honor, when the *new heaven,* the *new earth,* and the *new Jerusalem* all come down from heaven at the time when all things are made new by our heavenly Father, there shall be seen lying beneath the city wall twelve foundation stones, each made of a different jewel, and on each stone there shall be the names of the twelve apostles (reference Matthew 19:27–29; also read Revelation 21:14 regarding the twelve foundation stones of the church).

THE BOOK OF REVELATION AND THE BIBLE
AS NEVER EXPLAINED BEFORE

BUT DO YOU TRULY BELIEVE IN GOD?

This is another question that has long troubled me into the night as I see how the world today, through Satan's deception, has been given a false understanding of what it truly means to believe in God. Millions of people all over this world think that they are born-again Christians simply because they said yes to God one day and acknowledge his existence as the basis of their belief and salvation while they continue doing the same things as they had done them before. If that were the case, then Satan and all his fallen angels would also be saved, born-again Christians. They not only believe in God, but they go to church every Sunday, subverting and perverting his gospel, and can quote and misquote the scriptures as well as they please. But they do not do the will of God nor are they obedient to his commandments.

For the truth of the matter is this: to believe is to have faith and to have faith is to have completed works and also to strive toward understanding every word that proceeds out of the mouth of God. To strive toward understanding every word that proceeds out of the mouth of God is to become obedient to his commandments and to have repented from one's participation in the deadly sins of the world; to have repented from the deadly sins of the world is to be transformed into a newborn creation in Christ through the baptism of the Holy Spirit, which, because of this person's new spiritual makeup and change of heart, must now begin the struggle toward the inward perfection of God's love. In becoming obedient to this charge every Christian is expected, at some point in his or her walk or struggle in life, to ultimately achieve this goal. It is from this achievement that holiness comes, as the very Spirit or presence of God comes to dwell within him or her in all humility. The same shall be true for anyone else who claims to be a Christian or who is to be called one of God's chosen people. Once a convert makes this ultimate transformation into the Spirit of Christ, he can no longer return to his former sinful and lustful

49

ways of the world, as a dog always returns to its own vomit, or else he will become cutoff from any inheritance in the kingdom of God and destined for the lake of fire. Finally, to have the inward perfection of God's love and the outward glow of holiness is to be ready when Jesus comes for his chosen people. For this is truly what it means to believe and also what Jesus meant when he commanded us to be perfect and holy, even as his Father in heaven is perfect and holy. Otherwise, though it may be virtually impossible for us to be perfect in everything that we do, nevertheless, it is still God's wish and commandment that we never stop trying. Reference the King James Version of Matthew 5:48 regarding the commandment for us all to be perfect by Jesus, and 1 Peter 1:15 regarding the Lord's commandment for us all to be holy, as our Father in heaven is holy.

THE PERFECTION OF LOVE

But what is love, and, most importantly, how are we to become perfected in love if we don't really know what God means by it? The answer to this question comes to us by two means: first, by the account the Apostle Paul gives to us in 1 Corinthians 13, where he gives to us the basic attributes that comprise his spiritually inspired concept of what the word *love* means. Whereby he states: "Love is always patient and kind; love is never jealous; love is never boastful or conceited, it is never rude and never seeks its own advantage, it does not take offense or store up grievances. Love does not rejoice at wrong doing, but finds its joy in the truth. It is always ready to make allowances, to trust, to hope, and to endure whatever comes" (1 Corinthians 13:4–7, TNJB). He finishes by telling us that his love will always be there for us without fail and that it shall endure forever. Whereas, it is certain, that all the other things of this world will not.

Second, I believe that in conjunction with what the Apostle Paul is saying here in 1 Corinthians 13, we can get an even further understanding of what God means by his love when we

THE BOOK OF REVELATION AND THE BIBLE
AS NEVER EXPLAINED BEFORE

view the life that his son, Jesus Christ, lived for us while on earth. Only then can we see this concept in its true and perfected state. I now present this concept to you in the form of what I have come to call the twelve attributes of God's love, as viewed through the life of Christ, and after these I will then present to you the seven virtues of his love. It should also be pointed out that some of these twelve attributes of God's love may very well be thought of by some as virtues in and of themselves, but for the sake of this explanation, I have chosen to divide them into these two groups.

The first attribute of God's love is *humility*. The first thing that Jesus showed us by his life here on earth was that he loved his Father and each and every one of us so much that he was willing to leave behind his most exalted place in high heaven to be born to us here on earth in a manger in all humility. From this, we can see that *the foundation of God's love is humility* and learning how to perfect our lives in it is one of the greatest things we will ever achieve in our lifetime, as opposed to the futility of seeking self-righteous exaltation either from within the church or from without. For Jesus said: "But he who is greatest among you shall be your servant. And whoever exalts himself will be humbled, and he who humbles himself will be exalted" (Matthew 23:11–12, NKJV). Jesus also said, "Assuredly, I say to you, unless you are converted and become as little children you will by no means enter the kingdom of heaven" (Matthew 18:1–4, NKJV).

The second attribute of God's love is *obedience*. Jesus showed us through his life here on earth just how devoted he was to living his life in obedience to his Father's will as he went out to teach the world his Father's gospel. For Jesus said this to his disciples: "He who has My commandments and keeps them, it is he who loves Me. And he who loves Me will be loved by My Father, and I will love him and manifest Myself to him" (John 14:21, NKJV). Here it is clear to see that being obedient to the commandments of the Lord is critical to knowing the

51

very basics of what it takes for each of us to become perfected in God's love and also to winning his favor; for God has absolutely no use for those people who pay him lip service but whose hearts are far from him in everything else that they do. Disobedience will never have a place in the kingdom of God.

The third attribute of God's love is *faith*. Jesus showed us through his life here on earth how he remained faithful to the purpose for which his Father had sent him. That purpose was, in part, to teach the world that to have faith in him was not only critical to their individual healings along with the many blessings that followed, but it was also a necessary part of what it would eventually take for all of us to gain our salvation, as it is only through our faith in God, along with all the rest of those attributes that make up the perfection of his love, that anyone will ever enter into the royal house, which is the highest level attainable within the kingdom of God.

It is also written, "So then faith comes by hearing and hearing by the word of God" (Romans 10:17, NKJV), or better still, by every word that proceeds out of the mouth of God. It also follows that God did not give us his every word so that we could just pick and choose the ones that we like best to suit our fancy. Rather he has given us his every word so that we may be better able to both worship him in spirit and truth and to more comprehensively understand his will through our faith in him. But I also know that God has given us his every word so as to be justified in holding us accountable to it on the great Day of Judgment.

The last two points I wish to make concerning faith comes first from the Apostle James when he states that the most important aspect about faith is this: "—that faith without works is dead" (James 2:20, KJV). The Apostle Paul also gives a very good explanation of what faith is when he says that, "Faith is the substance of things hoped for, by the evidence of that which is unseen" (Hebrews 11:1, KJV). All throughout the life of Christ we can see just how important this one attribute of faith was to himself and his Father as he performed countless miracles on the sick and the afflicted in the mission fields of his ministry.

The fourth attribute of God's love is *hope*. It was out of Jesus' sheer love for us that no matter how much he suffered before and after he was hung on the cross, he never gave up the hope that his death and resurrection would bring the salvation of the world. In this way, Jesus taught us that we too could have this same hope in a life after death with him when his millennial kingdom finally does come down to earth where we shall reign with him for a thousand years and in the next world have eternal life.

The fifth attribute of God's love is *charity*. For God so loved the world that he gave his only begotten son as both a gift to the poor and as a living sacrifice for the forgiveness of sins so that whosoever would just believe in him would be saved. Also, Jesus, out of this same love shown by his Father, continued to give to all those in need of his blessings the many miracles that he performed on the sick, the blind, the lame, and the poor, both feeding and healing the multitudes without discrimination to their race, creed, or color. In this same way, we too must share our gifts of the spirit with others and give generously to the poor around us without discrimination, and one day we may even find ourselves helping an angel of the Lord disguised as an old beggar.

The sixth attribute of God's love is *truth*. Wherever Jesus went, he always boldly bore witness to the truth, even at great risk to his own safety. With regard to the *truth:* The truth is perhaps the most important attribute of all and the most easily overlooked. For Jesus said, "God is Spirit, and those who worship Him must worship in spirit and in truth" (John 4:24–25, NKJV). It follows then that all other worship of him that is not in spirit and in truth must be in vain. The Gospel of Matthew puts it this way when quoting the prophet Isaiah: "These people draw near to Me with their mouth, and honor Me with their lips, but their heart is far from Me. And in vain they worship

Me, teaching as doctrines the commandments of men" (Matthew 15:8–9, NKJV).

We can see from this that to merely say that we love God, or for that matter, even singing the praises of how much we love God in church every Sunday, is not what God wants if we are not, first of all, living our lives in obedience to his commandments. But what is just as important is that we take the time to come to know God through his inspired Word as it is contained within the many different books of the Bible. These are all the Holy Scriptures that have been handed down to us by his prophets of the Old Testament and by his Son and some of his apostles in the New Testament. These Holy Scriptures have been given to us for our edification and for our understanding of all that God wants for us and our children to do to be ready when his kingdom finally does comes down to earth. But it is only when we strive to gain a comprehensive understanding of the truth, as God's Word tells it, that the Holy Spirit will then reveal to us the hidden truths and mysteries that are also contained within this extraordinary book we call the Bible. Why else would God the Father have taken such pains through the sacrifice of his only Son to deliver all this information to us if he didn't want us to come to understand it and how much more to worship him in it?

The seventh attribute of God's love is *showing compassion*. Wherever Jesus went, he always looked upon the people with such great compassion from his heart as he very patiently took his time attending to their needs. In the same way we need to be compassionate to others and demonstrate this same quality of love to all whom we meet who are in need of it, even when there is no justification for it. It is only in this way that we can show our love to others and become the closest thing to Christ that the poor and the down trodden of this world will ever see. For this is yet another great example of what it truly means to be a Christian or once again Christlike.

THE BOOK OF REVELATION AND THE BIBLE
AS NEVER EXPLAINED BEFORE

The eighth attribute of God's love is *kindness*. This attribute follows close behind this last one as *showing compassion* and *kindness* really go together, and Jesus made no distinction between either as he would go forth to demonstrate both of these attributes to even those Romans who would be so bold as to approach him in their hour of need. In the same way, we are to go forth and show all whom we meet this same kind of loving compassion and kindness as Jesus showed us while he was here on earth. We must especially be compassionate and kind to those who would otherwise hate and despise us or else be hated and despised themselves.

The ninth attribute of God's love is being *fearless or otherwise being courageous* especially in the face of the enemy. All throughout Jesus' ministry he was continually faced with the death threats of the Jewish supreme council, but he never let any of them deter him from his Father's mission. Even in the face of death by crucifixion as he was brought before Pilate, the Roman governor, Jesus showed no fear but willingly gave his life for our salvation. In the same way, we must also go forth and boldly proclaim the truth about his gospel no matter who it might offend or even if it should put our very lives in danger. God is looking for the humble as well as the courageous and the bold to serve his cause. There will be no place for the cowardly in his kingdom.

The tenth attribute of God's love is *self-sacrifice*. This attribute is perhaps the greatest one of all, as Jesus showed us that the true meaning behind his self-sacrifice was that he loved us all so much that he was willing to lay his life down for our salvation. For it is written: "Greater love has no one than this, than to lay down one's life for his friends" (John 15:13, NKJV). Although this form of self-sacrifice represents the extreme, it is still possible to attain to a lesser level of this attribute by simply putting the needs of others before your own and sacrificing your own time, money, or special gifts and helping others who are less fortunate than you. But it is still possible that one day even you too will be presented with the ultimate test of your faith when the man the book of Revelation calls the beast comes to give you the choice of either to take his mark and live or die for your belief in Christ, just as it was for those Christians who chose to die in the Roman Coliseum during the reign of Emperor Nero. This is the other ultimate form of self-sacrifice.

The eleventh attribute of God's love is *forgiveness*. Finally, after being crucified and suffering untold pains and agonies at the hands of the Romans under the direction of the high priest and the Jewish supreme council, Jesus said, "Father forgive them, for they know not what they do" (Luke 23:34, KJV). After which, Jesus committed his spirit into his Father's hands and with his final words, "It is finished," he died.

This is the one attribute that without which there can be no hope of salvation for any of us. Jesus made this point very clear to us in the Lord's Prayer where he, in essence, stated that if we wish God to forgive us for our trespasses, then we must first forgive all those who have trespassed against us, no matter what they might have done. It is only in this way that we ourselves can be forgiven. At this point, Jesus had, for the most part, demonstrated to all of us what it truly means to be perfected in his Father's love, where it is also written, "It is good to give thanks to the Lord, for his love *endures* forever" (Psalm 118:1, TNEB), which then brings me to the last attribute.

The twelfth attribute of God's love is *endurance*. Jesus, by his own sacrificial death on the cross, had shown to all of us that he was willing and able to endure the pains and sufferings of this world to the end. In the same way and by his own perfect example, he had shown to all of us who claim to be Christians that we too must also endure the pains and sufferings of this world until the end if we truly wish to enter into his kingdom and receive a golden crown of glory by which to rule by. Likewise, it was the Apostle Paul who had also told us that we must finish the race if we wish to obtain the prize of salvation, for who has ever been awarded a medal without having first completed the race?

These then are the twelve attributes of God's love as viewed through the life of Christ, but they are still not complete without an understanding of the seven virtues of God's love being added to them. It is through these next seven virtues that a true mastery of one's self comes and, as such, puts the finishing touches on what it truly means to be perfected in his love.

The first virtue of God's love is *patience.* This is first because it is only through patience that God teaches us also how to control ourselves and, most importantly, our anger that is too often brought about by our impatience with mechanical things or else the people in our lives or even our pets. It is through patience that God will also come to test our resolve just to see if we will remain faithful to him and steadfast to his command that we love one another before he will grant our special requests, or, for that matter, even listen to any of our prayers. How many times have you asked God for something and then expected him to get it for you the next day, just like a spoiled child, only to find that God made you wait sometimes one, two, even three years or beyond before that special someone or something was finally delivered to you? Sometimes God will make you wait because of the time and preparation required before some deliveries can be made ready for you. But other times it may very well be God waiting on you to get yourself ready for them. We have all heard the sayings "Good things come to those who wait" or "Easy come, easy go." So if you really want that special someone or something to last throughout the test of time, patience is the first virtue you must master. Such is the case when asking God for a new home or a husband or even a wife to share your new home with. Too often, when we try to jump off into things without first allowing God the time to properly prepare us, the results can be disastrous. If you really want to know how to win God's heart over in granting you such things as these, then first strive to perfect yourself in both the twelve attributes of his love and also these seven virtues, but never forget the importance of patience. Then God will put you at the top of his list and bring to you the desires of your heart and bless you with them.

On the other hand, we must also learn to have patience with one another as God has taken so much of his time being patient with us. We must especially learn to have patience with our children as we teach them to wait on us and their preparation before they too can be ready to win from us the desires of their hearts. Only then will this virtue return back to us full circle as we see in our children what God sees in us.

The second virtue of God's love is *tolerance.* Tolerance is important because without it God's love could not be complete. God would have simply destroyed us all a long time ago for the lack of it. But it is only because of his tolerance that the wicked have any hope of salvation if they would only turn from their wicked ways and humble themselves and then pray for his forgiveness. In the same way, we too must be tolerant of the wicked, as we can only bear our testimonies to them, and if we are not able to do that, then we at least should be able to let our light shine upon them so that one day they too may be able to see the error of their ways and find salvation in Christ Jesus.

The third virtue of God's love is *understanding.* This is important because without understanding, the Word of God would be meaningless to us, and without which we could never have any hope of appreciating the wisdom of God in all the things within the universe that he has created. But because God has given us understanding, we must use it to fathom the unfathomable and to reach the unreachable star. Above all, we must use it to appreciate God and one another for our differences so that they may all be used for the glory of God and the good of mankind.

The fourth virtue of God's love is *honesty.* This is another great virtue that we as Christians must come to perfect early on in our lives if we wish to have any place in the kingdom of God. Dishonesty may be an acceptable lifestyle with the wicked, but it is not acceptable in God's true church or especially in his king-

THE BOOK OF REVELATION AND THE BIBLE
AS NEVER EXPLAINED BEFORE

dom that is to come. We as Christians must also be true to our words as we live our lives as righteous examples for all the world to see, so that in all of this we may be found trustworthy to both God and men. It is only in this way that we bring honor to both ourselves and to God, for we are his representatives here on earth.

The fifth virtue of God's love is *cleanliness*. And David said, "Wash me thoroughly from mine iniquity and cleanse me from my sin. For I acknowledge my transgressions, and my sin is ever before me" (Psalm 51:2–3, KJV). He went on to say, "Create in me a clean heart, O God, and renew a right spirit within me" (Psalm 51:10, KJV). David prayed this prayer of repentance because he had committed a grievous sin in killing Uriah the Hittite for his wife, Bathsheba.

In the same way, just as David prayed for a clean heart and a right spirit for his sins with Bathsheba, so must we pray for our sins that we may also be given a clean heart and a right spirit for God, for we have all sinned and fallen short of the glory of God at one time or another in our lives. But we as Christians have been commanded by God to strive toward perfection and holiness and at some point in our lives to actually achieve it. David committed this one grievous sin before God and was forgiven for it, but it is only because he went on from there to live a life that was totally devoted to the perfection of God's love. In doing this, he proved to God that he was truly repentant of his sins and not just paying him lip service for his forgiveness as so many people who call themselves Christians are doing today. David went on to be regarded by God as the most righteous man who ever lived and, as such, has become another one of the truly great examples for each of us to follow after. For it is only in this way, as demonstrated by the life and this one subsequent prayer of repentance by David, that our hearts will ever be made ready for the Lord's Holy Spirit to come and dwell within. And just as our hearts are to be made clean for God, how much more should our own physical bodies and the very places in which we

59

dwell with our families also be made clean and kept that way? For cleanliness is next to godliness.

The sixth virtue of God's love is *purity*. As God's newly chosen people, not only are we to keep our hearts clean, but we are also to keep them pure as well. But purity goes even beyond the condition of our hearts, as we are to not only keep our thoughts, our words, and our deeds pure, but our bodies pure as well. It is because of the new covenant that our bodies are now supposed to be the new holy temples of God. With respect to this, that means that we are not to desecrate our bodies with tattoos or scarring. We especially are not to abuse them with gluttonous eating and drinking or infuse them with addictive drugs and cigarette smoke. Living our lives in a balance and with moderation is the key that brings nourishment to our bodies and a long healthy life; never should there be any overindulgence. Rather, our bodies and hearts are to be kept clean, pure, and holy, as would be fit for a royal king to find as a place for refuge and inner sanctuary.

And for those young girls not yet given in marriage, this virtue also applies to them, as they are to maintain their purity through their virginity. In so doing, they bring honor to their husbands to be and also to themselves, as marriage is a holy union and a blood covenant relationship joined together by God and consecrated through the blood of the bride's virginity on her wedding night. But Satan has come and corrupted God's institution of holy matrimony and caused it to become an abomination in his eyes with the advent of state-sponsored gay marriage. But as Christians, we must hold on to this virtue and maintain our purity even in the face of this evil onslaught that has become so welcomed by the world.

The seventh virtue of God's love is *devotion*. Devotion is the highest and the most heartwarming of all the other virtues because it denotes a total commitment of one's heart, soul, mind, and strength to the loving service of another. Such was the kind of love that Jesus had for his Father and each and every one of us when he died on the cross, and it is to this end that we have all been commanded to love our heavenly Father as well. But how much better is it when we as Christians can truly come to love our heavenly Father not because we have been commanded to do so but instead because of our undying appreciation and understanding of all that the Father and his Son have both given up for our salvation? The Father first, because he gave his only Son as the ultimate sacrifice for the forgiveness of our sins, and the Son second, because he willingly allowed himself to suffer and die on the cross for us as the sacrificial Lamb of God by whose blood we are all cleansed from those very sins so that whosoever would just believe in him would be saved.

In the same way, and second only to this kind of devotion, are wives supposed to be devoted to their husbands and husbands to their wives, and both are supposed to be devoted to their children's upbringing so that they too may come to know what it truly means to love one another.

This then is the true meaning behind what is meant by our being perfected in God's love. It is only through the perfection of God's love that holiness comes. How unfortunate it is that to the rest of the world love is but a feeling or a four-letter word we pay in lip service to one another without the slightest understanding of what it truly means to love. To the world there is a thin line between love and hate, but to God where there is love, there can be no hate, and neither can there be any fear—not from the evils of this world and especially not of God. For with this kind of love there comes only the peace of knowing that all of those who achieve it will share a place with the Lamb of God in his royal house. But if a man says he loves God while hating his brother, he makes himself out to be a liar, and such a man will never enter the kingdom of God, neither shall any man who is afraid to venture forth and do the will of God at the risk of insult, injury, or even the loss of his own life (reference 1 John 4:18–20).

But what about mercy? A dear friend once asked me this question as I was sharing with him about the twelve attributes and seven virtues of God's love. I replied, after taking a moment to consider his question, mercy is something that goes along with justice and is rendered by all those who shall sit in the judgment seat to decide the punishment of others who have either broken the law or else have ignored their call to salvation. Mercy and justice are also those things that constitute the heart of the law as handed down to us through Moses. However, we as Christians are not supposed to judge anyone outside of the fellowship, and truly it is better for us not to pass any kind of judgment at all, but rather, we have been commanded by God to love one another, and wherever the attributes of forgiveness, compassion, and kindness may be found, there in the midst you will also find mercy.

HEBREW OR ISRAELITE?

This is another misunderstanding that I would like to clarify here before I move on to the next section of my book that has to do with where the basis for the name Hebrew comes from, which was the name given by Pharaoh as another name used to describe the Israelites. The name Hebrew is used for the first time in the Bible in the book of Genesis in Genesis 14:12–13 when a fugitive came and called Abram the *Hebrew,* for he dwelt in the plain full of the terebinth trees of Mamre, the Amorite (which, plain of terebinth trees, was also called *Hebron*), and told him that the four kings had just carried off his nephew Lot with all his flocks and herds. Historians can only speculate as to where this name has its origin in spite of the context that is being used here in Genesis 13:18 and also in Genesis 14:12–13. Their best guess is that it comes from one of Abraham's fore-fathers, whose name was Eber, a descendant of Shem, who was also one of the three sons of Noah, which makes no sense whatsoever. It becomes even worse when they try to say that Eber may have been pronounced Heber.

The truth of the matter is this: Abraham is for the first time regarded as a Hebrew after he is shown a preview of all the land that God is going to give to him and all his descendants forever in the land of Canaan (Genesis 13:14–17). This is, in fact, the same Promised Land that will be given as an everlasting possession through the everlasting covenant that is to be drawn up just a little while later between God and Abraham in Genesis 15:1–21. But just before this covenant is drawn up, Abraham goes into this same land that God has just promised to him and all his descendants and settles in the *land of Hebron,* by the terebinth trees of Mamre. Once there he goes to set up the altar of the Lord (reference Genesis 13:18). It is on this basis that Abraham is regarded as a *Hebrew* for the first time in the Bible. Just as our founding forefathers who came to settle in the land of America were also called Americans, or as also the Philistines, who today have become known to us as the Palestinians, had their name derived from the land of Philistia, which bordered Israel at that time. Though it appears that in some cases the name given to the land may have its origin with the people, or a forefather, as is the case with the nation of Israel and as it was with the land of Canaan, in this case it comes from the land whose name preceded Abraham's coming and remains Hebron to this day. Also God's covenant began with Abraham and included no one else before him, for it was God who said that I am the God of Abraham, Isaac, and Jacob. Nowhere is the name Eber or Heber to be found in that alliance.

THE RECORD OF PAUL

The rest of Acts speaks of the works and travels of the Apostle Paul, along with some of his companions as he continued his outreach ministry unto the Gentiles. We are shown here how Paul always followed a similar pattern of preaching, going first to the Jewish synagogues where he invited both Jews and Gentiles alike to hear the gospel of Jesus Christ as he traveled throughout the region (reference Acts 17:1–3). His ministry ranged all throughout various regions of the Mediterranean in what has been more classically described as his four missionary journeys. But he especially traveled through the inner regions of Asia where these seven churches were located. We are actually told that he spent a number of years in this region of Asia. *Ephesus* is one of those churches that he helped to foster while in Asia before being called back to Jerusalem. While in Ephesus, he preached to the Jews and Gentiles alike so that both would hear the gospel of Jesus Christ and receive the baptism of the Holy Spirit. What is interesting about Ephesus is that when Paul later returned to the city, he was amazed to see that some of the people had only heard of John the Baptist's ministry. We are then told that Paul went on to explain the good news about the gospel of Jesus Christ to John's followers and afterward he baptized them in the Holy Spirit as well, in Acts 19:1–7.

But his final calling, which was in fulfillment of the commission already given to him by Jesus himself, was that he take the gospel into Rome. He was finally taken to Rome by an appeal he made to King Agrippa during his trial in Jerusalem. Once in Rome, he too would be very instrumental in laying the spiritual groundwork for the coming of the great Roman Catholic Church. Emperor Nero eventually would put him to death in AD 67 for his faith in Christ as it is also believed that the apostle Peter had been killed before him. While in and out of prison, the Apostle Paul is accredited for having written the greater part of the New Testament.

THE RECORD OF JOHN

The Apostle John, who is also referred to as John the Evangelist, was perhaps the most loyal of all the apostles. He was the son of Zebedee, a fisherman by trade. His brother James was also one of the twelve apostles. John was one of the first of the apostles to join the company of Jesus at the beginning of his ministry. He accompanied the Lord at the raising of Jairus' daughter, the transfiguration, and during the agony in the garden of Gethsemane. John's steadfast belief in Jesus as being the Messiah and his emotional temperament sometimes caused him to say things that brought a quick reprimand from the Lord (reference Luke 9:49–56), but as the biblical record has shown, he would also become known to us as the one to whom he loved, as written in the Gospel of John.

John also attended the trial of Jesus. He was present at the crucifixion and accepted the responsibility of caring for Mary, Jesus' mother (reference John 19:25–27). He was among the first to investigate the tomb on Easter morning to find it empty. Following Pentecost, he preached and taught with Peter in Jerusalem until the time of the great persecutions. It was during that time that King Herod attacked certain members of the church and had John's brother James beheaded. This was also the same time that Peter was arrested and thrown into prison and later made his miraculous escape. We last hear of the Apostle John in the book of Acts at the big council of all the apostles and elders of the church in Jerusalem when they were trying to resolve the issue over circumcision.

In John's later years, the biblical record tells us that he was eventually exiled to the Isle of Patmos and stayed there for a while preaching the gospel, and it was from there that he recorded the message of the seven churches and the book of Revelation as it was revealed to him by God through Jesus Christ. The Apostle John is also accredited with having written the fourth gospel and the three Epistles. He is the only one of the twelve apostles who died a natural death.

65

DECIPHERING THE HIDDEN MESSAGE OF THE SEVEN CHURCHES

It is important to understand that up to now all that I have said has come purely by way of the historical as well as the biblical record, but after this point, I will be deciphering the truth by way of the Holy Spirit and supporting this with scriptural affirmation. Otherwise, this historic and biblical perspective as it has been presented was necessary as a preparation for what I am about to say next as I begin to decipher the hidden truths contained in this message to the seven churches and also to the rest of the book of Revelation that was given by Jesus Christ through his beloved servant John. The following are the seven levels of understanding given to me by the Holy Spirit after first laboring greatly in prayer and meditation over a period of several weeks before finally being given the understanding to this very powerful message.

The first level of understanding: This is the obvious understanding, and shows how this message appears to have been written for these seven churches alone to ponder and to take heed to all the things that were being said to them by Christ. For here we see seven churches that had been especially selected by Christ to serve as an example for the others to learn from, because of all the internal problems that some of these churches were having at that time that were unique to themselves. Where we are shown how five out of the seven churches had allowed themselves to become both infiltrated and corrupted by Satan while the other two did not. Of the other two churches, the one church of Smyrna was forcibly overtaken by Satan's synagogue and persecuted unto death. Only the one church of Philadelphia had not allowed either situation to happen. They are shown here to be the only church out of the seven who kept God's commands and who did not disown his name. Because of this, the church of Philadelphia, which means *the church of brotherly love*, was then set apart and given power over Satan's synagogue as an example to the rest of how God's perfected church should be.

If you are to just focus on this aspect of the message, it is very easy to assume that because this message was written on a single scroll and sent directly to these seven churches and nobody else that it was only intended for those congregations alone to see and to understand. But this is not the case, as Jesus clearly states to John in the first chapter of Revelation, where it is written: "Write the things that you have seen, and the things which are, and the things which will take place after this" (Revelation 1:19, NKJV). With this verse we are given the one clue that tells us that there is a lot more to this message than meets the eye. This then brings me to the next level of understanding.

The second level of understanding: We see from this one clue that this message was not just meant for the eyes and ears of these seven churches, but it was also meant as a warning to

THE BOOK OF REVELATION AND THE BIBLE
AS NEVER EXPLAINED BEFORE

all God's churches past, present, and to those churches yet to appear in our not too distant future. For here we are given six examples of just how easy it was for Satan to infiltrate God's church, even in its infancy. We are also shown how very success-ful he was in corrupting all but one of these six churches whom he had managed to infiltrate. But more importantly, we are also shown the six methods that Satan had used in this example and will use in the future to try to subvert the gospel of Jesus Christ right out of any church that will not take heed to this message.

The following are the six methods that Satan will use to infiltrate God's churches:

1. The first method as shown in the church of Ephesus is where Satan will come into a church of God and with great subtlety begin to create problems that will test the congregation's abil-ity to judge fairly within the fellowship as they strive to keep holiness in and the evildoers out. With this command that Paul preached, we are warned by Jesus not to become so over-zealous in this quest that we lose our love for one another. For as Paul also said, "Though I speak with the tongues of men and angels, but have not love, I have become sounding brass or a clanging cymbal. And although I have the gift of prophecy, and understand all mysteries and all knowledge, and though I have all faith, so that I could remove mountains; but have not love, I am nothing" (1 Corinthians 13:1–3, NKJV). That is why Jesus said to this one church if they did not repent of this loss of love for one another he would come to remove their lamp from its place (reference Revelation 2:1–7).

2. The second method as shown in the church of Smyrna is where Satan will forcibly come into a church of God by the powers that be and remove that congregation and throw them into prison. There they will be tortured cruelly and finally put to death as the ultimate test of their faith (refer-ence Revelation 2:8–11).

69

This actually speaks of a great many times in history when Christians have become martyrs for Christ. But symbolically, it speaks of both the time of Nero and of the time of the end when Christians will once again become martyrs for Christ by the testimonies they bear of him, as mentioned in the fifth seal of Revelation, where I believe the world is presently standing (Revelation 6:9–11). Otherwise, this method is also symbolic of the time immediately following the sixth trumpet and leading up to the second coming of Christ when the *beast* will cause everyone who is left on the earth to either take his mark on his or her right hand or forehead or be tortured and killed. For these are the other company of God's chosen people spoken of in Revelation 7:9–10, 13–15 who are called the *great multitude* that no one could count. These are also those of God's people who shall be left behind just before the sixth trumpet is sounded because they were simply unable to attain to the same level of perfection and holiness as the hundred and forty-four thousand had before them and, as such, must endure the *beast's great reign of terror* until they are either killed by the beast or live to see the second coming of the Lord for their deliverance. Here it is that many of God's people will be lead like lambs to the slaughter as the beast gives them the ultimate test of their faith (Revelation 20:4–6).

That is why this distinction is made between them and the church of Philadelphia. Smyrna was not faithful to God's command or the hallowing of his name as the church of Philadelphia was then, and so they had to suffer all the way through that *great ordeal* brought about by Nero, as many millions of Christians are going to have to suffer in our not too distant future when the beast's great reign of terror that was prophesied in the book of Revelation suddenly comes upon them.

This method is also representative of any number of thousands of righteous men and women who right now are being persecuted, imprisoned, tortured, or killed for the sake of God's Word and the testimonies that they bear. Even now as I write this, we are seeing the reality of this method as it is being used

THE BOOK OF REVELATION AND THE BIBLE
AS NEVER EXPLAINED BEFORE

in the greater part of the Muslim world as it was in China not too long ago and the former Soviet Union.

3. The third method as shown in the church of Pergamum is where Satan will come into an unsuspecting church and begin to pour out all manner of evil practice and temptation under the ancient disguise of the doctrine of the Nicolations, or, as it is better known today, as the doctrines of political correctness. Within these doctrines is also cloaked the ancient lie that man is the center of the universe, where all things, including his god or however many gods he decides to fashion out of his own two hands, are here to serve him at his convenience. This doctrinal way of thinking is better known today as humanism. With these two doctrines we can see just how perversely effective Satan has been at gutting all the laws of holiness and the teachings of Paul right out of a great many Christian churches, both Catholic and Protestant (reference Revelation 2:12–17).

Over the last thirty years, I have witnessed the evolution of political correctness and humanism within the church from the perspective of one searching to find the one true church of God from among many different churches and denominations. I have witnessed for myself how a great many pastors, priests, as well as other Christian preachers and evangelists have worked very hard at preaching messages that did not offend the other liberal members of the congregation and their ever-evolving humanistic political agenda. At the same time, this liberal movement from within the church has been working very hard at casting God out of all state and federal government and, even worse, from all our public schools. Meanwhile, all the good Christian people of the church for years have sat around and done nothing because they were just too afraid that if they said anything that it might offend somebody or, worse, expose them for being out of step with the ever-changing times of political correctness.

71

At Pergamum you will notice that Jesus first compliments this church for not denying their faith in him even as the Lord's faithful servant Antipas is killed bearing witness to him in their city, which is the home of Satan. This is not untypical of how so many other Christian churches are situated in similar cities all throughout the United States or even in the world. But afterward, Jesus brings up the small matter of how Satan has been allowed to bring this method, along with its accompanying agenda, into the very midst of their fellowship without any complaints and then very subtly begins the slow process of subverting his gospel right out of their church.

Today, we can see that Satan has been very hard at work all across the United States using this same method and has been doing so for at least the past fifty years, as I have witnessed it. At first Satan began watering down the church's stand on marriage and divorce by legalizing the no fault divorce process for ending a marriage, making adultery legally acceptable. Then he turned to popularizing fornication with the slogan, "Make love not war." Along with this came birth control and his new "sex, drugs, and rock and roll" approach to having a better and fuller life, teamed together with the Age of Aquarius and "What sign are you?" Then he popularized his next perverse idea with this question why get married when you can just live together with someone of either the same sex or opposite sex? It's all just a matter of choosing which lifestyle you wish to indulge yourself in. Next, came *Roe v. Wade* and the legalization of abortion, along with its counterpart, partial birth abortion, and the slogan that makes it all sound so right, "pro choice." Then came the corrupt issues of separation of church and state and the laws that made having prayer in our public schools suddenly illegal.

All this came, and some of it was even made into law, and then all of it was accepted within the church fellowship while the church stood by and did nothing. In fact, it was by the vote of thousands of so-called Christian church members all across this country that this whole politically correct agenda came into being. It took September 11 and finally hearing the liberal atheists actually spelling out how they would not rest until they had removed any and all mention of the word God from off all our currencies and further making it illegal for the word God or prayer or any suggestive idea about God to be used in either our public schools or state assemblies under the pain of either expulsion or imprisonment before the church finally woke up! This was and continues to be the liberal atheist's ultimate dream and vision for our nation.

On the other side of this issue has come the complete perversion to the idea of what our forefathers meant by freedom of religion, as we are now being forced to accept any and every form of idol worship and false god that man can dream up, all of which has been done in an effort to offend the one true God by whom this nation of ours was truly made great as this new humanistic renaissance of ancient Rome kicks into full swing.

In April 2004, a decision was handed down by the First United Methodist Church in Ellensburg, Washington, by a panel of 13 ministers, who after three days of deliberations, acquitted the Rev. Karen Dammann of the charges that because she was a self-avowed practicing Lesbian she should not be allowed to stand before the congregation and preach the word of God as it was an alleged violation of United Methodist Church Law. She was acquitted on a technicality leaning toward liberal interpretation of the Church law and remains a Pastor to this day. However in all fairness, it should also be mentioned that on October 31, 2005, in another jurisdiction of the church, another decision was also handed down by the United Methodist Court, in an official response to the first, involving the Rev. Irene Elizabeth "Beth" Stroud from Germantown, PA. In this decision the Rev. Stroud was officially stripped of her ministerial credentials after disclosing that she too was a self-avowed practicing lesbian during a sermon in 2003, but not before two other court battles had ensued. First, in the lower court where she first lost her credentials in December 2004, by a 12 to 1 vote;

and second, in the appeals court where they were reinstated in April 2005, by a 8 to 1 vote. Finally, in October 2005, by an undisclosed vote that came from the Church's highest judicial body, the Judicial Council, she was officially stripped of her credentials in an effort to put an end to this matter. But the church remains divided to this day over whether or not homosexuality should be allowed and accepted within both the fellowship and the clergy as the liberals continue to press for change.

As a final note: These court battles, regarding the Rev. Stroud, occurred in the Church's Northeastern Jurisdiction as a part of the Eastern Pennsylvania Conference. The final case was decided in the Stansbury Building of the Westchase Campus of the First United Methodist Church in Houston. The Rev. Dammann's court case occurred in a Northwestern Jurisdiction in Washington State, and as such, was not within the Judicial Council's jurisdiction to change that ruling.

Along with this many other Christian churches have now begun the drive to have gay and lesbian marriages legally consummated within the house of the Lord. Thus fulfilling what both Paul and John warned would happen if those of us who have been entrusted with the responsibility of watching over his sheep let our guards down or, worse, allow the purposeful watering down of the gospel so as not to offend the liberal members of the congregation. And at the same time avoiding any hell fire messages that might otherwise lead to their salvation but most probably would only drive them out of the church where they belong. All of this is being done for the sake of appeasement so as to keep the popularity and membership of the churches up while at the same time keeping the tithes and offerings coming in. In doing this, these wolves in sheep's clothing have not only sold God out, but they have also forsaken his Son's sacrifice for their sins.

They have also forgotten Jesus' command that we should keep his Father's everlasting name, Jehovah, (or Yahweh) holy and worship him in spirit and in truth no matter who it might

THE BOOK OF REVELATION AND THE BIBLE
AS NEVER EXPLAINED BEFORE

offend or what the consequences might be for it. Regarding the everlasting name of Jehovah (reference Exodus 3:14–16). But what is the truth, you may ask? The truth is that faith comes by hearing and hearing comes by every word that proceeds from the mouth of God, whether it is from the Old Testament or the New. It, however, is not to be found in the one or two or more verses that so many Christians have come to found their faith upon while they so conveniently misinterpret these verses to conform to their very busy and politically correct ways of life. Most importantly, Jesus said that if you truly loved him, then you would keep his commandments. For just as his father in heaven is holy, so are we to be holy here on earth, keeping our spiritual temples clean and purified as we dutifully wait on the Lord, doing all the things that he has commanded us to do, as faith without works is dead. Unfortunately, God, to a greater number of people who claim to be Christians and who have otherwise become lost in this whole politically correct and very humanistic way of believing, has become nothing more than just another idol fashioned out of wood or stone.

4. The fourth method as shown in the church of Thyatira is where Satan will come into an unsuspecting church of God with false prophets, either male or female, to accomplish his mission. This method works hand in hand with the third method as the victim church must first welcome in the compromise of political correctness before Satan can then be able to lure them gradually into the deeper dark secrets of satanic worship itself (reference Revelation 2:18–29).

Here in the church of Thyatira we see just how effective one false prophetess has been at luring many within the congregation into fornication and the eating of food sacrificed to the idols from off the altar of one of Satan's many temples built for him at the time where sacrifices were burned on almost a daily basis. It appears from the historical record as mentioned by David

75

Nunn in his Video: "The Seven Churches of Revelation Rediscovered," that Thyatira was perhaps one of the greater centers for satanic worship that existed at that time, which proved to be a real problem for this particular church, as it was trying to worship the Lord and conduct its church activities nearby. I'm also sure that this particular false prophetess didn't just spring all these deeper dark secrets of satanic worship upon this congregation overnight.

Today, as I look out upon all the scattered churches of God that Satan has scattered and divided to his heart's content, I remember how it was not too long ago that I was asking God the question: but where are all your prophets that Jesus, your Son, said would be a part of his church? Even the Mormon Church had what it claimed to be the only living prophet of God leading its church. So if the Mormon Church was not in fact the true church of God, then why was it that they were the only Christian church out of all the others, to include the Catholic Church, to claim to have a single living prophet? In pondering this question about the prophets I couldn't help recalling the words of the apostle Paul as he was addressing this matter concerning prophets along with the other gifts of the Spirit with the Ephesians. Whereas it is written: "And He Himself gave some to be apostles, *some prophets,* some evangelists, and some pastors and teachers, for the equipping of the saints for the work of ministry, for the edifying of the body of Christ" (Ephesians 4:11–13, NKJV).

Still, the Apostle Paul elaborates even more on the many different kinds of gifts that God the Father, through his Holy Spirit, will make manifest in each of us for some useful purpose. I paraphrase Paul's words in this way: one man has the gift of wise speech, another, by the Spirit, can put the deepest knowledge into words, another is granted faith, and another the gifts of healing; still another, by the Holy Spirit, has miraculous powers while another by this same Spirit has the gift of prophecy, and yet another the ability to distinguish between

THE BOOK OF REVELATION AND THE BIBLE
AS NEVER EXPLAINED BEFORE

true and false spirits while another, by this same Spirit, has the gift of ecstatic utterance while still another has the ability to interpret it. But all these gifts are the work of one and the same Spirit, distributing them separately to each individual at will (reference 1 Corinthians 12:7–11). Then in 1 Corinthians 14:1–12 Paul breaks down the difference between ecstatic utterance and prophecy; most importantly, he emphasizes how prophecy by far is the greater between the two because the words of the prophet have the power to build, to stimulate, and to encourage, but above all they build up the Christian community. The man speaking in ecstatic utterance serves only himself unless there is someone there to interpret it for the benefit of those standing around him. Prophecy then comes second only to love. For an even greater understanding of this concept, read the rest of 1 Corinthians 14:13–33.

So as I asked God, "Where are all your prophets?" I noticed that there were none except for the two prophets that represented each division of the Mormon Church. Both of them claimed to have a direct line to God and to be the one and only, true, living prophet of God's one true church that was now the divided Church of Jesus Christ of Latter Day Saints. The only difference in name between the two was that one was called the Reformed Church of Jesus Christ of Latter Day Saints. But the two prophets were also at direct odds with each other over the direction that they said God was telling them to take this church that Joseph Smith founded upon the Book of Mormon on April 6, 1830.

But I would like to say this to the two self-proclaimed living prophets of God today and to all the people from within both divisions of the Mormon Church: You have all forgotten that since Jesus came, the role of the prophet has changed, as the Apostle Paul put it so eloquently to the Corinthians. No longer are we to follow a single man claiming to be the one and only true living prophet of God as was Moses. That day has passed forever because that is exactly who Jesus is. By his birth, his life,

77

by the gospel he preached, by his sacrifice, and by his resurrection, Jesus lives and has become our all in all, but he especially has become our one and only, true, living prophet of God, who is our ultimate Savior and Deliverer all in one, whom we are to follow and to emulate through each and every day of our lives, and with this truth and in this Spirit we are to worship him.

But the question I raised remained unanswered for almost twenty-five years, and now of late there are prophets and prophetesses springing up all over the place, which, on one hand, is good, but on the other hand, I am disturbed by something that no one else seems to be catching. Yes, their messages are encouraging and inspiring and seem to give cause for joy in the Christian community. But they are not telling the truth about the time that lies just ahead of us, as has been foretold by almost every prophet since Samuel. Nor are they trying to prepare God's people for this great time of tribulation that is soon to be upon us. Instead they are telling everybody that a time of complete restoration lies just around the corner. They are telling God's people that Satan has already been defeated and how very soon he is going to be forced to give them back everything that he has ever stolen from them because the time of restoration is at hand.

I don't know what Bible or prophecies they have been reading, but I know this: I don't want anything back that Satan has had his perverted hands on. Not the wife that I once had and not one other thing that he has ever stolen or cheated me out of. No! To all the people of God, I say this: that very soon all the things of this world are going to be passing away and consumed by fire. I believe in the words of Jesus when he said do not store up for yourself treasures here on earth that can only rust and corrode away or be burned by fire but rather give generously to the poor, live your lives in humility, keeping your faith in God, sowing seeds of peace and love wherever you go, and then God will store up for you treasures in heaven that will never pass away. I believe that with all my heart. But I know this too: the time that lies just ahead of us is the time of our testing, which is the time when many will be lead like lambs to the slaughter and where many who had professed to be followers of Christ will lose their faith and begin to follow the beast rather than lose their lives (reference Romans 8:36–37 and also Revelation 6:9–11).

The other problem I have with all these new prophets and prophetesses of late is that they are not telling the people about this message of the seven churches so that they may be shown how greatly they have been deceived within the church by this fourth method of Satan. Otherwise, if they had not been so lulled by all these make-you-feel-good prophets and prophetesses, they might have seen the terrible plight that they were truly in and take the advice of Jesus and repent of their wicked ways.

But as I previously stated, this method goes one step farther by actually luring some of the members of the congregation into the deep, dark secrets of satanic worship. I have only heard of these practices from men being interviewed on television in a documentary concerning satanic worship. I remember this one high priest from a satanic order of men unknown to me claiming to have received his initial training from within the Catholic Church. He further claimed that this was the usual practice of all priests aspiring to get into this particular satanic priesthood order. I found this claim made by this particular high priest of Satan to be both profound and shocking. *How could this be,* I asked myself? But then I remember even my mother who was a devout Catholic was into witchcraft and astrology for many years until she finally turned away from these evil practices in her later years and returned to God for her salvation.

In having said all this, I am not by any means suggesting that every priest who has entered into the various priesthood orders within the Catholic Church is about satanic worship. I know that this is simply not true. However, the fact remains that the Catholic Church, like so many other churches, has become heavily infiltrated by Satan as he uses both the liberal members of its clergy and congregations to continue to press the newly elected pope for change as he had the previous pope.

If the previous pope would have relented and given into this call for change by its liberal members, it would have prepared the way for Satan's onslaught. But Pope John Paul II remained steadfast to the gospel even up until the time of his death. Because of this, Pope John Paul II has shown himself to be both a great and remarkable man whose example of love and humility shines bright as a model for every Christian to follow after. He will not be forgotten, not by God nor by the thousands of his faithful followers who have chosen to remain steadfast to the Lord's command that we love one another as we must also love the Lord our God with all our heart, soul, mind, and strength, and take his gospel given to us through his Son, our Lord and Savior, Jesus Christ, and preach it even unto the ends of the earth.

5. The fifth method, as shown in the church of Sardis, is where Satan will bring complacency and the spirit of procrastination into an unsuspecting church of God and use it to drain the life and Spirit of God right out of it until ultimately it is seen by God as being dead. God's message here is plain. Any church that thinks it can take the blessings of God that have made it great in both the size of its building and its congregation and then just sit back on its laurels and rest, thinking that its good name and the love it bears for one another alone will assure its place in the kingdom of God is in for a rather rude awakening when God's kingdom finally does come to this earth. For God is looking for both faith and works from his churches and congregations, amongst a few other things, but not just works that sound good when you speak about them but, most importantly, works that are completed and serve God (reference Revelation 3:1–6).

Paul did remind us in Galatians 5:6 that the only thing that matters is faith active in love. But here Jesus breaks it down to us by explaining just what exactly being active in love really means and that is that faith without *completed works* (and we can add to this *born out of love*) is dead. So let it suffice to say that it is true for the church, for the congregation, to the man and to the woman of God, that faith with even the most loving, half-completed works is still dead to God. Also, read Hebrews 11:1–40 for a greater rendition of this concept.

Jesus then finishes his remarks to the deceived members of this church by telling them to wake up and remember the teachings that they received and then to repent. Otherwise, they may find themselves caught off guard when he suddenly comes upon them like a thief in the night.

6.   The sixth method as shown in the church of Laodicea is where Satan will come into an unsuspecting church of God and bring upon its congregation the most nauseating spirit of all, the spirit of lukewarmness. Jesus had this to say to them and to any such church:

> "And to the angel of the church of the Laodiceans write, 'These things says the Amen, the Faithful and True Witness, the beginning and the creation of God: "I know your works, that you are neither cold nor hot. I could wish you were cold or hot. So then, because you are lukewarm and neither cold nor hot, I will vomit you out of My mouth. Because you say, 'I am rich, have become wealthy and have need of nothing'— And do not know that you are wretched, miserable, poor, blind, and naked—I counsel you to buy from Me gold refined in the fire, that you may be rich; and white garments, that you may be clothed, that the shame of your nakedness may not be revealed; and anoint your eyes with eye salve, that you may see. As many as I love, I rebuke and chasten. Therefore be zealous and repent. Behold, I stand at the door and knock. If anyone hears My voice and opens the door, I will come

in to him and dine with him, and he with Me. To him who overcomes I will grant to sit with Me on My throne, as I also overcame and sat down with My Father on His throne.

"He who has an ear, let him hear what the Spirit says to the churches!' "

Revelation 3:14–22 (NKJV)

The third level of understanding: This is the understanding that shows how these seven churches, which are symbolized by the seven golden lamps and seven angels of God, also symbolize the one true church where God's *authority* and *holiness* will rest and be centered on earth until his elect and his chosen people have each been taken up into heaven. This is also the church that Jesus said would be built upon the rock of Peter that the gates of hell would not be allowed to prevail against. Saint Peter's Basilica, when it was first built in 325 by Constantine on the foundation of Saint Peter's tomb, had become God's legal and authoritative representation of his kingdom here on earth, and the revelation that Jesus had proclaimed to Peter was there and then fulfilled.

It must also be pointed out that at that time there was but one church on the face of the earth, and its denomination was Christianity. It is, in fact, the mother church from which every other Christian church on the face of the earth can trace its roots back to. The only exceptions to this finding are the Church of Jesus Christ of Latter Day Saints and to some extent the Jehovah's Witnesses. Then in 313, Christianity was declared by Constantine to be the official religion of the entire Roman Empire, and its church became known as the Universal Church of Rome. This literally meant that the Universal Church of Rome, or the Roman Catholic Church as it has become know today, was in fact the official universal church of the world; this did not happen by chance or by accident. It all happened under God's direct intervention. It was Jesus that appeared to Paul in Acts 23:11 and told him to have courage and that he must go

THE BOOK OF REVELATION AND THE BIBLE
AS NEVER EXPLAINED BEFORE

back to Rome and affirm the truth about him there as he had done in Jerusalem. Paul gives another very interesting perspective on his feelings about this with his opening remarks in his letter to the Romans. You should also notice how he refers to the Romans here as his friends and the Lord's dedicated people and how he expresses such a deep desire to be with them again. It was also no coincidence that Paul was sent into Rome at the same time that Peter was there. For God had it planned all along that he was going to use the two of them together to affect his one purpose of laying the underground network toward his up and coming universal church and church center.

Peter, on the other hand, was also directed by God to be in Rome during this crucial time in the church's history. In the Gospel of John, Jesus gives Peter his first hint of this by telling him:

"In all truth I tell you, when you were young you put on your own belt and walked where you liked; but when you are old you will stretch out your hands, and somebody else will put a belt round you and take you where you would rather not go" In these words he indicated the kind of death by which Peter would give glory to God. After this he said, "Follow me." John 21:18–19 (TNJB)

Peter returned to Rome somewhere in about AD 64, where it is believed that he was very instrumental in laying the authoritative groundwork for Christ's underground church in the catacombs of Rome. He would be crucified upside down at his own request during the great persecutions of Emperor Nero in AD 67. The location of his death and burial are believed to have been very close to where his tomb lies in state beneath the Saint Peter's Basilica, and it remains there to this day.

To finalize my argument concerning Saint Peter's Basilica's authenticity as being the Lord's center of authority on earth, let me recant the same argument Jesus used when he was defending his own authority against the Pharisees proclaiming him to be a false prophet, where he said to the Pharisees: "It is also

83

written in your law that the testimony of two men is true" (John 8:17–19, NKJV). Then Jesus went on to cite the two witness's who bore their testimonies about him as being first himself and then his Father, but earlier he cites the first witness as being John the Baptist and the second as being his Father by the very miracles that he had performed (reference John 5:31–37). So it is that the testimonies of Peter, Paul and Constantine bear witness to the fact that it was Jesus himself that directed them to labor unto death toward the completion of this one church in Rome, whereas it was Jesus that first proclaimed the destiny of this church to the Apostle Peter; thus it was also Jesus that saw to its completion through the Emperor Constantine in 325.

The fourth level of understanding: This is the understanding that shows how these seven churches are also symbolic of God's universal church as it was then and as it exists today across the face of the earth in its broken and fragmented state. The seven angels, who are also the seven spirits of God, represent the power and authority of God as it is networked out to all those churches whose congregations have elected to remain faithful and attached to this one true center of God's authority and his holiness, Saint Peter's Basilica. These seven angels are also God's chief administrators or facing angels who report directly to God to do his will. They are also the same seven angels that blow the seven trumpets and pour the seven bowls full of the seven plagues in the book of Revelation.

Now because of Satan's disruption to the divine order of things, and because God is a merciful and just God, it appears that God has elected to show his mercy and still bless those other scattered flocks long since severed from his true vine of authority. It also appears from the evidence that God will even show his love and favor to anyone whose heart is pure and striving toward perfection regardless of what church he or she belongs to. The ultimate decision rests with God as he has always been about the inward condition of our hearts.

This then begs the question: If this is all true, then what difference does it make if we are Catholic or Protestant, Jehovah's Witnesses or Mormon, or, for that matter, Jew or Gentile? The answer is very profound: the difference is not so easily noticed at the congregational level but becomes extremely noticeable at the level of the priesthood, more particularly the holy royal priesthood.

You will recall earlier how I spoke about Jesus coming in the succession of Melchizedek, which replaced the old Aaronic priesthood order with the new holy royal priesthood. I also mentioned that this was all constituted by way of the new covenant that Jesus sacrificed himself to bring, which caused Melchizedek to step down from office and made Jesus the new and everlasting high priest in heaven. As such, the office of high priest on earth was now and forever rendered obsolete, as its service was no longer needed.

Along with all this came the geographical issue of where his new holy city was to be relocated. Keep in mind that in the old covenant order Jerusalem was his holy city and Solomon's Temple was his holy dwelling place. But now with the new covenant, Jerusalem was displaced by Rome, and Solomon's Temple was displaced by the inner sanctuary of our own hearts. What is important to understand in all of this is: where God's authority is centered on earth, there also is his holy city. Likewise, where Satan's dominion is centered on earth, there also is his unholy city. When the Jews rejected Jesus as their Messiah and then finally cast his church out of his holy city as well, Jerusalem became cutoff. Then God went out, and as a poetic gesture to the Jews, decided to make Rome his new holy city and center of his authority. This meant that Satan was being basically kicked out of his own unholy dwelling place and made to go off in search of a new one. I will be getting into this subject in a lot more detail later when I get to that chapter of my book entitled "The Great Whore of Babylon."

Now, I have said all that so I could say this: What the Catholic Church has that all the other churches do not is, first of all, God's *authority* and secondly, the holy royal priesthood. The loss of God's authority has left the various other churches of the world in a constant state of turmoil as they struggle against the ever-changing tides of political correctness and manmade doctrine. The Catholic Church has the pope, and with respect to today's ongoing church scandal, he is supposed to keep all these things in check as it is his assigned duty given to him by God. But the other churches only have one another and the various other charismatic leaders and prophets who are not always in agreement with one another or God.

The loss of holiness in the church, on the other hand, has created an entirely different kind of problem, for Jesus commanded us all to be holy as his Father in heaven is holy (1 Peter 1:14–16). But we must also understand that holiness comes out of the perfection of God's love, but only after God comes to recognize that perfection within us and then comes to dwell within us as we dwell within him. It is important to understand that it is God himself that makes us holy and not anything else found within us or from without, whether it be by an appointed church position or even a priesthood that we may hold, as we are all born from a sinful nature. For it is written, "For you alone are holy" (Revelation 15:4, NKJV). Otherwise, this holiness can also only come through humility, which is the foundation of his love. With it, there can be no room for self-righteous pride or arrogance.

The other profound thing to understand about holiness is that without it we will never be allowed to enter Jerusalem, his holy city, which can only be found within the kingdom of God. Neither can we be a part of the royal house or one of that number the book of Revelation calls the hundred and forty-four thousand, who are the priests of God that are also called his elect. These specially appointed priests of God can only be found within the Catholic Church for reasons that I will explain later in greater detail. Otherwise, it is unfortunate to have to

THE BOOK OF REVELATION AND THE BIBLE
AS NEVER EXPLAINED BEFORE

note that the other thing that has become so lost in all these other churches of the world, which have separated themselves from this one true church, with the only exception being that of the Eastern Orthodox Church, is this concept of the holy royal priesthood. For a more detailed understanding of this concept, read 1 Peter 2:4–10.

With regard to the seven angels, they also administer or network the gifts of the Holy Spirit to everyone within God's church. But all gifts of the Spirit are sent forth from the Father upon special request of the Son. These gifts are then administered through the seven facing angels who in turn network God's emanating Holy Spirit through to all the individual guardian angels who are assigned to each of us, who then serve as our advocates and God's helpers when we become born again. Our guardian angel then becomes God's Holy Spirit within us and helps to instruct us in doing the will of God, not by his own authority but by the authority of the Father who sent him and by whose Spirit dwells within them, whereby all the gifts of the Father are then bestowed upon us through them. In essence these holy angels of God are an example to each of us of how it is that we too shall become one in being with the Father, through holy matrimony, when Christ comes for his "Bride." That is why Paul says, "And do not grieve the *Holy Spirit* of God, by whom you were sealed for the day of redemption" (Ephesians 4:30, NKJV).

Also, though there may be myriads upon myriads of these guardian angels assigned to each and every one of us, as the Father's emanating Holy Spirit is sent through them to us, they become one in being with the Father and also each other through their holiness with God. Hence, the Holy Spirit from God's way of thinking is, in fact, one Spirit—just as the Father and the Son are one; and also as the twelve apostles are one with the Father, the Son, and the Holy Spirit; just as two people, a man and a woman, when they get married through the blood covenant of a woman's virginity also become one flesh and share

87

the same name. Even though they are two people, they are still considered one by God. The same is true with each of us as we strive to achieve God's inward perfection of love and thereby his holiness; we too become one with the Father, the Son, and the Holy Spirit, who will then come to dwell within us as we dwell within them by the emanating Spirit of love that comes from the Father. For a greater understanding of this concept, reference John 17:11–12 and also John 17:20–23.

The fifth level of understanding: This is the understanding that shows how these six churches and the one perfected seventh church are symbolic of the six great divisions that would occur within God's one true church and also the subdivisions that would spring forth from them. Starting with the Photian Schism in the 800s, leading up to the division of the Eastern Orthodox Church in 1054, going through all the antipopes and the conflicts that arose from them, starting in 217 and going all the way up to the 1400s to the Great Schism of the West in 1378 to 1409, leading up to the Protestant Reformation in the 1500s and all the denominations and divisions that have sprung forth from that movement.

The Mormons, more formally referred to as the Church of Jesus Christ of Latter Day Saints, although not a part of these six great divisions, however still do regard themselves as Christians. But they are very different from the others in that they put their faith, hope, and trust in a man called Joseph Smith and his other so called gospel of Christ—The Book of Mormon. Their church was established by Joseph Smith and his associates on April 6, 1830.

With regard to the Book of Mormon: It appears that this book has many witnesses to the fact that angels as well as other personages of a supernatural kind had appeared before them, but on most occasions only before Joseph Smith who on some occasions had Oliver Cowdery in his company. In his personal testimony, Joseph Smith describes these different personages as being from God as they had the ability to illuminate his room,

THE BOOK OF REVELATION AND THE BIBLE
AS NEVER EXPLAINED BEFORE

or other places where they were seen, to a brightness which was greater than that of the noonday sun. These personages ranged from: one being a resurrected man called, Moroni, who made several visitations to him and is the one who led him to the actual gold plates from which he later translated the Book of Mormon; to another called John the Baptist who ordained him with the authority of the Aaronic priesthood, to others called the apostles Peter, James, and John who gave him the keys of the kingdom and ordained him with the authority of the Melchizedek priesthood; to those who called themselves the prophets: Moses, Elias, and Elijah, to finally God the Father himself with Jesus by his side. But the one witness that they do not have, is the word of God itself. It is this very word of God, as I have quoted it all throughout this book that in explanation after explanation bears witness against the Book of Mormon and especially the other book which accompanies it called the Doctrine and Covenants.

To be fair with the people of the Mormon Church, who some of which are my friends, I must say that in reading the Book of Mormon and the other books associated with it as they suggested, I found that there were a number of things written within them that were just too incredible to believe. First and foremost is Joseph Smith's assertion: that because the plain and precious truths once contained within the Bible had, over time and bad translation, become lost to the world, he had been chosen by God to restore them through his translation of the Book of Mormon. So in studying the Book of Mormon and the Doctrine and Covenants as I have, I noticed that almost ninety percent of everything that is written within them, with regard to the restoration of the so called lost gospel of Jesus Christ, is in fact a plagiarized reiteration of those very truths that are still, in fact, present in the Bible. But what is even more amazing to me is how the remaining ten percent of these so called restored truths that Joseph Smith is given such credit for, do not restore anything, but rather, come into direct conflict with

89

the actual word of God as it remains written. To put it even more plainly: it appears that the Mormon Church along with its founding prophet Joseph Smith have gone to great lengths to restore the old covenant order of things after, Jesus Christ, by his self-sacrifice and ultimate resurrection from the dead had rendered many of the things found within that covenant obsolete. For that is exactly what Jesus meant when he said I now bring you a new covenant and with it a new commandment that you love one another.

And perhaps one of the most bizarre passions that seem to drive this church on, is its obsession with the dead and the endless genealogies associated with them through an ordinance they have come to revive, after its banning in the 4th century by the Catholic Church, which is called the "Baptism for the Dead." This baptismal rite is now being performed within their temples with a sense of great urgency and it is being performed despite the fact that even within their own church doctrines as recorded in the book of Mormon, in Alma 34:35–36, this high priest and judge of the Nephite people, not only speaks in contradiction to all such practices but he also speaks of its vanity. Although there is a lot more that can be said about all of these things, it is not the purpose of this book to speak about them now, but it will be one of many subjects written about in my next book that will be entitled: "Satan: He Who Has Led the Whole World Astray."

The Jehovah's Witnesses, on the other hand, constitute the sixth division. And although they are considered to be Christians, they completely disassociate themselves from all Christendom. They use the Watch Tower Bible and the Tract Society as their governing body and devote themselves entirely to the service of Jehovah the Father. Their organization was started in Pennsylvania in the 1870s by Charles Taze Russell. The Watch Tower Bible and the Tract Society were later incorporated in 1884 with Russell as president.

THE BOOK OF REVELATION AND THE BIBLE
AS NEVER EXPLAINED BEFORE

I have studied with the Jehovah's Witnesses, as I have with so many other denominations, and I have seen that there are many good people among them just as there are in the Mormon Church; unfortunately, they have become lost, like so many others within the Christian churches, including the Catholic Church, which still maintains God's true center of authority here on earth, in their traditions, manmade doctrines and personal or otherwise denominational interpretations of God's word; or as is the case with so many of the other denominations, by the liberal movement that has been allowed to enter in. The truth of the matter is this: that these are all still a part of God's one true church that has now become very broken, fragmented, and scattered across the face of the earth with each fragmented part having created its own set of barriers against the other. Where it is now that most all are either lost in all these things or else they are suffering from the very perversions of Satan as he has been allowed to infiltrate them as is the case now within the Catholic Church.

But with regard to the Jehovah's Witnesses who consider all of Christendom to be the great whore of Babylon, God does not care whether or not we celebrate our own birthdays or color Easter eggs on Easter or even if we put up a Christmas tree on Christmas, along with all the rest of the things that they tell their followers they cannot do, as long as we keep God first and foremost in these celebrations. What God is most concerned about is the inward condition of our hearts and, along with this, that through our hearts we become perfected in his love for him and for one another, and from there shall the spirit of his holiness come to dwell within us. The Jehovah's Witnesses, although meaning well in what they do, have forgotten that it is only through humility that this kind of love and holiness may be attained or that any shall even enter and then be exalted within his kingdom when it is finally brought down to earth. For God has made it only too clear that self-righteousness, along with all the rest of the evils of this world, will never possess his kingdom.

On the other hand, one of the most tragic things I have encountered in my Christian walk with Christ is all those people I have met who claim to be saved born again Christians who are still thinking and speaking the same vile thoughts and words as they had before. They even take the Lord's name in vain, using it as a common expression, while listening to the same old satanic rock and roll. Without a second thought they continue to live their lives as they had before, looking more like the devil than the devil himself. And though they do not know it, they are more lost now in their sins than they were before. They tell me that they know they are saved because they believe in God and further because they know that no matter what sins they commit they will be forgiven for them because God loves them and will accept them into his kingdom just the way they are. In vain, I try to teach them the truth as it is contained within the rest of the gospel of Christ, but they would rather believe what all the superstars preaching from within the megachurches have told them: "It is by grace alone that you are saved. Only say yes to God today, and you shall forever more be saved. Never mind about perfection and holiness; these things are impossible to achieve so don't even bother. The life of Christ is but to live your life in a constant state of sin and repentance."

The sixth level of understanding: This is the understanding that shows that these seven churches are symbolic of the different distinctions made between God's created people and the seals of their deliverance, which are: the chosen elect, the saved by the blood of the Lamb, the saved by the grace of God, the forgiven by his own holy name sake, and the damned. To clarify these distinctions, I must say that it is not that some of us cannot be both saved and chosen or, for that matter, forgiven by the grace of God and also by the blood of the lamb, but I chose these different titles of the groupings to help illustrate this level of understanding that there are in fact five different categories of deliverance

THE BOOK OF REVELATION AND THE BIBLE
AS NEVER EXPLAINED BEFORE

and four different seals that each of these different groups shall be delivered by, before and after, the Lamb of God finally makes his triumphant return to the earth. They are as follows:

The chosen elect (also called God's elect): These are the hundred and forty-four thousand. As I mentioned earlier, these are a very special priesthood order of men appointed by God whom shall be chosen from among the twelve tribes of Israel and later ransomed as the first fruits of humanity at their appointed time of deliverance. They alone, out of all the inhabitants of the earth, through their steadfast dedication and devotion to God, shall be found perfected in his love when the angel comes to deliver their seal, and through this perfection they shall be made holy by God's emanating spirit. These are also the only ones to receive the seal of God on their foreheads and will also bear the fleshly seal of circumcision because they are also bound by the everlasting covenant made between Abraham and God in Genesis 17:7–14.

The saved by the blood of the Lamb: These are the Christian Gentiles as well as the other Christian Israelites who are marked by the seal of the Holy Spirit for their deliverance because of their great love and faith in the Father and his Son, Jesus Christ. These also constitute the great multitude. Though they were not as steadfast in the perfection of God's love as the hundred and forty-four thousand , they will be able to achieve holiness later on in their Christian lives through it by the emanating power of the Holy Spirit as it also comes to dwell within them. Then shall they be washed and atoned of their imperfections by the blood of Jesus and thereby made ready for their deliverance either at the last trumpet or at the time of their resurrection, as these are also those that gave their lives bearing their testimonies to the truth about his gospel and that also died refusing to take the mark of the beast. The Israelites here will also bear the fleshly seal of circumcision.

The saved by the grace of God: These are the survivors of all Israel who will be saved, also a part of that group known as,

93

"the remnant of Israel who will be saved." They will be saved purely by the grace of God and his own holy namesake after Christ's second coming and the armies of the beast and the false prophet have been destroyed. Then shall these who are the only ones left from all Israel to survive the beast's great reign of terror be gathered from all the nations, coasts, and islands of the world and finally brought home to Zion and his holy mountain. There they shall fall on their faces as they see that the one to whom they had pierced and rejected is also the same one who is now calling them home to this ancient land once promised to Abraham, Isaac, and Jacob and all their descendants. This is the land of Zion, which is also called Israel. Then after a great time of mourning and grieving has been concluded, they shall all be reconciled back unto the Lord their God and finally come to dwell in peace in this land that for so long had become such a curse to them. They will be sealed and delivered by the fleshly seal of circumcision.

The forgiven by his own holy namesake: These are the whole house of Israel, and they shall be raised back from the dust after the one-thousand-year reign of Christ and the judgment day is over. They shall also be saved by his own holy namesake, just as the survivors of all Israel will have been saved before them, for there is no other cause for their salvation than this. And so it will be as it is written: "But many who are first will be last and the last first" (Mark 10:31, NKJV). They will also be known to God by the fleshly seal of circumcision, for without this seal they cannot be called Israelites and will otherwise be completely cut off from God.

Finally, the dammed: These are those who take the mark of the beast and worship him. This mark of the beast, or otherwise the number 666, which is the numerical value of the beast's name as computed by an Israeli alphabetical numbering system, is also the seal of damnation. All those with this seal on either their right hand or forehead shall drink the wine of God's wrath poured undiluted into the cup of his vengeance. All these shall

THE BOOK OF REVELATION AND THE BIBLE
AS NEVER EXPLAINED BEFORE

be cast into the lake of fire during the great Day of Judgment where they will be tormented in sulfurous flames before the holy angels and before the Lamb. The smoke of their torment will rise forever and ever, and there will be no reconciliation or forgiveness for anyone who worships the beast and its image or has the mark of its name placed upon them (Revelation 14:9–12).

At this point, it is very important to understand that the lake of fire is a real place and is not meant as a metaphor depicting some other realm or outer darkness as so many Christian faiths, as well as the Jehovah's Witnesses, would have you believe. Just imagine being cast naked and alive into the surface of the sun. The lake of fire will be just as real and horrifying a place, and all those with this seal will suffer this second, very painful, physical as well as a spiritual death in it. The spiritual death, to be clearer, is the realization that your spirit and eternal soul are now and forever cut off from God's without any hope of reconciliation throughout all eternity as you burn in unending torment in this place of eternal fire. The only exceptions to this second physical death will be with Satan, his fallen angels, and the false prophet.

Satan, along with his angels, were each created as immortal beings and as such will be unable to experience a physical death; however, with their fall from grace and ultimately heaven itself, they lost their beauty along with their initial spiritual forms and became grotesque spiritual entities left to roam the earth; hence the demons, devils, or unclean spirits as Jesus always refers to them, are all synonymous with Satan's fallen angels. Another way to look at this is that the unclean spirit of Satan is the perverse opposite of the Holy Spirit of God. In both cases, this can signify either great multitudes of angels or the singular spirits of either Satan or God himself. For a greater understanding of this explanation study John 14:7–11, 18–21, and 26 regarding how the Holy Spirit actually represents a multitude of God's holy angels sent by God to dwell in each of us and how we will all eventually become one in being with the Father, just as the Son and all

95

his holy angels are one in being with him now, hence the Holy Spirit; reference Mark 5:1–13 regarding how the unclean spirit can sometimes denote legions of fallen angels.

So these fallen angels of Satan, when they are finally judged and sentenced to the lake of fire, will only be able to suffer the second spiritual death as they, along with Satan, are each cast into this place of eternal torment. The false prophet, on the other hand, is the only being to experience a single physical death as he is sent directly from his existence on earth to the lake of fire. He differs from the beast in that he is not a resurrected being brought up from the abyss but is created solely for the purpose of preparing the way for the beast who, upon its arrival, the false prophet will cause all the inhabitants of the earth, except those whose names have been written in the Lamb's Book of Life, to worship the beast and receive its mark. What the beast and the false prophet do share in common is that they are the first two beings from amongst all those who are to be dammed, to be cast into the lake of fire at the end of the great battle of the Armageddon.

With the exception of Satan, the fallen angels, and the false prophet, all the rest of these who are to be sentenced to the lake of fire and sulfur will suffer the second physical death, as the beast had a thousand years before them, as their newly resurrected bodies are each consumed by the flames. Here all their eternal souls will live on as they will be tormented day and night forever, for this shall be their eternal punishment (Revelation 19:20–21, Revelation 20:7–15, and Revelation 21:8). The lake of fire is also described by Jesus as being both a place of fire and brimstone and the place of wailing and gnashing of teeth (reference Matthew 13:36–43 and 49–50, Hebrews 10:26–28, and also 1 Thessalonians 5:9–10).

The seventh level of understanding: This is the understanding that shows that the church of Philadelphia is symbolic of God's perfected church, as it was in the beginning and as it shall be at the time of the end just before Christ comes for these who

THE BOOK OF REVELATION AND THE BIBLE
AS NEVER EXPLAINED BEFORE

are called his elect, which again is synonymous to the perfected church. The church, as used in the general context of being the bride of Christ, is not to be confused with the perfected church, although this particular bride of Christ is still composed of both groups, but for the purpose of this explanation, these two groups that make up God's one church must be distinguished from each other.

The first group is those of whom the Apostle John describes to us in the fourteenth chapter of the book of Revelation as the hundred and forty-four thousand; they are also the same ones who alone will have the seal of God placed upon their foreheads. As I mentioned earlier, they will be gathered from every nation of the world, twelve thousand from each of the twelve tribes of Israel, as the first fruits of humanity to be ransomed.

On the other hand, the church of Smyrna is also symbolic of the great multitude, which is the Christian Gentiles as well as the other Christian Israelites who, for the most part, constitute the church. Some of the Christian Israelites here will also be from the ten lost tribes of Israel, but all of these, whether Israelite or Gentile, will have the seal of the Holy Spirit placed upon them. These are also all those who were not able to obtain to this higher level of perfected love and holiness as the hundred and forty-four thousand will have done at their time of deliverance, but they will still manage to hang on to their faith in Christ during their time of testing when the beast shall reign over the earth. Some of these will, however, eventually reach this perfected state just prior to their time of deliverance at the last trumpet. It will be during this time that the beast will test many of these, even unto death. This will fulfill the scripture that says, "You will be betrayed even by parents and brothers, relatives and friends, and they will put some of you to death; and you will be hated by all for my name sake" (Luke 21:16–17, NKJV). They, together with the dead in Christ who shall rise first, will be caught up to mid-heaven to meet the Lord, along with his herald of angels, at the last trumpet. Then, in the twinkling of an eye, they will all be

97

changed into immortality, and from there, they will be taken up into heaven itself to join the Lamb for the celebration of his great wedding feast. For it is written, "Blessed are those who are called to the marriage supper of the Lamb!" And he said to me, "These are the true sayings of God" (Revelation 19:9–10, NKJV). This is where the church, which is also called the bride of Christ is to be spiritually united in holy wedlock with the Lamb of God, where the two shall become one.

It should also be understood that this last trumpet, which will occur during the time of the sixth bowl that shall be full of one of the seven plagues, as described in Revelation 16:14–16, is actually synonymous to the seventh trumpet that is blown in Revelation 11:15. What is important to understand here is that although the events occurring within the sets of seven revelations are sequential, the order of the sets themselves, are not always presented this way, as many of the revelations given after the seventh trumpet depict events that happen before it or between the fifth, sixth, and leading up to the seventh trumpet, such as those events regarding the two beasts, the two witnesses, and the seven bowls filled with the last seven plagues (with the exception of the seventh plague which comes after the seventh trumpet). For the scriptural affirmation of those events regarding the seventh and last trumpet, reference 1 Corinthians 15:50–57, 1 Thessalonians 4:15–18, Matthew 24:30–31. This contextual explanation is otherwise known to us as "the thief in the night harvest," or as most Christians have come to commonly refer to it as being called "the rapture."

THE SCROLL WITH THE SEVEN SEALS
(REVELATION CHAPTER FOUR)

After these things I looked, and behold, a door standing open in heaven. And the first voice which I heard was like a trumpet speaking with me, saying "Come up here, and I will show you things which must take place after this." Immediately I was in the Spirit; and behold, a throne sat in heaven, and One sat on the throne. And He who sat there was like a jasper and a sardius stone in appearance; and there was a rainbow around the throne, in appearance like an emerald. *Around the throne were twenty-four thrones, and on the thrones I saw twenty-four elders sitting, clothed in white robes; and they had crowns of gold on their heads. And from the throne proceeded lightnings, thunderings and voices.* Seven lamps of fire were burning before the throne, which are the seven spirits of God.

Before the throne there was a sea of glass, like crystal. *And in the midst of the throne and around the throne, were four living creatures full of eyes in front and in back.* The first living creature was like a lion, the second living creature like a calf, the third living creature had a human face like a man, and the fourth living creature was like a flying eagle. The four living creatures, each having six wings, were full of eyes around and within. And they do not rest day or night; saying: *"Holy, holy, holy, Lord God Almighty, who was, and is, and is to come!"*

Whenever the four living creatures give glory and honor and thanks to Him who sits on the throne, who lives forever and ever, the twenty-four elders fall down before Him who sits on the throne and worship Him who lives forever and ever, and cast their crowns before the throne, saying: "Thou art worthy, O Lord, to receive glory and honor and power; for You created all things, and by Your will they exist and were created!"

Revelation 4:1–11 (NKJV)

THE OPENING OF THE SCROLL WITH THE SEVEN SEALS (REVELATION CHAPTER FIVE)

And I saw in the right hand of Him who sat on the throne a scroll written inside and on the back, sealed with seven seals. Then I saw a strong angel proclaiming with a loud voice, "Who is worthy to open the scroll and to loose its seals?" And no one in heaven, or on the earth, or under the earth was able to open the scroll or look at it. So I wept much, because no one was found worthy to open and read the scroll. But one of the elders said to me, "Do not weep. Behold, the Lion of the tribe of Judah, the Root of David, has prevailed to open the scroll and to loose its seven seals."

And I looked, and behold, in the midst of the throne, and of the four living creatures, and in the midst of elders, stood

THE BOOK OF REVELATION AND THE BIBLE
AS NEVER EXPLAINED BEFORE

a Lamb as though it had been slain, *having seven horns and seven eyes, which are the seven Spirits of God sent out into all the earth.* Then he came and took the scroll out of the right hand of Him who sat on the throne.

Now when he had taken the scroll, the four living creatures and the twenty-four elders fell down before the Lamb, each having a harp, and golden bowls full of incense, which are the prayers of the saints. And they sang a new song, saying: "You are worthy to take the scroll and to open its seals; *for You were slain and have redeemed us to God by Your blood out of every tribe and tongue and people and nation, and have made us Kings and priests to our God; (or a royal house) and we shall reign on the earth."*

Then I looked, and I heard the voice of many angels around the throne, the living creatures, and the elders; and the number of them was ten thousand times ten thousand, and thousands upon thousands, saying with a loud voice: "Worthy is the Lamb who was slain, to receive power and riches and wisdom, and strength and honor and glory and blessing!"

And every creature which is in heaven and on earth and under the earth and such as are in the sea, all that are in them, I heard saying: "Blessing and honor and glory and power be to Him who sits on the throne, and to the Lamb, forever and ever!" Then the four living creatures said, "Amen!" And the twenty-four elders fell down and worshiped Him who lives forever and ever.

Revelation 5:1–14 (NKJV)

As a special note: It should be understood that the reason I have taken the time to quote chapters four and five out of the book of Revelation is because of the many different and especially important things that are being said here. It should also be understood that from this point on I will be using this same method of quoting chapters first out of the book of Revelation before giving their explanations afterwards. Here especially in chapters four and five I have elected to italicize those scriptures that I have found to be of special importance so that I can reference them more easily for the detailed explanation that I will be giving about them next. Otherwise, I will be using some of these very same scriptures as the basis for further explanation later as I begin to reveal the other hidden truths contained within the book of Revelation.

The first italicized scripture: *"Around the throne were twenty-four thrones, and on the thrones I saw twenty-four elders sitting, clothed in white robes; and they had crowns of gold on their heads"* (Revelation 4:4, NKJV). Here is a mystery that has troubled me for quite some time as I have often pondered over the different possibilities of who these twenty-four elders could possibly be. I have even heard some very reputable writers and theologians give their identities their best shot, but none of them have gotten them completely right. All seemed to be in agreement that the number twenty-four was divided into two sets of twelve and that the last set of twelve represented the twelve apostles in our dispensation, which is the third dispensation. The third dispensation, you should recall, is from the time of Christ to the present date, which in each dispensation is a period of about two thousand years, and there are only three dispensations. The first dispensation is from Adam to Noah. The second dispensation is from Noah to the time of Christ, and the third dispensation is from the time of Christ to the present date.

The problem arises with the question of who in the second dispensation could the first set of twelve be. Some have said that they number across all three dispensations, starting with Adam, Noah, Samuel, Nathan, Elijah, etc. Others have suggested that they begin with Abraham, Isaac, Jacob, Hosea, Amos, Micah, Joel, etc., and number up through all the prophets. But no matter how I would try to add these up, I could not get the number to equal twelve because there were a lot more than twelve prophets to choose from. In fact, there have been hundreds. So began the dilemma where I finally asked the Lord, in all earnest, to reveal this mystery to me. But as I lay there pondering the answer to

THE BOOK OF REVELATION AND THE BIBLE
AS NEVER EXPLAINED BEFORE

this mystery, a quiet voice that I have come to recognize as the voice of the Holy Spirit spoke to me once again, saying, "Just keep researching and studying my word as you had before and then shall I reveal this mystery to you." Then one day as I was studying the scriptures regarding God's holy city, the new Jerusalem, as it had come down out of heaven, the answer was finally revealed to me in this way; where it is written:

> Then one of the seven angels who had the seven bowls filled with the seven last plagues came to me and talked to me, saying, "Come, and I will show you the bride, the Lamb's wife." And he carried me away in the Spirit to a great and high mountain, and showed me the great city, the holy Jerusalem, descending out of heaven from God, having the glory of God. Her light was like a precious stone, like a jasper stone, clear as crystal. Also she had a great and high wall with twelve gates, *and twelve angels at the gates and names written on them, which are the names of the twelve tribes of the children of Israel:* Three gates on the east, three gates on the north, three gates on the south, and three gates on the west. *Now the wall of the city had twelve foundations (or foundation stones) and on them were the names of the twelve apostles of the Lamb.*
>
> Revelation 21:9–14 (NKJV)

I must have read this passage at least fifty times before and I was never able to see this connection until now. As soon as my eyes fell upon the words contained within these two italicized scriptures, I knew that I had finally been given the answer and that it was given to me by God. The names of the twelve tribes of Israel are none other than the names of the twelve sons of Jacob, who are also called the twelve patriarchs of Israel, and they come from the second dispensation. All Israel are the offspring of Jacob's twelve sons and their wives. Jacob's name was changed to Israel by God after he wrestled with him throughout the night and prevailed. During the wrestling match, God struck him in the hip and made him lame because he could not throw him; it is also believed that he may have done this to keep Jacob from running away from his bother Esau at the boundary of the river Jordan (reference Genesis 32:22–31.)

The names of the twenty-four elders whose thrones surround the throne of God are as follows. From the second dispensation, these are the names of those written on the twelve gates of the new Jerusalem, who represent the twelve tribes of Israel, whose origin may be traced back to the twelve sons of Jacob. In order of birth, they are as follows: Reuben, Simeon, Levi, Judah, Dan, Naphtali, Gad, Asher, Issachar, Zebulun, Joseph, and finally, Benjamin (Genesis 35:23–26).

From the third dispensation, these are the names of the twelve apostles, who are also regarded as the twelve foundation stones of the church. They are as follows: Simon, also called Peter, and his brother Andrew; James and his brother John; Philip and Bartholomew, Thomas and Matthew, the tax gatherer; James, son of Alphaeus; and Labbaeus, also called Jude, brother of James, Simon the zealot, and finally Paul, who was personally chosen by Jesus to replace Judas Iscariot, the man who betrayed him.

The second italicized scripture: *"And from the throne proceeded lightnings, thunderings, and voices"* (Revelation 4:5, NKJV). Here we are given the one clue that helps us to unlock the mystery behind the seven thunders that were momentarily revealed to John in chapter 10 of the book of Revelation, and then soon after he was told to seal them up. From this one scripture, we are shown that whenever God issues forth a command from his throne to his seven facing angels, the power of his command is always sent first, along with that angel who has received his command, and seen as flashes of lightning, followed by peals of thunder as the sound of his voice always follows in quick succession. I will be speaking about this subject in greater detail when I get to that section of my book called "The Seven Thunders."

The third italicized scripture: *"—and in the midst of the throne and all around the throne, were four living creatures full of eyes in front and in back."* (Revelation 4:6, NKJV). These are

THE BOOK OF REVELATION AND THE BIBLE
AS NEVER EXPLAINED BEFORE

four very special angels called seraphim by the prophet Isaiah and cherubim by the prophet Ezekiel. They were created by the Father to stay continually in his presence and attend to his divine will. Here they must perform the various duties assigned to them, of which one is to call upon all heaven and earth to give praise and worship to himself, the most high God, for he is worthy of their praise and worship, because he is the creator of all things in both heaven and on earth. Another duty that each one of the four living creatures has is the calling forth of the four horsemen in that section of the book of Revelation called the Seven Seals (Revelation 6:1–8).

It is interesting to note that the book of Revelation is not the only place where these four living creatures are described in the Bible. In chapter 6 of the book of Isaiah, the prophet Isaiah describes them this way:

> In the year that King Uzziah died, I saw the Lord sitting on a throne, high and lifted up, and the train of His robe filled the temple. Above it stood seraphim; each one had six wings: with two he covered his face, with two he covered his feet, and with two he flew. And one cried to another and said: "Holy, holy, holy is the Lord of Hosts; the whole earth is full of His glory!" And the posts of the door were shaken by the voice of him who cried out, and the house was filled with smoke.
>
> So I said: "Woe is me, for I am undone! Because I am a man of unclean lips, and I dwell in the midst of a people of unclean lips; for my eyes have seen the King, the Lord of Hosts." Then one of the seraphim flew to me having in his hand a live coal which he had taken with the tongs from the altar. And he touched my mouth with it, and said: "Behold, this has touched your lips; your iniquity is taken away, and your sin is purged."
>
> Isaiah 6:1–7 (NKJV)

But the most detailed description of all is given by the prophet Ezekiel in the first chapter and then once again in the tenth chapter of his prophetic book where he identifies them as cherubim. In the first chapter of his book, he opens with these remarks:

> Now it came to pass in thirtieth year, in the fourth month, on the fifth day of the month, as I was among the captives by the river Chebar, that the heavens were opened and I saw visions of God. On the fifth day of the month, which was in the fifth year of King Jehoiachin's captivity, the word of the Lord came expressly to Ezekiel the priest, the son of Buzi, in the land of the Chaldeans, by the river Chebar (also spelled Kebar), and the hand of the Lord was upon him there.

> Then I looked, and behold, a whirlwind was coming out of the north, a great cloud with raging fire engulfing itself; and brightness was all around it, and radiating out of its midst like the color of amber, out of the midst of the fire. Also from within it came the likeness of four living creatures. And this was their appearance: they had the likeness of a man. Each one had four faces and each one had four wings. Their legs were straight, and the soles of their feet were like the soles of calves' feet, they sparkled like the color of burnished bronze. The hands of a man were under their wings on their four sides; and each of the four had faces and wings. Their wings touched one another. The creatures did not turn when they went, but each one went straight forward.

> As for the likeness of their faces, each had the face of a man; each of the four had the face of a lion on the right side, each of the four had the face of an ox on the left side, and each of the four had the face of an eagle. Thus were their faces. Their wings stretched upward; two wings of each one touched one another, and two covered their bodies. And each one went straight forward; they went wherever the spirit wanted to go; and they did not turn when they went.

THE BOOK OF REVELATION AND THE BIBLE
AS NEVER EXPLAINED BEFORE

As for the likeness of the living creatures, their appearance was like burning coals of fire, like the appearance of torches going back and forth among the living creatures. The fire was bright and out of the fire went lighting.

Now as I looked at the living creatures, behold, a wheel was on the earth beside each living creature with its four faces. The appearance of the wheels and their workings was like the color of beryl (or sparkling topaz), and all four had the same likeness. The appearance of their workings was, as it were, a wheel in the middle of a wheel, when they moved, they went toward any one of four directions; they did not turn aside when they went. As for their rims, they were so high they were awesome; and their rims were full of eyes, all around the four of them. When the living creatures went, the wheels went beside them; and when the living creatures were lifted up from the earth, the wheels were lifted up. Wherever the Spirit wanted to go, they went, because there the spirit went; and the wheels were lifted together with them, for the spirit of the living creatures was in the wheels. When those went, these went; when those stood, these stood; and when those were lifted up from the earth, the wheels were lifted up together with them, for the spirit of the living creatures was in the wheels.

The likeness of the firmament above the heads of the living creatures was like the color of an awesome crystal, stretched out over their heads. And under the firmament their wings were spread straight out, one toward another. Each one had two which covered one side, and each one had two which covered the other side of the body. When they went, I heard the noise of their wings, like the noise of many waters, like the voice of the Almighty, a tumult like the noise of an army; and when they stood still, they let down their wings. A voice came from above the firmament that was over their heads; whenever they stood, they let down their wings.

PETER J. DAVIS

And above the firmament over their heads was the likeness of
a throne, in appearance like a sapphire stone; on the likeness
of the throne was a likeness with the appearance of a man
high above it. Also from the appearance of His waist and
upward I saw, as it were, the color of amber with the appearance of fire all around within it; and from the appearance of
His waist and downward I saw, as it were, the appearance
of fire with brightness all around. Like the appearance of a
rainbow in a cloud on a rainy day, so was the appearance of
the brightness all around it. This was the appearance of the
likeness of the glory of the Lord.

Ezekiel 1:1–28 (NKJV)

In chapter 2, the Lord God speaks with Ezekiel from his
throne and brings a case against the Israelites whereby Ezekiel
is ultimately sent to deliver the word of the Lord to his rebellious and brazenly stubborn people. A little later on in chapter 2,
the four living creatures, propelled by their chariotlike vehicles,
carry the prophet Ezekiel away to the place where the Lord
would have him prophesy to his people in (Ezekiel 2:12–15).

What is interesting to note from each of these different
accounts given by the Apostle John and the other two prophets
of God are, first of all, where the similarities lie in their descriptions of the four living creatures and then where they do not.

In John's account, the four living creatures appear to have
four different faces, but with the addition of Ezekiel's account,
we see that they are actually identical, each having four different faces that face out in four different directions. The chariotlike vehicles having eyes all around the wheels inside and out
appears to be both symbolic and real. The chariots themselves
appear to be real as they are not always seen with them. The
eyes in the wheels, on the other hand, are purely symbolic as
they appear to change location from being seen within the
creatures in John's account to being seen within the wheels in
Ezekiel's account. Thus denoting that the four systems of eyes
found within each of the four seraphim, or cherubim, depend-

108

ing on whose account you wish to name them by, can only be symbolic of the all-seeing power of God as he keeps watch over the four quarters of the earth and the universe through them. Hence, the all-seeing eyes of the four living creatures, as John describes them, are always present whether they are seen within the creatures themselves or in the wheels of their chariots.

The six sets of wings on the seraphim are also real and apparently were not visible from Ezekiel's perspective, as the middle set of wings were drooped over the lower body of each of the four living creatures, covering the lower sets. Their synchronized movements are also characteristic of their oneness with one another and especially with the emanating Spirit of the Father that dwells within them.

The fourth italicized scripture: The four living creatures are then heard saying: *"Holy, holy, holy, Lord God Almighty, who was, and is, and is to come:"* (Revelation 4;8, NKJV). Here we are given the one Holy Scripture from which the beast makes his unholy comparison. Where it is written:

> The beast you have seen was once alive and is alive no longer; and is yet to come up from the abyss, but only to go to its destruction. And the people of the world, whose names have not been written since the beginning of the world in the book of life will be astonished when they see how the beast was once alive and is alive no longer, and is still to come.
>
> Revelation 17:8 (TNJB)

As we can see from this comparison of scriptures, the beast is in fact a man who was once alive and is now dead but who will, at the appointed time, be resurrected from the dead, just as Jesus was by the same power and authority of God. But instead of coming back to the earth with a herald of heavenly angels in clouds of glory, the beast will be returning from beneath the molten bowels of the earth in a hideous herald of fallen angels and dark smoke to deceive the world into believing he is the Messiah. That is why the world will be so astonished to see him when he comes back because when they see him they will recognize him as being the man who has been called "the great destroyer." I will be speaking in much greater detail later about this man that God symbolizes as the beast with the seven heads, ten horns, and ten diadems when I get to that section of my book called "The Beast and the False Prophet."

The fifth italicized scripture: "—and in the midst of the elders, stood a Lamb as though it had been slain, having *seven horns and seven eyes, which are the seven Spirits of God sent out into all the earth*" (Revelation 5:6, NKJV). In this scripture, it is important to understand that the seven horns and seven eyes that are seen by the Apostle John on the head of the Lamb are purely symbolic. The seven horns symbolize the sovereign dominion of the Lamb, who is King of kings and Lord of lords and reigns over the seven churches who represent his kingdom on earth as it is in heaven, which are also symbolized by the seven golden lamp stands, hence the seven horns.

The seven eyes of the Lamb are in fact symbolic of three different things. First, the seven eyes symbolize *the seven spirits of God* who are sent out over all the world. Second, the seven spirits of God also symbolize *the seven stars* that the One (Jesus) holds in his right hand. Finally, the seven stars also symbolize *the seven angels of God* who stand watch over the seven churches and who are also the same seven facing angels that I wrote about earlier; reference Revelation 1:20, Revelation 3:1, and also Revelation 2:1.

The sixth italicized scripture: "Thou art worthy to take the scroll and to break its seals, *for thou wast slain and by thy blood didst purchase for God, men from every tribe and language, people and nation; and make of them a royal house, to serve our God as priests who shall reign upon the earth*" (Revelation 5:10, TNEB). This scripture is important to understand because it encompasses a lot of things, and to understand it is to know where your place will be in the kingdom of God when it finally comes down to earth. But there is yet another place in the book of

THE BOOK OF REVELATION AND THE BIBLE
AS NEVER EXPLAINED BEFORE

Revelation that brings even more clarity to who most of these are who constitute this royal house of reigning priests. But even so, there are still two other groups that God keeps as a secret from us whom I will be revealing for the first time, by the power of the Holy Spirit, when I get to the end of this sequence of explanations. Whereas it is written:

> Then I saw thrones, where they took their seats, and on them was conferred the power to give judgment. I saw the souls of all who had been beheaded for having witnessed for Jesus and for having preached God's word, and those who refused to worship the beast or his statue (or his image) and would not accept the brand-mark on their foreheads or hands; they came to life, and reigned with Christ for a thousand years. The rest of the dead did not come to life until the thousand years were over; *this is the first resurrection*. Blessed and holy are those who share in the first resurrection; the second death has no power over them, but they will be priests of God and of Christ and reign with him for a thousand years.
>
> Revelation 20:4–6 (TNJB)

To spell this out, there are three groups here who shall be priests of God and also constitute, for the most part, the reigning class of royalty in the kingdom of God, and they are:

The first group: Aside from Jesus Christ, who shall sit in the presiding judgment seat over those of the world and also those who will enter his kingdom, these shall be those to whom judgment is committed in this context. They are first, as stated by Jesus, the twelve apostles. Whereas it is written:

> Then Peter answered and said to Him, "See, we have left all and followed You. Therefore what shall we have?" So Jesus said to them, "Assuredly I say to you that in the regeneration, (or in the millennial kingdom) when the son of man sits on the throne of His glory, you who have followed Me will also sit on twelve thrones, judging the twelve tribes of Israel."
>
> Matthew 19:27–28 (NKJV)

This is not to mean that they will be the only judges over Israel; because they also sit in the company of the other twelve elders who together with them make up the twenty-four thrones that surround the throne of God. So it can be inferred from this that there will actually be twenty-four judgment seats that will preside over all Israel when the kingdom of God is finally brought down to earth. They are, as previously stated, the twelve patriarchs from the second dispensation and the twelve apostles from the third.

At another time, all those from within the royal house, who shall be called the priests of God, will also sit in this same judgment seat of Christ as all the angels who were cast out of heaven are brought before them. There, these angels will finally be brought to justice for all their crimes committed against God and his people, as they will be literally cast into the *lake of fire* at the conclusion of that time. These same priests will also sit in judgment over another group of angels who will be brought before them and who shall receive no less the same fate because of the fornication they had each committed with the women of the earth during the first dispensation. It is because of this sin committed so long ago that each of these angels will have been left bound beneath the dark molten bowels of the earth in everlasting chains, as they will on this same day also be brought to judgment. Reference 1 Corinthians 6:1–3 regarding God's people judging the world and the angels. Also, read 2 Peter 2:3–4 and Jude 1:6–7 regarding the fallen angels reserved for judgment. It is also written, "To him who overcomes I will grant to sit with Me on My throne, as I also overcame and sat down with my Father on his throne" (Revelation 3:21–22, NKJV).

The second group: These are the hundred and forty-four thousand who are symbolized by the church of Philadelphia. However, unlike the church of Philadelphia, who will be resurrected at this time, along with all the others who had died in their faith, these who are called the first fruits of humanity to be ransomed, will not be resurrected or even taste death for another

THE BOOK OF REVELATION AND THE BIBLE
AS NEVER EXPLAINED BEFORE

thousand years. These are those who will have been previously taken up into heaven and transformed into immortality at a time secretly appointed by God, which will come before all the rest who are being taken up into heaven here. Hence, that is why they are called the first fruits of humanity to be ransomed. Whereas it is written about the church of Philadelphia:

> I know your works. See, I have set before you an open door, and no one can shut it; for you (who) have a little strength, have kept My word, and have not denied My name. Indeed I will make those of the synagogue of Satan, who say they are Jews, and are not, but lie—indeed I will make them come and worship before your feet, and to know that I have loved you. Because you have kept My command to persevere, I also will keep you from the hour of trial which shall come upon the whole world, to test those who dwell on the earth. Behold, I am coming quickly! Hold fast (to) what you have, that no one may take your crown. He who overcomes, I will make him a pillar in the temple of My God, and he shall go out no more. *I will write on him the name of My God, and the name of the city* of My God, the *new Jerusalem*, which comes down out of heaven from My God. And *I will write on him My new name*.
>
> Revelation 3:8–13, (NKJV)

Notice how strikingly similar the description about the church of Philadelphia is to the criteria given later about the hundred and forty-four thousand by Jesus. Notice also how this church here does not actually receive *the seal of God* but only its promise if they are victorious; even then, that promise will not be fulfilled until after the time when all things are made new, which will not be until after the one-thousand-year reign of Christ has come to its completion. As I have already stated before, this is the time when the new heaven, and the new earth, and finally the new Jerusalem will be seen coming down out of heaven as the bride of Christ. Otherwise, both groups had, in the first instance, or will have in the second, achieved the status

113

of being called one of God's *chosen elect,* where neither Satan's synagogue nor the beast that has yet to appear, will be allowed to touch either of them. Out of all the other groups who are to be saved, these are the only ones who will achieve this elite status during their time on earth.

The third group: These are all the *men* from within the third dispensation called the *great multitude* who will have the *seal of the Holy Spirit* placed upon them. These are also those who either have been already or shall be in the future led like lambs to the slaughter for the sake of God's word and their testimony to Jesus, and also, all those of the faithful who will have resisted the beast and its mark, and lived to see the second coming of Christ for their deliverance. It is the latter part of this group that will also not taste death until the one-thousand-year reign of Christ has come to its end.

These then are the three groups, as mentioned in the book of Revelation, who will be called the priests of God and who will be transformed into immortality and made into a royal house in the kingdom of God.

As I mentioned at the beginning of this explanation of the royal house, there are still two other groups of Israelites whom the Lord keeps as a secret from us who will also come to reside here in the royal house. They are perhaps the most honored of all the groups. They are, in the first group, none other than Abraham, Isaac, and Jacob, as well as the hundreds of other men known to us as the prophets and messengers of the Lord who had been beaten, tortured, murdered, stoned, and their dead bodies mutilated for the witness they bore to their own people in behalf of the Lord their God.

In the second group, they are none other than the ten righteous kings and their families that may only be found from within the house of Judah. All the rest of the kings from either the house of Judah or the house of Israel corrupted themselves and did what was wrong in the eyes of the Lord. These are the names of the ten righteous kings by the order of their succession to the throne after King David: King Asa, who reigned forty-one years; King Jehoshaphat, who reigned twenty-five years; King Joash, who reigned forty years; King Amaziah, who reigned twenty-nine years; King Azariah, who reigned fifty-two years; King Uzziah, who reigned for fifty-two years, King Jotham, who reigned for sixteen years; King Hezekiah, who reigned for twenty-nine years, and finally King Josiah, the last righteous king from the house of Judah, who reigned for thirty-one years. All of these and also those previously mentioned, along with the twelve patriarchs who will be joined by the twelve apostles whose twenty-four thrones will surround the throne of God, will be the only ones out of all Israel who will come to reside in the royal house as priests of God and be transformed into immortality.

The survivors of all Israel who will be saved from the beast's great reign of terror at the second coming of Christ are the only other group out of all Israel who, although not allowed to enter the royal house, will be allowed to dwell within the inner kingdom as they live out the rest of their mortal lives in peace within the land that encompasses the holy city of Jerusalem. The holy city of Jerusalem will be completely restored to its earlier time of greatness after Christ's triumphant return as his kingdom begins its one-thousand-year reign of peace upon the earth.

It should also be noted that these priests of God who shall reside in the royal house are all men, as it is an abomination against God for any woman to enter the priesthood even though she may have been a prophetess. Having said that, it must also be mentioned that even though the book of Revelation makes no mention of any women or children being present in these three groups of the royal house, we still know that they have to be a part of this harvest called the *great multitude,* or otherwise those sealed with the *seal of the Holy Spirit.* This is primarily because there is no other seal by which they can be delivered and still be a part of that group called the faithful of God's chosen people.

Even so, I must confess that I was greatly troubled by this realization as it first occurred to me. So I asked the Lord to reveal its hidden meaning so that I might be able to write about it and ease the minds of all the women and children who will come to read this book and also to the few women chosen to be prophetesses, as well as all the other women who have served and dedicated their lives to the many different women's order of nuns only found within the Catholic Church and its counterpart, the Eastern Orthodox Church. Most notably the regular black and white order and the very special blue and white order founded by Mother Teresa in India. Although it has been pointed out to me that there are many other orders of nuns that do not wear either habits or colors and it is only right and proper that their service to God be recognized here as well.

The seventh italicized scripture: *"Then I looked, and I heard the voice of many angels around the throne, the living creatures, and the elders; and the number of them was ten-thousand times ten-thousand, and thousands upon thousands"* (Revelation 5:11–12, NKJV). This scripture is important to take notice of because it, first of all, depicts all those who constitute God's firstborn citizens of heaven, or, as they are more affectionately known to us as being called—his heavenly angels. Secondly, this scripture is important because it shows that these angels are also God's helpers who are sent out into the world to serve as our guardian angels who will come to dwell within each of us as we perfect ourselves in his love. Otherwise, they are also the ones who keep the record books up to date for God on everything that we say or do that is either good or evil. For the righteous, each angel becomes the seal of their deliverance as the time approaches when the Lord shall come like a thief in the night for his chosen and faithfully waiting people.

THE KINGDOM OF GOD

Once again, the question that I had asked in the previous chapter, of where all the women and children would be in the kingdom of God, came to mind. Then as I laid down in quiet meditation and awaited the Lord's answer, the Spirit of the Lord came upon me and began to explain its hidden meaning to me in this way. And the Spirit said that within the Lord's kingdom that is to be brought down to earth, whereby his Son, the Lamb of God, shall reign supreme over all the earth as the King of kings and the Lord of lords, there shall be many kingdoms given to those within the royal house. There, each king and lord shall have his own golden crown of glory and a throne to rule by, as it has been written. Accordingly, within those kingdoms there will be the palaces of all the founding patriarchs and apostles, from Abraham to Benjamin and from Peter to Paul. There too will be all the palaces of the prophets, from Abel to Ezra from the first and second dispensations and from John the Baptist to all the rest that have yet to come from the third dispensation, even up until the second coming of Christ. There will also be the palaces of the ten righteous kings of Judah, from King David to Josiah, but it is the throne of King David that will be set above all those who shall be called: "The survivors of all Israel."

Just as important to God will be the many palaces of the holy royal priests and of his other faithful servants who shall all be called the reigning priests of God. But there will also be many mansions and estates given to others who will have earned his favor according to their different levels of love, their works of faith, and by their different levels of self-sacrifice that they were each willing to make for the Lord's sake and his gospel as well. As it will be for all the rest of that group who were given the seal of the Holy Spirit not already mentioned, so it shall be that not everyone will be rewarded the same, whether they be man or woman, son or daughter, rich or poor, or great or small, or even among those who had been slaughtered in the womb. This is just as it is written in the parable about the bags of gold where some will even be cast out of his kingdom into the place of wailing and gnashing of teeth, as it is written in Matthew 25:14–30.

So it shall also be that within the kingdoms of the royal house, some will have great estates with many subjects and servants, and others will have lesser estates with not as many subjects and servants. Some will have vast kingdoms while others will have smaller kingdoms upon which to rule by. Some will have great treasures of gold and silver stored up for them within their palaces and mansions, and others will not have much at all. All will be rewarded according to the amount of favor that they had each earned from the Lord during their time on earth. Otherwise, all will be allowed to marry and be given in marriage and have children in this age that shall not end until after the one-thousand-year reign of Christ is over. But only those who were willing to sacrifice their most treasured possessions here

THE BOOK OF REVELATION AND THE BIBLE
AS NEVER EXPLAINED BEFORE

on earth for the Lord's sake and his gospel shall be rewarded a hundred times over for those very things in the Lord's millennial kingdom, as it is written in Mark 10:28–31. It is only when the eternal kingdom comes, after the one-thousand-year reign of Christ has ended, that men and women shall not be allowed to marry or be given in marriage. There they shall be as the angels are and become the glorified sons of God.

With regards to the mansions and palaces of the reigning priests of the royal house, it is within them that there shall be found all the women, the wives, the children, and especially all the unborn who had been slaughtered here on earth that the Lamb of God will give to each of them who are so deserving. Also in the royal house, it shall be that every royal priest will reign sovereign over his kingdom and show favor where he will show favor and render mercy and justice where he will render mercy and justice. All shall live and reign immortal with Christ for a thousand years.

Then shall heaven and earth pass away and all creation return back unto the Father as all these things from both heaven and earth, to include the Son of God, will vanish from existence and rest for seven days within the Father. Only the Father sitting upon his great white throne in a brilliant display of emanating light will be all that is left from within or without the entire universe. After the seven days of rest and silence have ended, then shall the final resurrection of the dead come that Jesus spoke about in the Gospel of Luke and after that the great Day of Judgment. Then when the great Day of Judgment is over, there shall come the eternal kingdom where men and women do not marry but become as the angels are, or otherwise, the glorified sons of God, as it is written in Luke 20:32–38.

All the rest who survive the beast's great reign of terror will be mortals. As such, if they are able to maintain their righteousness, they will only live to be a hundred years of age before they grow old and die. All of these will be allowed to marry and be given in marriage and have children as well, but they will not

119

be allowed to enter the royal house except as servants. However, they will be allowed to dwell and live in peace within the inner kingdom, which will encompass all the lands and mountains that surround the holy city of Jerusalem. Otherwise, the unrighteous will not even live to see the age of fifty, as their land, their lives, and their families will all be cursed by God, as it is also written in Isaiah 65:19–25 regarding the peaceful life and age the Lord will grant to the survivors of all Israel who are brought home to dwell with him in the land of Zion.

THE BRIDES OF CHRIST

Symbolically and spiritually speaking, especially from the context of the Old Testament, there have already been four brides of Christ. Within each marriage, a blood covenant was drawn up and marital vows were exchanged and a very loving relationship ensued for a short time. But as time would tell, two of these wives later became terribly unfaithful. As a result of this infidelity, the other two wives became defiled by the first two's repeated acts of adultery as they began to worship other gods in violation of the covenant they had each made with their husband, the Lord their God. Finally, after all attempts and pleas for reconciliation were ignored by each of the first two wives, two divorce decrees were issued. A separation notice was also issued to the other two wives until ultimately they would be divorced as well. Each wife was then ultimately cut off from the Lord by their own separate decree of divorce and remains so to this day.

You may well be asking, "But who were these early wives of the Lord?" You may also be wondering what has become of them. The answer to these two questions is very profound and will amaze you. Symbolically speaking, *the nation of Israel* was the first wife of the Lord and was consecrated unto the Lord through the blood covenant of Abraham and became the first wife of the Lord after the twelve sons of Jacob, also called Israel, became independent after his death.

The second wife of the Lord was Israel's sister, *Judah*. After the death of Solomon, the nation of Israel became divided, and Judah, her sister, also found herself married to the Lord by way of the same blood covenant of Abraham. Reference Jeremiah 3:6–10 regarding the many acts of adultery committed by both Israel and her sister Judah and the two subsequent divorce decrees that were issued to the two of them by the Lord. Then, years later, after a final plea for reconciliation was also rejected, two more divorce decrees were issued to the other two wives as well.

The third wife of the Lord was the *land of Zion*. In the book of Isaiah, we are told by the prophet Isaiah in a prophecy regarding the millennial reign of Christ that when the Lord reweds the reconciled survivors of all Israel, he will also rewed the newly restored land of Zion, (Isaiah 62:1–5).

The fourth wife of the Lord is found within the land of Zion itself and is none other than the *holy city of Jerusalem*, which at that time encompassed the holy temple of God. Jerusalem was supposed to be the most beautiful wife of all, but when Jesus came the first time in gesture of reconciling this symbolic marriage, he knew that he would be rejected and murdered instead by the very people he was coming to reconcile himself with and save from their sins. Because of this, God's holy city of Jerusalem remained defiled, and the rewedding of Jerusalem that could have been never happened.

Since that time, a new covenant has been made, and once again Christ has named his brides to be. They are similar to the first four with this one major difference. The nation of Israel, which was divided in two, has now in part been replaced by the *church of God*. Otherwise, after Christ's second coming, the other part of the nation of Israel, or more specifically, *the survivors of all Israel who will be saved*, and the *land of Zion* shall each be reconciled back unto the Lord and rewed after his second coming; in the meantime, they will remain cut off from God.

With regard to the city of Jerusalem: Originally I had thought that because Jerusalem had become so defiled by men over the ages that she would not be rewed by Christ as a consequence for this defilement, but after a closer look at the writings of the prophet Isaiah in chapter 54, I discovered something even more profound. The truth is: that when Christ comes in his second coming to establish his kingdom here on earth for a thousand years, he not only comes to reconcile himself with the survivors of the divided nation of Israel and the land of Zion, but he also comes back to rewed another wife who is actually regarded here by Isaiah as being synonymous with the other three which is none other than the city of Jerusalem. For though God through his prophets speaks of Israel symbolically as being four separate wives, it is important to understand that it was not this way in the beginning. But it was only because of the sins of the nation that they became divided, and as such, divorced by God. But in chapter 54 it is very interesting to note how Isaiah regards them all as being the one barren woman whom God has made his wife again. Once again showing how God does not see things as man sees things. So it is that the land, the city, and the divided nation of Israel, which constitute the four brides of Christ, shall all be made holy again and reconciled back to God as his one wife; because it is only through holiness that this reunion can occur as it will also be through holiness that we are all made one with God again as it was in the beginning before our creation. For a greater understanding of this explanation read (Isaiah 54:1–17). For another perspective on this restoration read (Isaiah 35:5–10) pay particular attention to the causeway that is called the, "Way of Holiness" which leads into the city of Jerusalem in verse 8.

But there is still one last bride of Christ that has yet to be mentioned here who is perhaps the most beautiful bride of all. She is made known to us in the last chapter of Revelation where we are told that after the one-thousand-year reign of Christ has come to pass away or at the time when the new heaven, the new earth, and the *new Jerusalem* are seen coming down out of heaven as all things are made new again, that here, his most treasured and glorious bride of all, the new Jerusalem, will be

THE BOOK OF REVELATION AND THE BIBLE
AS NEVER EXPLAINED BEFORE

taken and wed, (Revelation 21:9–11). How fitting it should be that it is not until then that Christ will have the one virgin bride and wife that he has so longed for throughout the ages—a bride and wife created by his father, perfect in beauty and gloriously adorned in priceless jewels for a Son who deserves nothing less for all that he has done to please his father and for the sacrifice he was willing to make for the salvation of the world.

It is important to remember at this point that these brides and their ensuing weddings are all spiritually symbolic unions, as most everyone in the kingdom of God will be allowed to marry or else be given in marriage. Otherwise, it should be pointed out that even though Christ does not actually tell us whether or not he will take for himself a physical wife or wives during his millennial reign, his own words make it very plausible. Where it is written: "There is no one (and the word no one should also include Christ himself) who has left house or brothers or sisters or father or mother or wife or children or lands, for My sake and the gospel's, who will not receive a hundredfold now *in this time* (or a hundred times as many of all these things during the time of Christ's millennial reign on earth)—houses and brothers and sisters and mothers and children and lands, with persecutions (the persecutions signify the end times that will precede the millennial reign)—and *in the age to come,* (or during the time when the new heaven, the new earth, and the new Jerusalem are created, which is also the beginning of the eternal kingdom) eternal life" (Mark 10:29–30, NKJV). How much more right will the King of kings and Lord of lords have to freely choose, as he has decreed for all the rest within the royal house, as many wives as a king should be allowed to have? I believe it shall be as it is written. For a slight hint of this possibility reference (Isaiah 53:10) regarding how the messiah will live to see his seed, or more clearly, his children's children during the millennium, which is inferred as the time when his Father's pleasure shall prosper in his hand.

As for the different orders of nuns who had lived their lives in total dedication to the Lord their God, I believe that if Christ is to have a part in his own decree, then it would be very fitting that they should have the very high honor of living within the most prestigious palace of all: the palace of the King of kings and Lord of lords, where they will be allowed to love, adore, and serve him as wives. Then if it should be the will of the Father, he will choose one from among them to be his queen because of her great love and adoration for the Lord that will have outshone all the rest. Some of the candidates might very well be starting with Mary of Magdala from the Lord's time on earth, or even Mother Teresa from our time. It is in this one area that the Spirit of the Lord has not chosen to make this answer known. However, a queen will be chosen by each of the other reigning kings within the royal house. Otherwise, here in these palaces of the royal house, it will become known that though many were called, only these few will have been chosen.

With regard to Mary the mother of God: It is written that she shall be called blessed by all generations, which will especially be true during the Lord's one-thousand-year reign on earth and perhaps even into eternity. Because of this, it is also very likely that she will have her own very special place in the royal house as the most exalted woman in all Israel. Reference (Luke 1:46–48), regarding her special blessing and (Revelation 12:1–2), regarding her exalted status being symbolized by the crown of twelve stars on her head, the sun wrapped around her, and the moon beneath her feet.

But then I inquired of the Spirit of the Lord, if these are all those which constitute the *holy royal priests of God*, who shall reside in the royal house and reign with Christ for a thousand years, then just who exactly is it that they will be reigning over? The answer came very simply, as I was directed by the Spirit to the very scriptures themselves. There I could see for myself what most all the prophets of the kings had been describing to us all along. As I read their accounts, I could see how they were each giving a uniquely different perspective of the same thing, as they described at great length why God exiled and abandoned his people to all the nations of the world. They're to be abused, hunted, and killed, and enslaved until their time of disgrace should be ended. But always as the time of their disgrace would come to its end, their time of restoration would follow. There, between the accounts given by the different prophets, is the restoration of Israel described in great detail, as the Lord is shown to come at the end of this age to call his exiled and abandoned people home to the land promised to them and their forefathers in the everlasting covenant. On this great and terrible Day of the Lord, all these prophets tell how the Lord shall destroy all the warring nations who will come against him and his heavenly host when he appears in his second coming to save Jerusalem and, after which, how there will only be two groups left on the earth. They are the survivors of all Israel, who will be saved, and the survivors of Gog and Magog, who are, in essence, all the surviving countrymen and family members of all the nations who came to wage war against the Lamb of God and his heavenly host.

It is written by the prophet Zechariah:

> It shall be in that day that I will seek to destroy all the nations that come against Jerusalem. "And I will poor on the house of David and on the inhabitants of Jerusalem the Spirit of grace and supplication; then they will look upon Me whom they pierced. Yes they will mourn for Him as one mourns for his only son, and grieve for Him as one grieves for a firstborn. In that day there shall be a great mourning in Jerusalem, like the mourning at Hadad-rimmon in the plain of Megiddo. And the land shall mourn, every family by itself: the family of the house of David by itself, and their wives by themselves; the family of the house of Nathan by itself, and their wives by themselves; the family of the house of Levi by itself, and their wives by themselves; the family of Shimei by itself and their wives by themselves; all the families that remain, every family by itself, and their wives by themselves.
>
> Zechariah 12:9–14 (NKJV)

In that day a fountain shall be open for the house of David and for the inhabitants of Jerusalem, for sin and for uncleanliness.

"It shall be in that day," says the Lord of Hosts, "that I will cut off the names of the idols from the land, and they shall no longer be remembered. I will also cause the prophets and the unclean spirit to depart from the land. It shall come to pass that if anyone still prophesies, then his father and mother who begot him will say to him, 'You shall not live, because you have spoken lies in the name of the Lord.' And his father and mother who begot him shall thrust him through when he prophesies.

"And it shall be in that day that every prophet will be ashamed of his vision when he prophesies; they will not wear a robe of course hair to deceive. But he will say, 'I am no prophet, I am a farmer; for a man taught me to keep cattle from my youth.'

Zechariah 13:1–5 (NKJV)

It shall come to pass in that day that there will be no light; the lights will diminish. It shall be one day which is known to the Lord—neither day nor night. But at evening time it shall happen that it will be light.

And in that day it shall be that living waters shall flow from Jerusalem, half of them toward the eastern sea and half of them toward the western sea; in both summer and winter it shall occur. And the Lord shall be King over all the earth. In that day it shall be—"The Lord is one," and His name one. All the land shall be turned into a plain from Geba to Rimmon south of Jerusalem. Jerusalem shall be raised up and inhabited in her place from Benjamin's Gate, to the place of the First Gate and the Corner Gate, and from the Tower of Hananel to the king's winepresses. The people shall dwell in it; and no longer shall there be utter destruction, but Jerusalem shall be safely inhabited. And this shall be the plague with which the Lord will strike all the people who fought against Jerusalem: Their flesh shall dissolve (or more clearly be consumed by fire) while they stand on their feet, their eyes shall dissolve in their sockets, and their tongues shall dissolve in their mouths.

THE BOOK OF REVELATION AND THE BIBLE
AS NEVER EXPLAINED BEFORE

It shall come to pass in that day that a great panic from the Lord will be among them. Everyone will seize the hand of his neighbor, and raise his hand against his neighbor's hand; Judah also will fight at Jerusalem. And the wealth of all the surrounding nations shall be gathered together: gold, silver, and apparel in great abundance. Such also shall be the plague on the horse and the mule, on the camel and the donkey, and on all the cattle that will be in those camps. So shall this plague be.

And it shall come to pass that everyone who is left of all the nations which came against Jerusalem shall go up from year to year to worship the King, the Lord of Hosts, and to keep the Feast of the Tabernacles. And it shall be that whichever of the families of the earth do not come up to Jerusalem to worship the King, the Lord of Hosts, on them there will be no rain. If the family of Egypt will not come up and enter in, they shall have no rain; they shall receive the plague with which the Lord strikes the nations who do not come up to keep the Feast of Tabernacles. This shall be the punishment of Egypt and the punishment of all the nations that do not come up to keep the Feast of Tabernacles.

In that day "Holiness to the Lord" shall be engraved on the bells of the horses. The pots in the Lord's house shall be like the bowls before the altar. Yes every pot in Jerusalem and Judah shall be holiness to the Lord of Hosts. Everyone who sacrifices shall come and take them and cook in them. In that day there shall no longer be a Canaanite in the house of the Lord of Hosts.

Zechariah 14:6–21 (NKJV)

The prophet Micah has this to say regarding the restoration of Jerusalem and the gathering home of the remnant of Israel:

Now it shall come to pass in the latter days that the mountain of the Lord's house shall be established on the top of the mountains, and shall be exalted above the hills; and peoples shall flow to it. Many nations shall come and say, "Come, and let us go up to the mountain of the Lord, to the house of the God of Jacob; He will teach us His ways, and we shall walk in His paths." For out of Zion the law shall go forth, and the word of the Lord from Jerusalem. He shall judge between many peoples, and rebuke strong nations afar off; they shall beat their swords into plowshares, and their spears into pruning hooks; nation shall not lift up sword against nation, neither shall they learn war anymore. But everyone shall sit under His vine and His fig tree. And no one shall make them afraid; for the mouth of the Lord of Hosts has spoken. For all people walk each in the name of his god, but we will walk in the name of the Lord our God forever and ever.

"In that day," says the Lord, "I will assemble the lame, I will gather the outcast and those whom I have afflicted; I will make the lame a remnant, and the outcast a strong nation; so the Lord will reign over them in Mount Zion from now on, even forever.

Micah 4:1–7 (NKJV)

Listen as the prophet Joel, in his account, describes the time leading up to and during the great and terrible Day of the Lord and thereafter the calling home of the remnant of Israel to Mount Zion:

"And it shall come to pass afterward that I will poor out my spirit on all flesh; your sons and your daughters shall prophesy, your old men shall dream dreams, your young men shall see visions. And also on My menservants and on My maidservants I will poor out My Spirit in those days.

"And I will show wonders in the heavens and in the earth: blood and fire and pillars of smoke. The sun shall be turned into darkness, and the moon into blood, before the coming of the great and awesome Day of the Lord. And it shall come to pass that whoever calls on the name of Lord shall be saved. For in Mount Zion and in Jerusalem there shall be deliverance, as the Lord has said, among the remnant whom the Lord calls.

Joel 2:28–32 (NKJV)

THE BOOK OF REVELATION AND THE BIBLE
AS NEVER EXPLAINED BEFORE

For behold, in those days and at that time, when I bring back
the captives of Judah and Jerusalem, I will also gather all
nations, and bring them down to the Valley of Jehoshaphat;
and I will enter into judgment with them there on account
of My people, My heritage Israel, whom they have scattered
among the nations; they have also divided up My land. They
have cast lots for My people, have given a boy as payment for
a harlot, and sold a girl for wine, that they may drink.

Joel 3:1–3 (NKJV)

Proclaim this among the nations: "Prepare for war! Wake up the
mighty men, let all the men of war draw near, let them come up.
Beat your plowshares into swords and your pruning hooks into
spears; let the weak say, 'I am strong.' " Assemble and come,
all you nations, and gather together all around. Cause Your
mighty ones to go down there, O Lord. "Let the nations be
weakened, and come up to the Valley of Jehoshaphat; for there
I will sit to judge all the surrounding nations. Put in the sickle,
for the harvest is ripe. Come, go down; for the wine press is
full, the vats overflow—for their wickedness is great." Multitudes, multitudes, in the Valley of Decision! For the Day of
the Lord is near in the Valley of Decision. The sun and moon
will grow dark, and the stars will diminish their brightness.
The Lord also will roar from Zion, and utter His voice from
Jerusalem; the heavens and earth will shake; but the Lord will
be a shelter for His people, and the strength of the children of
Israel. "So you shall know that I am the Lord your God, dwelling in Zion My holy mountain. Then Jerusalem shall be holy,
and no aliens shall ever pass through her again."

And it will come to pass in that day that the mountains shall
drip with new wine, the hills shall flow with milk, and all
the brooks of Judah shall be flooded with water; a fountain
shall flow from the house of the Lord and water the Valley of
Acacias. "Egypt shall be a desolation, and Edom (Lebanon)
a desolate wilderness, because of violence against the people
of Judah, for they have shed innocent blood in their land. But
Judah shall abide forever, and Jerusalem from generation to

generation. For I will acquit them of the guilt of bloodshed, whom I have not acquitted; for the Lord dwells in Zion" Joel 3:9–21, (NKJV).

The Apostle John explains this great battle to us this way in the book of Revelation:

Now I saw heaven opened, and behold, a white horse. And He who sat on him was called Faithful and True, and in righteousness He judges and makes war. His eyes were like a flame of fire and on His head were many crowns. He had a name written that no one knew except Himself. He was clothed with a robe dipped in blood, and his name is called the Word of God. And the armies in heaven, clothed in fine linen, white and clean, followed Him on white horses. Now out of his mouth goes a sharp sword, that with it he should strike the nations. *And He Himself, will rule them with a rod of iron.* He Himself treads the winepress of the fierceness and the wrath of Almighty God. And He has on His robe and on His thigh a name written: King of kings and Lord of lords.

Then I saw an angel standing in the sun; and he cried with a loud voice, saying to all the birds that fly in the midst of heaven, "Come and gather together for the supper of the great God, that you may eat the flesh of kings, the flesh of captains, the flesh of mighty men, the flesh of horses and those who sit on them, and the flesh of all people, free and slave, both small and great."

And I saw the beast, the kings of the earth, and their armies, gathered together to make war against Him who sat on the horse and against His army. Then the beast was captured, and with him the false prophet who worked signs in his presence, by which he deceived those who received the mark of the beast and those who worshiped his image. These two were cast alive into the lake of fire burning with brimstone. All the rest were killed with the sword which proceeded from the mouth of Him who sat on the horse. And all the birds were filled with their flesh.

Revelation 19:11–21 (NKJV)

THE BOOK OF REVELATION AND THE BIBLE
AS NEVER EXPLAINED BEFORE

Listen now to the prophet Ezra, the last prophet of the Israelites from the house of Judah after their return home from exile in Babylon to Jerusalem in 536 BC. It was in the time of 516 BC, just after they had rebuilt the temple of God and the following consecration ceremonies were completed, that they began to corrupt themselves in ways even worse than before, and it is because of this that they are finally abandoned by God and left to the cruelty of all the other nations.

In his first book, the first book of Esdras, the prophet Ezra details their return and the rebuilding of the temple. Later, in his second book, the second book of Esdras, he calls them to account for their many grievous transgressions made against their God after he had shown them such mercy, but because Ezra has found such favor with the God Most High, he is shown and then has explained to him some of the most startling revelations of the Bible, revelations as no other prophet had ever received. There will not be another prophet of God after him until John the Baptist comes to prepare the straight way for the coming Messiah in AD 26. This account was written during the reign of King Artaxerxes of Persia, when the Persian and Medes Empire ruled the world from 536 BC until 330 BC.

It should also be noted that this account that I am about to quote comes from the second book of Esdras that is found within the compilation of books from The New English Bible, called the Apocrypha. Where it is written:

> The seven days passed; and the next night I had a dream. In my dream, a wind came up out of the sea and set the waves to turmoil. And this wind brought a human figure rising from the depths, as I watched this man came flying with the clouds of heaven. Wherever he turned his eyes, everything that they fell on was seized with terror; and wherever the sound of his voice reached all who heard it melted like wax at the touch of fire.
>
> Next I saw an innumerable host of men gathering from the four winds of heaven to wage war on the man who had risen

131

from the sea. I saw that the man hewed out a vast mountain for himself, and flew up on to it. I tried to see from what quarter or place the mountain had been taken from, but I could not. Then I saw that all who had gathered to wage war against the man were filled with fear, and yet they dared to fight against him. When he saw the hordes advancing to attack he did not so much as lift a finger against them. He had no spear in his hand, no weapon at all; only, as I watched, he poured what seemed like a stream of fire out of his mouth, a breath of flame from his lips, and a storm of sparks from his tongue. All of them combined into one mass—the stream of fire, the breath of flame, and the great storm. It fell on the host advancing to join battle, and burnt up every man of them; suddenly all that enormous multitude had disappeared, leaving nothing but dust and ashes and a reek of smoke. I was dumbfounded at the sight.

After that, I saw a man coming down from the mountain and calling to himself a different company, a peaceful one. He was joined by great numbers of men, some with joy on their faces, others with sorrow. Some came from captivity; some brought others to him as an offering. I woke up in terror, and prayed to the Most High. I said, "You have revealed these marvels to me, your servant, all the way through; you have judged me worthy to have my prayers answered. Now show me the meaning of this dream also. How terrible, to my thinking, it will be for all who survive through those days! But how much worse for those who do not survive! Those who do not survive will have the sorrow of knowing what is in store in the last days and yet missing it. Those who do survive are to be pitied for the terrible dangers and trials which, as these visions show, they will have to face. But perhaps after all it is better to have endured the dangers and reach the goal than to vanish out of the world like a cloud and never see the events of the last days."

"Yes," the angel replied, "I will explain the meaning of this vision, and tell you all that you ask. As for your question about all those who survive, this is the answer: the very person from

THE BOOK OF REVELATION AND THE BIBLE
AS NEVER EXPLAINED BEFORE

whom the danger will then come will protect in danger those who have works and fidelity laid up to their credit with the Most High. You may be assured that those who survive are more highly blessed than those who die.

"This is what the vision means: the man you saw rising from the depths of the sea is he whom the Most High has held in readiness through many ages; he will himself deliver the world he has made and determine the lot of those who survive. As for the breath, fire, and storm you saw pouring from the mouth of the man, so that without a spear or any weapon in his hand he destroyed the hordes advancing to wage war against him, this is the meaning: The day is near when the Most High will begin to bring deliverance to those on earth. Then men will be filled with great alarm; they will plot to make war on one another, city on city, region on region, nation on nation, kingdom on kingdom. When this happens, and all the signs that I have shown you come to pass, then my son will be revealed, whom you saw as a man rising from the sea. On hearing his voice, all the nations will leave their own territories and their separate wars, and unite in a countless host, as you saw in your vision, with a common intent to go and wage war against him. He will take his stand on the summit of Mount Zion, and Zion will come into sight before all men, complete and fully built. This corresponds to the mountain which you saw hewed out, but not by the hand of man. Then my son will convict of their godless deeds the nations that confront him. This will correspond to the storm you saw. He will taunt them with their evil plottings and the tortures they are soon to endure. This corresponds to the flame. And he will destroy them without effort by means of the law—and that is like the fire.

"Then you saw him collecting a different company, a peaceful one. They are the ten tribes which were taken off into exile in the time of King Hosea, who Shalmaneser king of Assyria took prisoner. He deported them beyond the river and they were taken away into a strange country. But then they resolved to leave the country populated by the Gentiles

133

and go to a distant land never yet inhabited by man, and there at least to be obedient to their laws, which in their own country they had failed to keep. As they passed through the narrow passages of the Euphrates, the Most High performed miracles for them, stopping up the channels of the river until they had crossed over. Their journey through that region, which is called the Arzareth (China or also all of Asia), was long, and took a year and a half. They have lived there ever since until this final age. Now they are on their way back, and once more the Most High will stop the channels of the river to let them cross.

That is the meaning of the peaceful assembly that you saw. With them too are the survivors of your own people, all who are inside my sacred boundary. So then, when the time comes for him to destroy the nations assembled against him, he will protect his people who are left, and show them many prodigies."

"My lord my master," I asked, "explain to me why the man I saw rose up out of the depths of the sea?" he replied: "It is beyond the power of any man to explore the deep sea and discover what is in it; in the same way no one on earth can see my son and his company until the appointed day. Such then is the meaning of your vision. This revelation has been given to you and to you alone, because you have given up your affairs and devoted yourself entirely to mine, and the study of my law. You have taken wisdom as your guide in everything, and called understanding your mother. That is why I have given this revelation to you; there is a reward in store for you with the Most High."

2 Esdras 13:1–56 (TNEB)

As we can see from what the prophets are telling us here in the Bible, the remnant of Israel, who have been for almost the last two thousand years cut off from God, shall once again be called his people as the Lord shall once again become their God, and with this, a new covenant shall be made between them. This new covenant relationship will remain in effect both during the one-thousand-year reign of Christ and also thereafter. In his millennial kingdom, they will be allowed to dwell throughout his inner kingdom and also to enter in through the gates of his holy city as freely as they choose where they will come to pay homage to the Lord, whom they had rejected and crucified. They will do this on all feast days, Sabbaths, and as often as it is required, but they will not be allowed to enter the royal house, except as servants and courtiers. They will further be distinguished from the reigning royal house by their mortality as opposed to the immortality of God's holy royal priests. Here in this land called Zion is where they will come to live and raise their children after being called back from the four quarters of the earth. Here also is where they will finally come to dwell in peace and grow their crops all throughout the seven holy mountains of his kingdom, as their time in exile will now and forevermore be over.

The land where these seven holy mountains shall be is the same land that was given to Abraham by God as an everlasting possession that was made a part of the everlasting covenant in Genesis 17:7–8. This is also the same land that was called the land of Israel and the Promised Land by Moses. This is not in any way, shape, or form to be confused with or even associated with the land of America or more precisely the land of the United States of America.

For a greater understanding of this restoration of the land and reconciliation of the people called the remnant of Israel who will be saved, read Ezekiel 34:1–31; also read Isaiah 54:1–17.

The survivors of Gog and Magog, on the other hand, will reside at the lowest level of God's outer kingdom, or otherwise be in effect the peasant class. And they will not be allowed to enter in through the gates of his inner kingdom except during those times when they must come to pay tribute and homage to the Lord of hosts for his continued blessings, or else once every year during the pilgrim Feast of Tabernacles. Otherwise they will live in the outer lying regions of the earth and will be lorded over by the different members of the reigning royal house. Their descendants are also those who shall be as countless as the sands of the sea at the end of the one-thousand-year reign of Christ. This will also be the same time when Satan is finally let loose from his chains and brought up out of the abyss to seduce these descendants of the survivors of Gog and Magog one last time. Where it is written:

> Now when the thousand years have expired, Satan will be released from his prison and will go out to deceive the nations which are in the four corners of the earth, Gog and Magog, to gather them together to battle, whose number is as the sand of the sea. They went up on the breath of the earth and surrounded the camp of the saints and the beloved city. And fire came down from God out of heaven and devoured them. The devil, who deceived them, was cast into the lake of fire and brimstone where the beast and the false prophet are. And they will be tormented day and night forever and ever.
>
> Revelation 20:7–10 (NKJV)

But there is one other attachment to this group of which the Lord promises will also have the lowest place in his kingdom, and these are all those who teach that the Law and the prophets have been done away with, especially any part of the Law in even its least part (Matthew 5:17–20).

Otherwise, Paul quotes the prophet Joel when he says, "For 'whoever calls upon the name of the Lord shall be saved' " as quoted from Joel 2:32 (Romans 10:13, NKJV). But the Apostle Paul goes on to explain that this is still not possible without first having faith in the Word of God as it had been previously preached by those who had been sent under the authority of God to do so. In conjunction with this, we already know that faith without works is dead as we are told in the letter of James. Even so, Paul reminds us of this scripture, which makes it very clear that if anyone should call upon the name of either Jehovah

THE BOOK OF REVELATION AND THE BIBLE
AS NEVER EXPLAINED BEFORE

(God's everlasting name for all generations) also pronounced Yahweh, or Jesus (I am, or which also means the Savior), he shall be saved (Exodus 3:13–16). It would seem to follow then, as so many Christians have come to believe, that anyone shall be saved who shall call upon the name of the Lord, even if they do so at the end of their wicked lives, having no completed works of faith to offer God, and it is true. But if this should be the case of a person's belief in salvation, the Word of God makes this very clear as well. At the time of God's first judgment for those about to enter his millennial kingdom, if anyone should come before his judgment seat having no record of completed works or a return in interest for the gifts that he had given them, he shall be thrown out of his inner kingdom and made to reside in the outer lying regions of the earth along with the survivors of Gog and Magog.

These outer lying regions of the earth are also referred to by Jesus as the place of wailing and gnashing of teeth and are symbolic of two things. First, it denotes outer darkness, which defines the state of one being forever cut off from the light of God, or otherwise one living in a permanent state of spiritual damnation as the survivors of Gog and Magog will be then, and second, it denotes the lake of fire, which shall be revealed to all men during the great Day of Judgment after the Lamb of God's millennial reign comes to an end. The lake of fire is, for the most part, the future destination of all those who reside here, especially all those who had taken the mark of the beast and yet still survived because they were not present at the battle of the Armageddon. But even so, for those who have not taken the mark of the beast, it will still be possible for some of them to earn a place in God's eternal kingdom if somehow they can prove themselves worthy through their devotion and self-sacrifice to God during their limited stay in the Lord's millennial kingdom. But it will be extremely difficult given the kind of company they will have to keep, as they live here at the lowest level of God's kingdom. This is also where this scripture derives the second part of its three-part meaning: "And He Himself will rule them with a rod of iron" (Revelation 19:15, NKJV).

In the first instance, this scripture denotes the wrath of God during the battle of the Armageddon when all the warring armies of the beast and the rest of the world come together to wage war on the Lamb of God as he takes his stand on top of Mount Zion, along with his entire heavenly host. All these warring armies of the world, along with the warring armies of the beast, constitute Gog and Magog.

In the second instance, this scripture denotes the time during the millennial reign of Christ when he shall reign supreme as the King of kings and the Lord of lords over all the other kings, lords and royal subjects of the earth, to include the survivors from the great hosts of Gog and Magog.

Finally, in the third instance, which shall come at the end of the one-thousand-year reign of Christ, this scripture denotes the time as I had just mentioned when Satan is to be let loose from his dungeon one last time to seduce the nations from the four quarters of the earth and from there to muster them for battle. Yes, the scripture tells us they are the hosts of Gog and Magog, countless as the sands of the seas, who shall march over the breadth of the land and lay siege to the camp of God's people and the city he loves. But fire shall come down on them from heaven and consume them all, and soon after, Satan, their seducer, will be flung into the lake of fire and sulfur, where the beast and the false prophet had been flung before him, and there he and all the rest of his company who are to be judged shall be tormented day and night forever, just as it is written in Revelation 20:7–10 as quoted earlier in this chapter.

THE SEVEN SEALS
(REVELATION CHAPTER SIX)

- The first seal:

   "Then I watched as the Lamb broke the first of the seven seals; and I heard one of the four living creatures say in a voice like thunder, 'Come!' And there before my eyes was a *white horse;* and he was given a crown and a bow with which to ride forth conquering and to conquer."

   Revelation 6:1–2 (TNEB)

This symbolizes the coming of the many false prophets and false messiahs who we were told would come to deceive the world, but especially the church, where even some of God's own people will be led astray and even murdered for their mistaken beliefs. But in the extreme sense, this seal symbolizes the time when many will come trying to conquer God's people and thereafter forcefully imposing their own religious beliefs upon them with the consequence of death for any who will refuse to accept these religious beliefs (Matthew 24:3–6, 11–12). I will tell you now that this seal has come and is now upon us as I present the following examples as evidence to this claim.

Charles Manson and the Family is a cult group that was formulated somewhere during the late 1960's and continues on to this day from behind prison bars even after the horrific murders of Sharon Tate and her friends at the Tate mansion by some of Manson's family members in 1969. These were not the only murders perpetrated by the Manson family, but they are the ones most remembered. Manson's motives in all of these ordered murders, though varied, are to a greater extent taken from his twisted and perverted understanding of the book of Revelation and especially from what he perceived the final battle of the Armageddon to be all about. He then blended this perversion of the truth in with the lyrics to the Beatles song "Helter Skelter" and from there concocted his perverse message that would lead all who would listen to him to commit some of the most horrendous murders ever seen at that time. A total of eight people at four different crime scenes would ultimately be murdered by the Manson family before their capture.

Jim Jones and the People's Temple was founded in Indiana in the early 1950s and ended in 1978 when 914 interracially mixed men, women, and children all died in Jonestown, Guyana, most committing suicide while some were murdered either by lethal injection or gunshots to the head on the order of Jim Jones and carried out by his subordinate church leaders and security guards. This event occurred because the people chose to put their faith in a man rather than in Jesus Christ, the everlasting high priest and prophet of God, where they were ultimately led astray and into a place that they could not return from, and it cost them their lives.

David Koresh and the Branch Davidians were a splinter group that evolved from the Seventh Day Adventists Church in Waco, Texas, which brought the deaths of 130 of its members

THE BOOK OF REVELATION AND THE BIBLE
AS NEVER EXPLAINED BEFORE

in 1993 by its controversial, fiery self-destruction that was influenced to some extent by law enforcement. Here, the Branch Davidians believed that David Koresh was the messiah and that to die with him would lead them up into heaven as the battle of the Armageddon was about to begin outside their door.

Marshall Applewhite and Heaven's Gate were UFO believers in a cult that was founded in California in 1975 and ended with the suicides of twenty-one women and eighteen men on March 23, 1997. Two months later, another member, Charles Humphrey, joined them, and in February 1998, alone in the Arizona desert, the last member, Wayne Cooke, also killed himself, making the total number of suicides for this cult forty-one.

Heaven's Gate followed a syncretistic religion that blended their own interpretations about the Word of God, especially the book of Revelation, with unusual beliefs about the nature of UFOs and astrology, and from this they concocted a very elaborate story about UFOs and the extraterrestrials that fly them. Out of this, they then created the basis from which to believe that they were an elite group destined for the kingdom of heaven. They believed that by committing suicide on Easter, which was also timed to the Hale-Bopp comet's close proximity to earth, that somehow their souls, upon leaving their bodies, would be translated aboard a spaceship that was hiding behind the comet and from there they would be taken up into heaven in their new spiritual bodies to become one of God's elect, or else, as the book of Revelation states, a member of the hundred and forty-four thousand. This spaceship, according to their beliefs, was the same one that brought the first two visitors from heaven two thousand years before, who were none other than Jesus Christ and, unbelievably, a female companion, who he called his heavenly Father. This concocted tale goes on and on and ultimately led them all to their deaths. They thought that by committing suicide they could force the hand of God and become one of the elite members of the royal house. But the Word of God states that he who shall destroy his own body,

141

or as the scriptures refer to all Christians as being God's new holy temple, shall himself be destroyed (1 Corinthians 3:16–17).

Make no mistake; it is not by men's hands that the different harvests of Revelation shall be commanded, but by God's alone; and it shall be done in his own time and not in ours or any other man's. That is why Jesus warned us repeatedly not to be misled by the many men who would come in the last days claiming to be the messiah or as one of the many other false prophets who he also said would come, for like lightning flashing from as far as east is from west shall be the sign that heralds the second coming of Christ. Reference Matthew 24:1–27 for a complete and comprehensive explanation of this concept given by Christ himself.

The Movement for the Restoration of the Ten Commandments of God was founded in Karlungu, Uganda, by various excommunicated Catholic priests and two nuns in 1989 to 1994 and ended on March 17, 2006, when 530 men, women, and children were burned alive inside their church by an intentionally set fire that was perpetrated by its leaders who then ran off with all the money gained from the selling of all the possessions of its impoverished believers. Another 308 bodies were later found buried in mass graves hidden in various places within the church compound. Once again, these poor people were deceived into believing that by committing suicide or by allowing themselves to be murdered by their church leaders that this would somehow allow them an early entrance into the kingdom of God, cutting short their time of misery and suffering on earth.

The Solar Temple was founded in France by Luc Jouret in 1984 and ended with two different dates for their believers either being murdered or committing mass suicides. The first occurred in October 1994, with fifty-three of its members either being murdered or committing suicide to begin the early transfer to a better world to escape the fiery end they believed was coming soon to this world with the coming of the biblically prophesied battle of the Armageddon. The second murder-suicide occurred on November 16, 1995, with twelve of its remaining members committing suicide and one woman and three children being murdered before them as they struggled for their lives.

The Aum Shinri Kyo, which means the supreme truth, was a cult founded in 1987 by Shoko Asahara and was a combination of beliefs taken from the scriptures found within the book of Revelation and the writings of the sixteenth century Christian astrologer Nostradamus. It ended in 1995 with some of its members being indicted for the murder of others within the cult and still others for the spreading of microbes and germ toxins from rooftops and convoy trucks driving through different cities of Japan. Later Asahara himself would be indicted for the distribution of the nerve gas Sarin into a Tokyo subway station heavily populated with patrons. Of this crime, twelve passengers were killed and five thousand were injured. In all of this cult's criminal actions, the members believed they were preparing the way for the coming of the great battle of the Armageddon as described to us in the book of Revelation.

What is remarkable to note here is that within all of these different cults were leaders who either claimed to be Jesus Christ or who claimed to be prophets of God who, in the end, would either murder their followers or lead them to their deaths or to the deaths of others outside their cult with this deceit and their perversions of the truth. This is yet another reason why I have been given the authority to write this book at such a crucial time as this, and it is in keeping with the purpose that I have already stated in my introduction, which is to ensure that all who shall come to read this book will know the truth as God intended it to be understood and in so doing not be deceived by all those who have yet to come to interpret the Bible and especially the book of Revelation as they have here that, in the end, cost all these people their lives.

On the extreme side of this understanding, we have the Islamic militants of the various terrorist organizations ranging from Hezbollah, Hamas, al-Qaeda, and the Taliban. All have claimed an Islamic jihad (or holy war) on Israel and its chief allies, the United States and Britain, as each of these groups murder and kill indiscriminately over the forceful imposition of their religious beliefs upon the rest of the world who are nonbelievers in Islam. It has become the terrorists' ultimate dream to first destroy the United States and then afterward Britain and Israel and from there to conquer the rest of the world with their religious beliefs—all in the name of Allah and his great false prophet Mohammed.

- The second seal:

 "When the Lamb broke the second seal, I heard the second creature say, 'Come!' And out came another *horse all red*. To its rider was given the power to take peace from the earth and make men slaughter one another; and he was given a great sword."

 Revelation 6:3–4 (TNEB)

This symbolizes the time of wars and rumors of wars that Jesus warned would come during the last days as a prelude to the great tribulation where the time of our testing will occur (Matthew 24:6–7).

Since the dawning of the industrial revolution nearly 100 years ago, world history has witnessed the beginning of a new era in warfare. It was the industrial age that ushered in the two Great Wars—World War I and World War II, and with them came the technologies to develop weapons that were then the predecessors to today's smart bombs and nuclear weapons of mass destruction that have since come to mark the final age of man as the book of Revelation tells it. Along with this, and all the other wars that have since followed these two, have come the rogue nations who are now desperately seeking to establish their own nuclear weapons programs so that they too might have a sense of world power. With this, it should not be too difficult to see how the present world has suddenly become a very dangerous place to be living in. But most importantly, how right before our very eyes, the stage is

THE BOOK OF REVELATION AND THE BIBLE
AS NEVER EXPLAINED BEFORE

being built that, upon its completion, will host the final battles of this age, and will ultimately end as a battle between the beast and the Lamb of God. With this, there should be no doubt, that this seal too has already come and remains a sign of the times that is presently glaring at us.

• The third seal:

> When he broke the third seal I heard the voice of the third creature say, "Come!" And there, as I looked, was a *black horse;* and its rider held in his hands a pair of scales and I heard what sounded like a voice from the midst of the four living creatures say, "A whole day's wage for a quart of flour, a whole day's wage for three quarts of barley-meal! But spare the olive and the vine."
>
> Revelation 6:5–6 (TNEB)

This symbolizes the time of famine and great economic hardship that will be brought upon the world. But God's anointed people will not be hurt during this time, hence the sparing of the olive and the vine. This time has also come and is presently upon us as great famines scorch the earth and millions are losing their jobs and homes all over the world, but especially here in America because of the economic collapse of the world market, just as it was prophesied nearly two thousand years ago in the book of Revelation. This is aside from the millions of homes and lives that are also being lost due to the ever-rising number of great disasters that are raging throughout America and the world.

• The fourth seal:

> And when he broke the fourth seal, I heard the voice of another creature say, "Come!" And there, as I looked, was another *horse, sickly pale;* and its rider's name was Death, and Hades followed close behind. To him was given power over a quarter of the earth, with the right to kill by sword, and by famine, by pestilence, and wild beasts.
>
> Revelation 6:7–8 (TNEB)

145

We are still reeling from the accumulative effects of these four horsemen, but as the signs of the times are already beginning to show, we are fast nearing the time of the fifth seal, which I will be speaking about here shortly. For now, our peace and stability exists only by the grace of God, which is only because there are still those within our government and our nation who are still trying to preserve the blood covenant that our forefathers made with God that had caused our nation to be blessed above all other nations. Even so, God's judgments are falling upon this nation as never before for the grievous sins that are being committed by the ungodly. It is only for the sake of the righteous and all of the other signs and wonders that must also be fulfilled that the Lord is staying his mighty hand over this nation's total destruction.

But as we can see from the international news reports, the world of late is suffering as never before from all its wars, famines, and plagues. Plagues such as the Ebola virus, HIV/AIDS, the West Nile virus, malaria, the Asian bird flu, the swine flu, influenza and now from a new blend of the swine flu that has just emerged, having strains of bird, swine, and human flu viruses all joined together. It first appeared in Mexico City, in April 2009, and is spreading with pandemic speed into the United States as well as a growing number of other countries around the world. Most of these diseases to date have no vaccine and no cure and are claiming millions of lives each year, especially in the most impoverished countries of the world such as in Africa.

Wild animal attacks from hippopotami, crocodiles, elephants, water buffaloes, rhinoceroses, lions, Bengal tigers, grizzly bears, polar bears, black bears, mountain lions, great white sharks, and bull sharks, to name the most dangerous of these animals, are all on the rise as well, with the hippopotamus being the number one animal killer of humans on the earth followed closely by the crocodile, the water buffalo, and the Bengal tiger. To see the statistics for the attacks of each of these animals on humans, go to Google and type in "statistics for (name of animal) attacks on humans." The culmination of all these events will lead us into the fifth seal.

- The fifth seal:

> When he broke the fifth seal, I saw underneath the altar the souls of those who had been slaughtered for God's word and for the testimony they bore. They gave a great cry: How long, sovereign Lord, holy and true, must it be before thou wilt vindicate us and avenge our blood on the inhabitants of the earth? Each of them was given a white robe; and told to rest a little while longer, until the tally should be complete of all their brothers in Christ's service who were to be killed as they had been.
>
> Revelation 6:9–11 (TNEB)

This seal describes the time that both precedes the coming of the beast and especially the time thereafter when the beast's great reign of terror shall begin. It will be in the latter part of this time period, or more clearly, in the fifth trumpet, that the beast shall ascend out of the shaft of the abyss, and after his true purpose for coming back into the world has been exposed, he will be given full power over all the inhabitants of the earth for a period of three and a half years. This power will be given to him by God himself. It will be during this time period that the beast will be allowed to wage war on God's people and to defeat them (Revelation 17:8, Revelation 13:5–8). Where it is written, " 'Happy are the dead who die in the faith of Christ! Henceforth,' says the Spirit, 'they may rest from their labors: for they take with them the record of their deeds' " (Revelation 14:13, TNEB).

Unfortunately, when the beast's great reign of terror finally does come upon the inhabitants of the earth, thousands of people who had previously claimed to be Christians will lose faith and fall away from believing in the Lord. This will be because while they were on that wide and spacious highway prepared for them by the megachurches, they were lulled into believing that Satan and his entourage of fallen angels were already defeated and that the road to heaven was going to be a rich and peaceful experience from there on out. Their pastors said never mind all those scriptures that foretold of this time and warned us to be on our guard. Preach only the good news, for we wouldn't want to turn anyone away that might cause our great numbers to diminish even by one. Rather, let us preach to them that God is good and would never let anything bad happen to them.

It is for this failure of God's churches, whether they be great or small, that God will call the leaders of these churches to account because they did not prepare his people for this time that he had warned us all would come. Reference Matthew 24:15–25 regarding the falling away of his chosen; also reference Revelation 13:9–18 regarding the time when the beast and the false prophet will deceive the peoples of the world to include great numbers of God's people and cause them to worship and follow the beast into damnation.

- The sixth seal:

   I looked when he opened the sixth seal, and behold, there was *a great earthquake;* the sun became black as sackcloth of hair, and the moon became like blood. And the stars of heaven fell to the earth, as a fig tree drops its late figs when it is shaken by a mighty wind. Then the sky receded as a scroll when it is rolled up, and every mountain and island was moved out of its place. And the kings of the earth, the great men, the rich men, the commanders, the mighty men, every slave and every free man, hid themselves in caves and in the rocks of the mountains, and said to the mountains and the rocks, "Fall on us and hide us from the face of Him who sits on the throne and from the wrath of the Lamb." For the great day of His wrath has come and who is able to stand?"

   Revelation 6:12–17 (NKJV)

   After these things I saw four angels standing at the four corners of the earth, holding the four winds of the earth, that the wind should not blow on the earth, on the sea, or on any tree.

THE BOOK OF REVELATION AND THE BIBLE
AS NEVER EXPLAINED BEFORE

Then I saw another angel ascending from the east, having the seal of the living God. And he cried with a loud voice to the four angels to whom it was granted to harm the earth and the sea, saying: "Do not harm the earth, the sea, or the trees till we have sealed the servants of our God on their foreheads." And I heard the number of those who were sealed. One hundred and forty-four thousand of all the tribes of the children of Israel were sealed:

Of the tribe of Judah twelve thousand were sealed; of the tribe of Reuben twelve thousand were sealed; of the tribe of Gad twelve thousand were sealed; of the tribe of Asher twelve thousand were sealed; of the tribe of Naphtali twelve thousand were sealed; of the tribe of Manasseh (or more correctly Dan) twelve thousand were sealed; of the tribe of Simeon twelve thousand were sealed; of the tribe of Levi twelve thousand were sealed; of the tribe of Issachar twelve thousand were sealed; of the tribe of Zebulun twelve thousand were sealed; of the tribe of Joseph twelve thousand were sealed; of the tribe of Benjamin twelve thousand were sealed.

After these things I looked, and behold, a great multitude which no one could number, of all nations, tribes, peoples, and tongues, (were) standing before the throne and before the Lamb, clothed with white robes, with palm branches in their hands, and crying out with a loud voice, saying: "Salvation belongs to our God who sits on the throne, and to the Lamb!" All the angels stood around the throne and the elders and the four living creatures, and fell on their faces before the throne and worshipped God, saying:

"Amen! Blessing and glory and wisdom, thanksgiving and honor and power and might, be to our God forever and ever. Amen."

Then one of the elders answered saying to me, "Who are these arrayed in white robes, and where did they come?" And I said to him, "Sir, you know." So he said to me, "These are the ones who come out of the great tribulation, and washed their robes and made them white in the blood of the Lamb.

149

Therefore they are before the throne of God and serve Him day and night in His temple. And He who sits on the throne will dwell among them. They shall neither hunger anymore nor thirst anymore; the sun shall not strike them, nor any heat; for the Lamb who is in the midst of the throne will shepherd them and lead them to living fountains of waters. And God will wipe away every tear from their eyes."

Revelation 7:1–17 (NKJV)

Here in the sixth seal is where God makes his awesome power known to the world through all of these great heavenly, as well as earthly, signs that he causes to happen here, and yet here is also another very good example of how God uses his angels, in this case, four, to stand guard over the earth at its four corners. Notice how they have been given complete power and control over the four winds and use that power to cause great damage to the land and the sea upon his command. Here, the scriptures show once again that it is not because of global warming, all the hurricanes, tropical storms, and tornados are striking this nation, but rather it is because we have broken our blood covenant with the Almighty and decided to go our own way as a nation as all the rest of the world. Now instead of receiving his wonderful blessings, we have invited the very plagues and curses of God to come upon us just as he promised they would. Except for the righteous few that still remain during this time does God spare our nation from total destruction.

Also here is where the *seal of God*, which bears both the Son's name and the name of his Father, is placed on the foreheads of God's elect, the hundred and forty-four thousand. It is important to note that only the hundred and forty-four thousand receive this particular seal and no one else (Revelation 7:3–8, Revelation 14:1–5). They will also bear the fleshly *seal of circumcision* because they are still bound by the everlasting covenant made between God and Abraham as well (Genesis 17:9–14).

It must also be mentioned that the *seal of God* must not be mistaken for the other seal of deliverance that God has reserved

150

THE BOOK OF REVELATION AND THE BIBLE
AS NEVER EXPLAINED BEFORE

to mark the rest of his chosen people who are faithfully ready and waiting at the last trumpet, and that is the *seal of the Holy Spirit* (Ephesians 4:30–31).

In this next passage, this group is referred to as the great multitude, as there are actually two companies of God's people who are momentarily revealed to us here. They are, as I have just mentioned above, the *hundred and forty-four thousand* who will be ransomed from the twelve tribes of Israel as the first fruits of humanity and the *great multitude* that no one could count who have passed through the great tribulation but whose robes have been washed clean and made white by the blood of the Lamb. The gathering of the hundred and forty-four thousand will occur at about the middle of the great tribulation because of their great faith, purity, and obedience to God. They alone will be spared the last and most terrible half of the great ordeal (Revelation 3:10–11, Revelation 14:1–5).

The *great multitude,* as has already been mentioned a few times earlier, will not be delivered until after the last trumpet is sounded, which will not sound until after the sixth bowl is poured on the great river Euphrates during the time of the seven plagues. This is also the time when God comes like a thief in the night for his remaining chosen people. But only those who bear the mark of their faith and deliverance, which is the *seal of the Holy Spirit,* will be taken up to heaven at that time.

• The seventh seal:

Then the Lamb broke the seventh seal, and there was silence in heaven for about half an hour. Next I saw seven trumpets being given to the seven angels who stand in the presence of God. Another angel, who had a gold censer, came and stood at the altar. A large quantity of incense was given to him to offer with the prayers of all the saints on the golden altar that stood in front of the throne; and so from the angel's hand the smoke of the incense went up in the presence of God and with it the prayers of the saints. Then the angel took the censer and filled it from the fire of the altar, which he then hurled down onto the earth; immediately there came *peals of thunder and flashes of lightning,* and *the earth shook.*

Revelation 8:1–5 (TNJB)

Notice here how we are given the second clue as to what the seven thunders actually signify that John speaks about for a moment in chapter ten of the book of Revelation before he is told to seal them up. This clue comes to us in the form of this second sequence of peals of thunder and flashes of lightning with an earth quake that always follows as revealed to John, by Christ. There are a total of four of these sequences given in the book of Revelation and with these two given there are still two more to come. The third one may be found at the end of the seven trumpets in chapter eleven and the last one at the end of the seven bowls full of the seven plagues in chapter sixteen. Otherwise it is important to notice how all these events of the seventh seal then herald in the seven trumpets of chapter nine.

THE SEVEN TRUMPETS
(REVELATION CHAPTER EIGHT)

- The first trumpet:

  "The first angel blew his trumpet; and there came hail and fire mingled with blood, and this was hurled upon the earth. A third of the earth was burnt, including a third of the trees and all of the green grass" (Revelation 8:7, TNEB).

This is the beginning of the time when God shall cause great judgments to fall upon the earth to strike terror into the hearts and minds of all those who, up until now, still refuse to turn from their wicked ways and believe in the power of God to heal their land and save them from their sins. But the people of the world would rather continue on with their evildoings rather than humble themselves before the Lord and pray for his forgiveness so that they might otherwise be saved. This also marks the beginning of the time when loud audible trumpet blasts shall be heard all across the face of the earth from one end to the other, and they shall bring terror to all who hear them. It should also be understood that these seven angels are the same seven angels who blew their trumpets from on top of Mount Sinai when Moses received the Ten Commandments in the midst of peals of thunder, flashes of lightning, fire, and a great herald of red smoke as the Lord God, Jehovah, spoke these commandments to him and to the people of Israel in (Exodus 19:16–19).

- The second trumpet:

   "The second angel blew his trumpet, and it was as though a great mountain blazing with fire was hurled into the sea: a third of the sea turned into blood, a third of the living things in the sea were killed and a third of all ships were destroyed," (Revelation 8:8–9, TNJB).

This is clearly our worst nightmare come true as God sends a huge blazing asteroid the size of a mountain hurling into one of our great oceans as a punishment for all the evil occurring in the world at this time.

- The third trumpet:

   "The third angel blew his trumpet, and a huge star fell from the sky, burning like a ball of fire, and it fell on a third of all rivers and on the springs of water; this was the star called wormwood, and a third of all water turned to wormwood, so that many people died; the water had become so bitter" (Revelation 8:10–11, TNJB).

This description once again sounds like God delivering another one of our greatest nightmares to us in the form of a giant radioactive meteor or comet falling to the earth and hitting in a mountainous region that supplies water to a lot of rivers. These rivers would then become poisoned by the massive levels of radioactive fallout caused by the explosive impact of such a meteor or comet hitting the earth.

THE BOOK OF REVELATION AND THE BIBLE
AS NEVER EXPLAINED BEFORE

- The fourth trumpet:

  The fourth angel blew his trumpet; and a third part of the sun
  was struck, a third of the moon, and a third of the stars, so
  that the third part of all their light failed and went dark, both
  in the daytime and in the night.

  Then I looked and I heard an eagle calling with a loud cry as
  it flew in midheaven: Woe, woe, woe to the inhabitants of the
  earth when the trumpets sound which the three last angels
  must now blow!

  Revelation 8:12–13 (TNEB)

  This is another great and awesome judgment that God will
bring upon the inhabitants of the earth for all their vile and evil
practices being perpetrated against one another and especially
God's people during this time.

- The fifth trumpet:

  Then the fifth angel blew his trumpet, and I saw a star that had
  fallen from heaven onto the earth, and the angel was given the
  key to the shaft leading down to the Abyss. When he unlocked
  the shaft of the Abyss, smoke rose out of the Abyss like the
  smoke from a huge furnace so that the sun and the sky were
  darkened by the smoke from the Abyss, and out of the smoke
  dropped locusts onto the earth: they were given the powers
  that scorpions have on the earth: they were forbidden to harm
  any fields or crops or trees and told to attack only those people
  who were without God's seal on their foreheads. They were not
  to kill them, but to give them anguish for five months, and the
  anguish was to be the anguish of a scorpion's sting. When this
  happens, people will long for death and not find it anywhere;
  they will want to die and death will evade them.

  These locusts looked like horses armored for battle; They had
  what looked like gold crowns on their heads; and their faces
  looked human, and their hair was like women's hair, and teeth
  like lion's teeth. They had body-armor like iron breastplates,
  and the noise of their wings sounded like the racket of chari-

155

ots with many horses charging. Their tails were like scorpions' tails, with stings, and with their tails they were able to torture people for five months. As their leader they had their emperor, the angel of the Abyss, whose name in Hebrew is Abaddon, and in Greek Apollyon, (which means the Destroyer).

Revelation 9:1–12 (TNJB)

The *first woe* has now passed but there are still two more to come.

Here in this chapter, marked by the sound of the fifth trumpet, is where the beast makes his grand entrance back into the world's political arena, as the key to the shaft of the abyss is handed down to this star that had fallen from heaven to earth by an angel of the Lord. This star is none other than the former great archangel Lucifer, the morning star, who, after his fall from grace, was renamed Satan. And this rather hideous swarm of locustlike scorpions with the faces of humans, the hair of women, and the teeth of lions are none other than that same group of fallen angels who, in the first dispensation, were kicked out of heaven and bound beneath the darkness of the abyss in everlasting chains because they had committed fornication with the female inhabitants of the earth during the days of Noah. Here in a mockery of the second coming of Christ, these real hell's angels also precede their king in a massive herald of smoke and darkness as they ascend up through the shaft of the abyss, just as a great heavenly host will also precede the second coming of Christ. Next, we are given the name of this angel king of the abyss, who is the real scorpion king. His name in Greek is Apollyon, or the Destroyer. But this *destroyer* is none other than the *beast* himself who I will be speaking about in much greater detail a little later on in this book.

- The sixth trumpet:

  The sixth angel then blew his trumpet, and I heard a single voice issuing from the four horns of the golden altar in God's presence. It spoke to the sixth angel with the trumpet,

THE BOOK OF REVELATION AND THE BIBLE
AS NEVER EXPLAINED BEFORE

and said, "Release the four angels that are chained up at the great river Euphrates!" These four angels had been ready for this hour of this day of this month of this year, and ready to destroy a third of the human race. I learnt how many there were in their army: twice ten thousand times ten thousand mounted men, (or 200 million).

Revelation 9:13–16 (TNJB)

John then goes on to describe the horses and their riders in this way:

In my vision I saw the horses, and the riders with their breastplates of flame color, hyacinth-blue and sulfur-yellow; the horses had heads like lions' heads, and fire, smoke and sulfur were coming from their mouths. It was by these three plagues, the fire, the smoke and the sulfur coming from their mouths, that the one third of the human race was killed. All the horses power was in their mouths and their tails; their tails were like snakes, and had heads which inflicted wounds.

Revelation 9:17–19 (TNJB)

This description of John's actually sounds a lot like modern-day weapons of war similar to those used in the United States by the Third Armor Division's 155-track mounted howitzers, or could even be a battery of scud missiles or any number of other kinds of missile launchers with lion's heads painted on their war-heads. When either of these kinds of weapons are fired, it is well known among military personnel that the back blast can be just as lethal as the missile or round that is being fired. Again, what we are seeing here is a detailed description of modern-day weapons of war given by someone living in ancient times. This must have been a very frightening as well as a challenging sight for John to behold, as he then went on in the best way that he knew how to describe to the seven churches all that he had seen here.

I also believe that John was seeing some of the very same armies of the Middle East that had in 1967 gathered against Israel during the six days war and later in 1973 during the Yom

Kippur War, which was instigated by Egypt, and in English means the Day of Atonement. I further believe that what we had seen then in these two separate attacks on Israel—in conjunction with the whole extermination of Israel mentality, which emanates throughout the Middle East—are but the precursor for the final war that has yet to come as the book of Revelation describes it. But it will not be until after the last trumpet has sounded that this conflict will be decided once and for all. For here it must be stated that all those who war against Israel will, in the end, find themselves warring against God himself, the God of Abraham, Isaac, and Jacob.

We are then told that at the conclusion of this great battle caused by these four angels that despite the heavy casualties inflicted by their three plagues of fire, smoke, and sulfur, the rest of mankind still refused to stop abjuring and worshiping the gods that their hands had fashioned from every manner of stone, wood, or precious metal. Neither did they repent of their murders, their sorcery, their fornication, or their robberies (Revelation 9:20–21).

As for the four angels that were being held bound at the river Euphrates, they appear to be four holdovers from that same group of angels from the first dispensation who had abandoned their dominion given to them in heaven and began to follow unnatural lusts, as well as committing fornication with the inhabitants of the earth. All but these four were bound beneath the darkness of the abyss in everlasting chains before they too were released in the previous fifth trumpet as the herald of locustlike scorpions to plague mankind for five months. Reference Jude 1:6–7 for a better understanding of this correlation. Once again, this is another example of how God affects his purposes through both good and evil, as he has in this case used fallen angels instead of people to do this.

Then a lot of other things happen here, having to do with the *seven thunders* and *God's hidden purpose* being fulfilled after the seventh trumpet is sounded. I will be deciphering these

THE BOOK OF REVELATION AND THE BIBLE
AS NEVER EXPLAINED BEFORE

seven thunders as well as explaining God's hidden purpose within them in this next chapter entitled, "The Seven Thunders," but first I need to finish the seven trumpets.

Next the temple of God and his altar are measured as the beast and his army of Gentiles come into the holy city and trample it under foot. The beast then sets up his throne in the sanctuary of the temple of God and for three and a half years mounts bombast and blasphemy against him. John, the revelator, goes on to describe the beast in this way:

> It was also allowed to make war against the saints and to conquer them, and given power over every race, people, language, and nation; and all people of the world will worship it, that is, everybody whose name has not been written down since the foundation of the world in the sacrificial Lamb's book of life.
>
> Revelation 13:7–8 (TNJB)

Then the *two witnesses* are sent down to Jerusalem from heaven, and the voice from heaven said:

> But I shall send my two witnesses to prophesy for twelve hundred and sixty days, wearing sackcloth. These are the two olive-trees and the two lamps in attendance on the Lord of the world. Fire comes from their mouths and consumes their enemies if anyone tries to harm them; and anyone who tries to harm them will certainly be killed in this way. They have the power to lock up the sky so that it does not rain as long as they are prophesying; they have the power to turn water into blood and strike the whole world with any plague as often as they like. When they have completed their witnessing, the beast that comes up out of the Abyss is going to make war on them and overcome them and kill them. Their corpses lie in the main street of the great city known by the symbolic names Sodom and Egypt, in which the Lord was crucified. (Jesus, as most every Christian knows, was crucified outside the city of Jerusalem.) People of every race, tribe, language and nation, stare at their corpses for three-and-a-half days not letting them be buried, and the

159

PETER J. DAVIS

people of the world are glad about it and celebrate the event by giving presents to each other, because these two prophets have been a plague to the people of the world.'

After the three-and-a-half days God breathed life into them and they stood up on their feet, and everybody who saw it happen was terrified. Then I heard a loud voice from heaven say to them, 'Come up here,' and while their enemies were watching they went up to heaven in a cloud. Immediately there was *a violent earthquake,* and a tenth of the city collapsed; seven thousand persons were killed in the earthquake, and the survivors, overcome with fear, could only praise the God of heaven.

Revelation 11:1-14 (TNJB)

Next we are told that the *second woe* has now passed and that the third one is yet to come.

With regard to the two witnesses who are sent down by God: These two prophets are the same two great prophets of the Lord that came down from heaven and spoke to Jesus at the top of the mountain during his transfiguration that was witnessed by the Apostles Peter, James, and John. These two prophets were, in fact, *Moses* and *Elijah.* Jesus then tells us that the prophet Elijah and John the Baptist are one in the same person in Matthew 17:1-13. It is also interesting to note just how similar the plagues that Moses brought upon Pharaoh are to the plagues that he at this time brings upon the beast and his followers.

- The seventh trumpet:

Then the seventh angel blew his trumpet, and voices could be heard shouting in heaven, calling, "The kingdom of the world has become the kingdom of our Lord and his Christ, and he will reign forever and ever!" The twenty-four elders, enthroned in the presence of God, prostrated themselves and touched the ground with their foreheads worshipping God with these words, 'We give thanks to you, Almighty Lord God, He who is, He who was, for assuming your great power

160

THE BOOK OF REVELATION AND THE BIBLE
AS NEVER EXPLAINED BEFORE

and beginning your reign. The nations were in uproar and now the time has come for your retribution, and for the dead to be judged, and for your servants the prophets, for the saints (or for God's elect) and for those who fear your name, small and great alike, to be rewarded. The time has come to destroy those who are destroying the earth.'

Then the sanctuary of God in heaven was opened, and the Ark of the Covenant could be seen inside it. Then came *flashes of lightning, peals of thunder* and *another earthquake* and violent hail.

Revelation 11:15–19 (TNJB)

Finally the *third woe* has passed.

This is clearly the end of the beast's three-and-a-half year reign of terror upon the earth and marks the beginning of Christ's, which shall be from this point on, an everlasting reign. But what is not mentioned here or anywhere else in the book of Revelation is the gathering and taking up into heaven of the *hundred and forty-four thousand* in fulfillment of yet another part of God's hidden purpose as it was briefly mentioned to us in the sixth trumpet. It is also important to understand that even though the *hundred and forty-four thousand* are a part of that group called the *remnant of Israel* who will be saved, there is still a great distinction that must be made between them and the survivors of all Israel. As I have already mentioned earlier, the hundred and forty-four thousand are the most elite group out of all God's people left on earth who will be the first fruits of mankind to be ransomed at a time secretly appointed by God somewhere between the fifth and the sixth trumpet. And the survivors of all Israel will be the last of those descendants originally chosen by God to be saved during the time of Christ's second coming, as it has been foretold by almost every prophet of the Old Testament who prophesied of their coming day of reconciliation. Their time is still not yet. But to know this is to understand in part why Jesus told the multitudes in the Sermon

161

on the Mount, "Do not imagine that I have come to abolish the *Law or the prophets;* I have come not to abolish but to complete. In truth I tell you, till heaven and earth disappear, not one dot, not one little stroke, is to disappear from the Law *until all its purpose is achieved"* (Matthew 5:17–20, TNJB).

This one scripture is also loaded with hidden meaning and to understand it is to not only gain a comprehensive understanding of the book of Revelation, but it is also to gain a comprehensive understanding of the Bible itself. In this next section of my book, of which I call "The Seven Thunders," I will be revealing for the first time those things that God told the Apostle John to seal up because mankind was not ready to handle the truth contained within them at that time.

THE SEVEN THUNDERS

These are actually the seven harvests of the book of Revelation that God momentarily revealed the secret meaning of to John in the form of *seven thunders,* and immediately following them he was told to seal them up. Why did he do this, you may ask? In part because to know the truth about the seven thunders for some will be almost too much to bear but for others to know the hidden meaning of the seven thunders will only cause complacency. Still, there are those for whom it really doesn't matter what you say or do to try to convince them of the truth. They will never believe because they have long since hardened their hearts against God. But to me, to know their hidden meaning is to have in my possession the key that unlocks the greatest mystery and three-dimensional puzzle man has ever known—the book of Revelation. I must say that I have labored long and hard over the understanding to these seven thunders and that it has also cost me many countless hours of prayer, meditation, and a great deal of biblical research. The following understanding is the result of that labor and is also the revelation I received from the Holy Spirit.

1. The first thunder: This is God the Father raising his son Christ Jesus back up from the dead as the first fruits of the harvest. Then God spoke, and there before the throne of God went forth flashes of lightning and peals of thunder. On earth a violent earthquake was also felt as Jesus, the sacrificial Lamb of God, was raised from the dead by his Father's call and given all power and glory in heaven and on earth. Because of his great sacrifice, he alone in all heaven was found worthy to open the scroll with the seven seals before the throne of God.

Then after the seventh seal was broken, there was silence in heaven for what seemed half an hour; this time was used to commemorate the Lamb's great sacrifice. Thereafter, the seven angels are given the seven trumpets, and the gold censer full of incense and the prayers of God's people are both offered up before the throne of God; then once again the Father sends forth flashes of lightning, peals of thunder, and another violent earthquake as the gold censer full of fire is cast down upon the earth as a final tribute to his Son's great victory and to begin the time of great signs and wonders. His resurrection symbolizes him as being the first fruits of the harvest of the dead (1 Corinthians 15:20–21). With this resurrection, Satan and his angels were finally defeated and cast out of heaven (Revelation 12:7–11). Satan is symbolized in the fifth trumpet as the star that fell from heaven to earth and all his angels, a third of the host in heaven, went with him.

2. The second thunder: This is the harvesting of the first fruits of humanity, also called God's elect, or otherwise, the *hundred and forty-four thousand*. Then God spoke and there before the throne of God went forth flashes of lightning and peals of thunder, and God said there shall be no more

THE BOOK OF REVELATION AND THE BIBLE
AS NEVER EXPLAINED BEFORE

delay, for now is the time for my dedicated people, those who have perfected themselves in my love and holiness and who have remained steadfast to my command to be brought up to heaven to stand before me. Then, in an instant, the *hundred and forty-four thousand* with the *seal of God* on their foreheads are summoned up into heaven to stand before the throne of God. There, they are given harps and a new song to sing that only they can sing at this appointed time and then all heaven is heard rejoicing and shouting praises at their coming (Revelation 14;1-2).

With regard to the hundred and forty-four thousand, though we are never actually told when the hundred and forty-four thousand are taken up into heaven in the book of Revelation, it is discernable by the very cleverly placed clues that the Lord does give to us. First, we know that the hundred and forty-four thousand are still on the earth at the time of the fifth trumpet when the beast makes his grand entrance back from the abyss. And that it is in the sixth trumpet, while the four angels are mustering the armies of the world for war, that the beast makes his surprise attack upon Israel and tramples Jerusalem underfoot as he takes control of the newly restored temple of God. Here is also where the two prophets of the Lord are sent down from heaven to prophesy against the beast in Jerusalem for the remainder of his three-and-a-half year reign of terror upon all the inhabitants of the earth. But what we don't know is that before the beast can take over Jerusalem and the newly restored temple of the Lord he must first wait until the Lord's untouchable ones, the hundred and forty-four thousand, are removed from off the face of the earth. This can only happen, as it has been revealed to me by the power of the Holy Spirit, within the sequence of events occurring between the fifth and the sixth trumpet. Otherwise, we next hear about them in chapter 14, which comes after the seven trumpets and the following two chapters concerning the woman and the great red

165

dragon and the two beasts of Revelation. Here they are standing with the Lamb on top of Mount Zion with the name of God (*Jehovah or Yahweh*) and the Lamb's new name written on their foreheads, which is also none other than the *seal of God,* where they are clearly in heaven, singing the new song that only they could sing and playing on their harps. Here again it is important to understand that there is only the time span between the fifth and sixth trumpet that they can be taken in, as the seventh trumpet is in fact synonymous to the last trumpet call where the great multitude are next taken up into heaven as a prelude to the second coming of Christ.

The fourteenth chapter of Revelation goes on to describe them this way:

> There before the throne they were singing a new hymn (song) in the presence of the four living creatures and the elders, a hymn that could be learnt only by the hundred and forty-four thousand who had been redeemed from the world. These are the ones who have kept their virginity and not been defiled with women; they follow the Lamb where ever he goes; they, out of all the people, have been redeemed to be the first-fruits for God and for the Lamb. No lie was found in their mouths and no fault can be found in them.
>
> Revelation 14:3–5 (TNJB)

In the seventh chapter of Revelation, they are described as being Israelites who are specially chosen to receive the seal of God from the twelve tribes of Israel. Here God gives their exact number as being twelve thousand from each of the twelve tribes of Israel. Hence, from this the *hundred and forty-four thousand* number is derived (Revelation 7:4–8).

I have often wondered, given this criteria, who the *hundred and forty-four thousand* are, as I have heard the Jehovah's Witnesses say that they can only be found within their church, and the Church of Jesus Christ of Latter Day Saints say that they can only be found within their church. Then in the Protestant

THE BOOK OF REVELATION AND THE BIBLE
AS NEVER EXPLAINED BEFORE

churches it is believed to be the sanctified who are the specially chosen ones making up this number. This is what the words to the song means when they sing, "I want to be in that number, when the saints go marching in."

With all of this misinformation coming from all the various churches and given all of the criteria from the book of Revelation, there was one thing that I was absolutely sure of, and that is, none of those claiming to be the one hundred and forty-four thousand were them. None of those even came close to meeting all the criteria given about them in the book of Revelation. But the question remained, as I have often pondered its answer: just who on earth could they possibly be? Even in prayer and quiet meditation I have often asked God to reveal their mystery to me. But each time as I would ask, the Holy Spirit would always answer me in the same quiet voice as he had so many times before. "Just keep studying the Word of God in its full context," he would whisper. "But most importantly, keep researching the truth and the facts from within the historic record, and then will I reveal this mystery to you."

Then one day as I was researching the history of when Jerusalem first came into being on Mount Zion, the Lord finally revealed the mystery of their identity to me. It began with the Jesuits and ended up with the hundreds of priesthood orders found within the Franciscans before God finally made the following understanding known to me.

The hundred and forty-four thousand will not be found in any one priesthood order founded by men, as I had first thought, but will be a spiritual order founded and appointed by God. They are God's elect, and they are the only ones who will have achieved holiness on earth at the time of their deliverance. They will be gathered twelve thousand from the twelve tribes of Israel from the descendants of all those who in part had been scattered by God since the time when King Nebuchadnezzar freed the ten tribes of Israel from the Assyrians in 598 BC. They will be gathered from all the nations of the world. They will

167

be founded in humility and be a specially recognized spiritual priesthood order of circumcised Christian men. They will have each taken a vow of *chastity, poverty,* and *obedience* that will remain in effect for the remainder of their born-again Christian lives. They seek no office, no promotion, but strive to live the life of Christ, in the total servitude of the poor and the downtrodden as dedicated servants of God. It is written that neither Satan nor the beast will have any power over them. They are symbolized by the church of Philadelphia. They will, in fact, be gathered from within all the different priesthood orders found within the Catholic Church who have taken these vows of chastity, poverty, and obedience. However, not all from within these different priesthood orders will be chosen, but only those who shall be recognized by God for their special devotion and holiness unto him. They alone will have the *seal of God* placed on their foreheads by an angel of the Lord and it will be placed there for all the world to see. This sealing will occur during the time of the sixth seal as described in the book of Revelation (Revelation 7:2–4).

Furthermore, these specially chosen Israelite priests are *holy* because they will be found perfected in God's love, and they are *royal* because they alone will have the *seal of God* placed upon their foreheads, and during the millennium they shall reside in the royal house and be regarded as the first holy royal priests of God. They are *Israelites* because they have been circumcised since birth, keeping the everlasting covenant made between God and Abraham, and their lineage will be traced back to one of the twelve tribes of Israel. They are *small in number* because few are they who can attain to their level of perfection and devotion toward God while keeping those vows that each and every one of them had to take in order to be chosen as one of God's elect and thereby being allowed to enter into the elite, first fruits of the harvest priesthood order of God. Finally, they are devoted to the service of God's one true church and remain under the authority of the pope who is God's official representative here

THE BOOK OF REVELATION AND THE BIBLE
AS NEVER EXPLAINED BEFORE

on earth. They are the one hundred and forty-four thousand and there is no one else on earth like them.

3. The third thunder: This is the thief in the night harvest, or otherwise the taking up into heaven of the *great multitude.* God spoke and there before the throne of God went forth flashes of lightning and peals of thunder, as lightning is seen flashing as far as the east is from the west and even unto the ends of the earth. Then with the call from Michael, the great archangel, the last trumpet is sounded. Then Jesus is sent down into midheaven (or into the clouds above the earth) by his Father to gather his chosen from the four corners of the earth. He first summons the Christian dead to rise and then those who are left alive will soon join them. Then, in a flash, in the twinkling of an eye, they will all be changed into immortality as they are summoned up from the earth by Jesus to join him in midheaven. From there, they will all be taken up into high heaven to be with the Lord and all his angels. Where it is written, "Blessed are those who are invited to the wedding feast of the Lamb," and he added, "These words of God are true" (Revelation 19:9, TNJB). The great multitude are symbolized by the church of Smyrna, as they both had to suffer through the great ordeal of their own time because neither could remain steadfast to the command of the Lord nor could they attain to the same level of holiness as the hundred and forty-four thousand, which rendered them untouchable, as was also the church of Philadelphia.

4. The fourth thunder: This is the first grape harvest, or otherwise the end of all the warring armies of the world who will come to do battle against the Lamb and his heavenly host during the great battle of the Armageddon. God spoke and there before the throne of God went forth flashes of lightning and peals of thunder, and the angel of the Lord,

who had just been in the presence of the Lord, came out of the heavenly temple with a sharp sickle, and he was commanded by yet another angel, who had authority over fire, that had just come from the altar of the Lord to bring in the earth's grape harvest, for its clusters were ripe. So the angel with the sharp sickle stretched forth his sickle to the earth and gathered in its grapes and took them outside the city where he threw them in the great winepress of God's wrath. For two hundred miles around, blood flowed from the press to the height of the horses' bridles (Revelation 14:17–20).

This symbolizes the time of Christ's second coming when Mount Zion will suddenly come into view before all men, raised up from the earth, high above all the other mountains, as they are brought low before it but not by the hand of man. He will be accompanied by a mighty heavenly host. These will include a countless host of angels, the hundred and forty-four thousand, and the great multitude, who, out of the last two groups, had all been taken up into heaven where they were each transformed into immortality. Then upon seeing this awesome sight, all the nations of the world will stop their individual wars and unite together to wage war against the Son of God and his mighty heavenly host who have come down to settle upon the Lambs holy mountain. Then the Lamb of God, upon seeing all those gathered around his holy mountain to wage war against him, will convict each and every one of them of their godless deeds. Then by the word that comes out of his mouth he will condemn them. His word will be very much like a stream of fire flowing from his mouth, and they, and all their hosts, will be consumed by it. Just as it is written: "—their flesh will rot (or be consumed) while they are standing on their feet; their eyes will rot in their sockets; their tongues will rot in their mouths" (Zechariah 14:12, TNJB).

5. The fifth thunder: This is the harvesting, or gathering in of the survivors of all Israel that scripture says will be saved.

THE BOOK OF REVELATION AND THE BIBLE
AS NEVER EXPLAINED BEFORE

Then God spoke and there before the throne of God went forth flashes of lightning and peals of thunder and the angel that had been in the presence of the Lord came out of the heavenly temple and in a loud voice commanded the fifth harvest to begin, for now was the time for reconciliation. Then Jesus called out to his firstborn children from on top of Mount Zion to return home to Zion and be received by him who was their true messiah. From there, they will be gathered from the four corners of the earth and from every nation of the world and island of the sea. It shall be in fulfillment of all the scriptures that foretold of this great day ever since the beginning of their abandonment and exile with regard to this third and final grouping of "the remnant of Israel who will be saved," and the scriptures that suggest how "the first shall be last and the last shall be first." These are the descendants of the disobedient ones from both the house of Judah and the house of Israel who had been scattered throughout the ends of the earth by God for all their abominable acts committed against him. They are, at this time, called back to his holy mountain that will have suddenly come into view before all men; there they will be reconciled back unto the Lamb of God, whom their fathers before them had crucified. Otherwise, it will not be for their sakes that they are saved, but it will be purely for the sake of his holy name. For they have suffered and been cut off long enough and now is the time for their reconciliation. They are the only survivors of all Israel to be left alive from the beast's great reign of terror at the time of Christ's second coming. These are also those that rejected Jesus as being their Messiah and held on to the belief that he had yet to come. Thus shall it be in fulfillment of all the scriptures that foretold of this great event: that when the nation of Israel sees the Lamb of God who was slain for their sins coming on the clouds of heaven in all power and glory, so shall they see the one to whom they had pierced. Then every knee shall bow and every tongue will confess that he is Lord, as the kingdom of heaven is finally brought down to earth with him and shall remain on earth, henceforth, for a thousand years.

6. The sixth thunder: This is the second grape harvest, or otherwise the end of the rebellious descendants of Gog and Magog. Then God spoke and there before the throne of God went forth flashes of lightning and peals of thunder, as he commanded the great archangel with authority over fire to go out from his heavenly temple and pour fire on all the hosts of Gog and Magog who had come to lay siege around his holy city and the people whom he loves. This is the final attempt by Satan to wage one last war against the Son of God before he and his countless hosts of the very wicked and evil hearted people from Gog and Magog are eventually judged and thrown into the lake of fire. This happens at the end of the one-thousand-year reign of Christ on earth, when Satan is let loose one last time from the abyss. It is here that he is finally allowed to fulfill his place in eternity, along with everyone else whose name was not found written in the Lamb's Book of Life.

7. The seventh thunder: This is the last harvest, and it will come when the whole house of Israel is finally resurrected from the dead. This is also the last resurrection of the dead that occurs at the time when all things are made new. Then God spoke and there before the throne of God went forth flashes of lightning and peals of thunder and he said to the angel that was standing in his presence, "Behold! I am making all things new. Now is the time for the rest of the dead belonging to the divided house of Israel to be brought back to life again under a single roof." Then Jesus spoke the word of his Father and behold all things were made new again and there was seen coming from the Father, a new heaven and a new earth, and then from on top of a high mountain of this new earth, the new holy city of Jerusalem was seen

THE BOOK OF REVELATION AND THE BIBLE
AS NEVER EXPLAINED BEFORE

coming down from heaven. It is at this time that the whole house of Israel shall be raised back to life again.

These are all those from the house of Judah and the house of Israel who had either long since died in their sins or more recently died in their sins, refusing to be both faithful or obedient to the doctrines and commandments of the Lord their God. In the second dispensation, these are all those who lived before the time of Christ under the old covenant brought forth by God through Abraham and Moses, which we may also describe as the time in BC. In the third dispensation, these are all those who had either lived during or since the time of Christ under the new covenant brought about by the Lamb of God's own self-sacrifice that had simply refused to believe that Jesus was their Messiah, even up until the time of his second coming, and died with that disbelief. Each dispensation equates to a period of about two thousand years. These are all finally brought back to life again and given new hearts with which to worship without ceasing the God to whom they had been so disobedient and unfaithful in the second dispensation and to whom they had rejected and had crucified in the third dispensation of their first lifetime. It is here that every sin and abomination against their God and their fellow man shall also be forgiven. For it is written: "Therefore say to the house of Israel, "Thus says the Lord God: "I do not do this for your sake, O house of Israel, but for my holy name's sake, which you have profaned among the nations wherever you went" (Ezekiel 36:22–23, NKJV).

For the complete understanding of all that God had said regarding this matter, read Ezekiel 36:16–32 and then read Ezekiel 37:1–28. Keep in mind that chapter 36 is speaking in regards to the remnant of Israel who will be saved at Christ's second coming, and chapter 37 is speaking in regards to the last resurrection of the dead, which is the whole house of Israel. Also notice in chapter 37 as you read down through verse 11 how the whole house of Israel is likened unto a valley of dry bones countless in number and cut off from God.

173

THE GREAT RED DRAGON
(REVELATION CHAPTER TWELVE)

Now a great sign appeared in heaven: a woman clothed with the sun, with the moon under her feet, and on her head was a garland of twelve stars. Then being with child, she cried out in labor, and pain to give birth. And another sign appeared in heaven: behold, a great fiery red dragon having seven heads and ten horns, and seven diadems (or crowns) on his heads. His tail drew a third of the stars of heaven and threw them to the earth. And the dragon stood before the woman who was ready to give birth, to devour her Child as soon as it was born. She bore a male Child who was to rule all nations with a rod of iron. And her Child was caught up to God and His throne. Then the woman fled into the wilderness, where she has a place prepared by God, that they should feed her there one thousand two hundred and sixty days (or three and a half years).

And war broke out in heaven: Michael and his angels fought with the dragon; and the dragon and his angels fought, but they did not prevail, nor was a place found for them in heaven any longer. So the great dragon was cast out, that serpent of old, called the Devil and Satan, who deceives the whole world; he was cast to earth, and his angels were cast out with him.

Then I heard a loud voice saying in heaven: "Now salvation, and strength, and the kingdom of our God, and the power of His Christ have come, for the accuser of our brethren, who accused them before our God day and night, has been cast down, and they overcame him by the blood of the Lamb and by the word of their testimony, and they did not love their lives to the death. *Therefore rejoice, O heavens, and you who dwell in them! (But) Woe to the inhabitants of the earth and the sea! For the devil has come down to you, having great wrath, because he knows that he has a short time.*

Now when the dragon saw that he had been cast to the earth, he persecuted the woman who gave birth to the male child. But the woman was given two wings of a great eagle, that she might fly into the wilderness to her place, where she is nourished for a time and times and half a time (or for three and a half years), from the presence of the serpent. So the serpent spewed water out of his mouth like a flood after the woman, that he might cause her to be carried away by the flood. But the earth helped the woman, and the earth opened its mouth and swallowed up the flood which the dragon had spewed out of his mouth. And the dragon was enraged with the woman, and he went to make war with the rest of her offspring, who keep the commandments of God and have the testimony of Jesus Christ.

Revelation 12:1–17 (NKJV)

From here we are told that the dragon goes to take his stand on the seashore.

THE BOOK OF REVELATION AND THE BIBLE
AS NEVER EXPLAINED BEFORE

This chapter begins by telling the story about the Virgin Mary giving birth to our Savior, and afterward it tells of all the troubles she had to endure because of it. But the woman who is depicted in this story is actually symbolic of a number of different things. First of all, she obviously represents the Virgin Mary in her struggle while on earth against the evil powers of Satan, who is himself symbolized by the great red dragon, having seven heads, ten horns, and seven diadems, of which I will be explaining the meaning of all these things a little later. But this woman is also symbolic of the nation of Israel, as women are often used to symbolize nations and cities in the Bible. But what makes this woman a nation instead of a city in this context is the crown of twelve stars that has been placed upon her head. The crown of twelve stars are actually symbolic of the twelve patriarchs of Jacob, whose name was later changed to Israel, whose twelve sons went on to father the twelve tribes of Israel, which ultimately became the nation of Israel; hence, the woman with the crown of twelve stars.

The duality of this story also suggests one other thing: that the Virgin Mary was chosen by God from amongst all the other women of Israel to be the mother of God because of her purity of heart and exceptional love for God, and because of this she shall be called blessed for all generations. All this was done in fulfillment of the prophecies. This is the other meaning behind the woman seen here wearing the crown of twelve stars. It is for this same reason that she wears a robe as brilliant as the sun and that she stands having the moon beneath her feet, as both of these symbolize the exalted status given to her by God. In the book of Genesis, one of the dreams that Joseph had used similar symbols to show how he too would become elevated above his other eleven brothers as he would eventually become the first "savior of the world," just as Samson and Moses, would become either a savoir or a deliverer after him, as they were each born to fulfill this same purpose for the sake of Israel. It is interesting to note how God used these three men in particular,

177

aside from all the other Deliverers of Israel that are also spoken about from within the book of Judges, as a symbolic gesture before sending his own Son later to become the ultimate Savior and Deliverer of both Israel and the Gentile world. Reference Genesis 37:9–10 regarding the symbols and also Genesis 45:5–8 regarding Joseph's chosen status.

From his birth, using symbolic terms, the story then goes on to tell of the crucifixion and death of Jesus and how afterward he is resurrected. This corresponds to how the child is then quickly snatched up into heaven, whereby Jesus returns to heaven to sit on the throne of his Father. Then, because of his great victory over death and the *great red dragon,* a war broke out in heaven and the dragon (Satan), along with all his angels, or as John puts it, a third of the stars in the sky, were ultimately defeated and thrown down to the earth, where he then decides to go after first the blessed mother of Jesus, but since she is taken safely away to Egypt in the first instance and then later into the outer lying lands after the great time of persecutions began on the church, in the second instance; Satan then turns his fury on the woman's offspring or else the faithful followers of the Lord from within the nation of Israel who strive to keep the commandments of the Lord. It is here that Satan then takes his symbolic stand on the seashore as he guards over his last dominion granted to him by God; where it is written: "Rejoice then you heavens and you that dwell in them! But woe to you, earth and sea, for the Devil has come down to you in great fury, knowing his time is short" (Revelation 12:12, TNEB).

Here is the reminder to all those who stand before the congregations of the megachurches and preach the great lie telling God's people that now is the time for celebration for Satan has already been defeated. Satan has not been defeated here on earth and will not be defeated until after the one-thousand-year reign of Christ has come to its end, where Satan will be let loose one last time to seduce the nations into waging war against God's holy mountain and his people dwelling peacefully upon

THE BOOK OF REVELATION AND THE BIBLE
AS NEVER EXPLAINED BEFORE

it. Here the advancing armies of the descendants of Gog and Magog will make their final attempt to plunder the peaceful and holy ones living within the kingdom of God. But fire shall come down on them from heaven and they shall be consumed. Only then will Satan, the great red dragon, be utterly defeated. But as for now, it is as the book of Revelation has said: Satan is spewing forth his vomit across the face of the earth like a great flood of water because he knows his time is short. We have only to look out across the face of the earth to see the terrible truth in this with all the murdering and killing that is going on. But for many within this country, we need not look so far out to see that Satan's spew lies all around us.

It is interesting to note how *Satan* is described here as a *great red dragon* having seven heads, ten horns, and who is also wearing seven diadems (or crowns) as opposed to the description that is later given of the beast.

The *beast,* on the other hand, who is seen rising out of the sea in the beginning of Revelation chapter 13, is described as being, first of all, a beast of several different types instead of a dragon, and then the rest of the description is quite similar to the dragon in that they both have seven heads and ten horns, but the difference is that the beast has ten diadems instead of the seven diadems of his father, Satan. Once again, a great description of both is given, and their mutual purpose for being here is made quite clear. It also mentions the precise amount of time that the beast will have to reign on this earth, which will be exactly forty-two months, or three and a half years. During this time, the *beast* will be allowed to mouth bombast and blasphemy against God and his holy dwelling, but also he will be allowed to wage war on God's people and to defeat them. If that were not enough, he will also be granted authority over every tribe and people, language, and nation. This authority comes to the beast from God himself and all will worship it, except those whose names have been recorded in the Lamb's Book of Life written there since the world was made.

179

THE BEAST AND THE FALSE PROPHET
(REVELATION CHAPTER THIRTEEN)

Then I stood on the sand of the sea. And I saw a *beast* rising up *out of the sea,* having seven heads and ten horns, and on his horns ten crowns, and on his heads a blasphemous name. Now the beast which I saw was like a leopard, his feet were like the feet of a bear, and his mouth like the mouth of a lion. The *dragon* gave him his power, his throne, and great authority. And I saw one of his heads as if it had been mortally wounded, *and his deadly wound was healed.* And all the world marveled and followed the beast. So they worshiped the dragon who gave authority to the beast; and they worshiped the beast, saying, "Who is like the beast? Who is able to make war with him?

And he was given a mouth speaking great things and blasphemies, and he was given authority to continue for forty-two months. Then he opened his mouth in blasphemy against God, to blaspheme His name, His tabernacle, and those who dwell in heaven. It was granted to him to make war with the saints and to overcome them. And authority was given him over every tribe, tongue, and nation. All who dwell on the earth will worship him, who names have not been written in the Book of Life of the Lamb slain from the foundations of the world.

If anyone has an ear, let him hear. He who leads into captivity shall go into captivity; He who kills with the sword must be killed with the sword. Here is the patience and the faith of the saints.

Revelation 13:1–10 (NKJV)

THE FALSE PROPHET

Then I saw another beast coming up *out of the earth;* and he had two horns like a lamb and spoke like a dragon. And he exercises all the authority of the first beast in his presence, and causes the earth and all those who dwell in it to worship the first beast, *whose deadly wound was healed.* He performs great signs, so that he even makes fire come down from heaven on the earth in the sight of men. And he deceives those who dwell on the earth by those signs which he was granted to do in the sight of the beast, telling those who dwell on the earth to make an image to the beast who was wounded by the sword and lived. He was granted power to give breath to the image of the beast, that the image of the beast should both speak and cause as many as would not worship the beast to be killed. He causes all, both small and great, rich and poor, free and slave, to receive a mark on their right hand or on their foreheads, and that no one may buy or sell except one who has the mark or the name of the beast, or the number of his name.

THE BOOK OF REVELATION AND THE BIBLE
AS NEVER EXPLAINED BEFORE

Here is wisdom. Let him who has understanding calculate
the number of the beast, for it is the number of a man: His
number is 666.

Revelation 13:11–18 (NKJV)

Here in chapter thirteen is where the book of Revelation makes
the appearance of both the *beast* and the *false prophet* known to
us. The first beast is shown to rise up out of the sea, and the second is shown to rise up out of the earth. This is all very symbolic
of the two very distinctly different ways in which these two men
shall make their grand entrances into the world's political arena
just before they seize complete power and control over it.

With regard to the first beast, the sea, as it is being used
here in this context, is symbolic of several things. First, it
denotes the supernatural power of God, but it also suggests the
very place from where the beast will make his return visit to the
earth, which I will be speaking about in more detail a little later
on in this chapter. Otherwise, there are those scriptures found
within the book of Revelation that suggest there is a port hole
that lies deep beneath the sea in an area of sea bottom oceanographers can only refer to as the abyss because of its great depths
that once opened, the scriptures say, leads into another spiritual realm, or more clearly, the spiritual abode of the dead and
damned that lies below this level of sea bottom as it transcends
deep into the molten bowels of the earth. Interestingly enough,
this is also the same place that the book of Revelation refers
to as the abyss. The presently sealed porthole that leads into
it is called the shaft of the abyss. It will be through this shaft
that the man referred to as the beast with the seven heads must
ascend, and this can only happen by the supernatural power and
authority of God as it is described to us in the fifth trumpet
(Revelation 9:1–11). It will also be by this same power that the
mortal wound that has yet to be inflicted upon the beast shall be
healed. This mortal wound will more than likely be caused by a
gunshot wound to the head and will be rendered by an assassin

183

from either Israel or the former Soviet Union at some unspeci-
fied time after the beast makes his grand entrance back into the
world's political arena.

With regard to the second beast, the earth, as it is being used
here in this context, denotes that the false prophet will come to
power by the natural earthly way of things. In other words, he
will be born of a woman and raised and educated by the natural
worldly systems but especially in the art of war. Then, by the
miraculous powers that will later be bestowed upon him by God
through Satan, he shall deceive the world in believing that he is
the great prophet Elijah come back to set all things right as it
has been prophesied and to proclaim to the world that the beast
with the seven heads is the rightful messiah that it has been
waiting for. His gospel will be a gospel of war, as opposed to the
Lamb's, which is a gospel of peace, where murder and killing for
the sake of power will be the only morality. The world will come
to love and worship the beast for his gospel, for it is the gospel
that they would rather believe in, as opposed to the other one
that was about peace, love, and forgiveness. The other gospel
was unnatural to the world, but the beast's gospel will seem
right to them because it will satisfy all their natural desires.

The first beast, who has sometimes been referred to as the
antichrist or son of Satan, is then described to us as having
seven heads and ten horns, whereupon each of his ten horns
there is a diadem (or crown). The body of the beast is like that
of a leopard, and its feet are like a bear's; the mouth on each of
the seven heads is like that of a lion. Finally, we are told that on
each head is written a blasphemous name. The following is the
deciphered meaning of all these things as it has been given to
me by the power of God's Holy Spirit and his Holy Word as it
is contained within the Bible.

In the book of the prophet Daniel, we are given several
clues as to what the beast with the seven heads and ten horns
signifies and also why it is depicted as having the body of a
leopard, the feet of a bear, the mouth of a lion, and ten horns on

its heads. Here in the seventh chapter of Daniel, he begins by telling us about the different dreams and visions he had during the first year of the reign of King Belshazzar, the son of King Nebuchadnezzar. The following is the record of one such dream of the prophet Daniel:

Daniel said, I have been seeing visions in the night. I saw that the four winds of heaven were stirring up the Great Sea; four great beasts emerged from the sea, each different from the others. The first was like a lion with eagle's wings and, as I looked, its wings were torn off, and it was lifted off the ground and set standing on its feet like a human; and it was given a human heart. And there before me was a second beast, like a bear, rearing up on one side, with three ribs in its mouth, between its teeth. "Up!" came the command. "Eat quantities of flesh!" After this I looked; and there before me was another beast, like a leopard, and with four birds wings on its flanks; it had four heads and was granted authority. Next, in the visions of the night, I saw another vision: there before me was a fourth beast, fearful, terrifying, very strong; it had great iron teeth, and it ate its victims, crushed them, and trampled their remains underfoot. It was different from the previous beasts and had ten horns.

While I was looking at these horns, I saw another horn sprouting among them, a little one; three of the original horns were pulled out by the roots to make way for it; and in this horn I saw eyes like human eyes, and a mouth full of boasting.

While I was watching, thrones were set in place and one most venerable took his seat. His robe was white as snow, the hair of his head as pure as wool. His throne was a blaze of flames, its wheels were a burning fire. A stream of fire poured out, issuing from his presence. A thousand thousand waited on him, ten thousand times ten thousand stood before him. The court was in session and the books lay open. I went on watching: then, because of the noise made by the boastings of the horn, as I watched, the beast was put to death, and its body destroyed and committed to the flames. The other beasts were deprived of their empire, but received a lease of life for a season and for a time.

I was gazing into the visions of the night, when I saw, coming on the clouds of heaven, as it were a son of man. He came to the One most venerable and was led into his presence. On him was conferred rule, honor and kingship, and all peoples, nations and languages became his servants. His rule is an everlasting rule which will never pass away, and his kingship will never come to an end.

I, Daniel, was deeply disturbed and the visions that passed through my head alarmed me. So I approached one of those who was standing by and asked him about all of this. And in reply he revealed to me what these things meant. "These four great beasts are four kings who will rise up from the earth. Those who receive royal power are the holy ones of the Most High, and kingship will be theirs forever and ever." Then I asked about the fourth beast, different from all the rest, very terrifying, with iron teeth and bronze claws; it ate its victims, crushed them, and trampled their remains underfoot; and about the ten horns on its head—and why the other horn sprouted and the three original horns fell, and why this horn had eyes and a mouth full of boasting, and why it looked more impressive than its fellows. This was the horn I had watched making war on the holy ones and proving the stronger until the coming of the One most venerable who gave judgment in favor of the holy ones of the Most High, when the time came for the holy ones to assume kingship. This is what he said:

"The fourth beast is to be a fourth kingdom on earth, different from all other kingdoms. It will devour the whole world, trample it underfoot and crush it. As for the ten horns: from this kingdom will rise ten kings and another after them; this one will be different from the previous ones and will bring down three kings; he will insult the Most High, and torment the holy ones of the Most High. He will plan to alter the seasons and the Law, and the saints will be handed over to him for a time, two times, and half a time, (or for a period of three

THE BOOK OF REVELATION AND THE BIBLE
AS NEVER EXPLAINED BEFORE

and a half years). But the court will sit, and he will be stripped of his royal authority which will be finally destroyed and reduced to nothing. And kingship and rule and the splendors of all the kingdoms under heaven will be given to the people of the holy ones of the Most High, whose royal power is an eternal power, whom every empire will serve and obey."

Daniel 7:2–27 (TNJB)

From this dream of Daniel's, we can see that the four beasts that are depicted here by Daniel and the beast with the seven heads and ten horns that is depicted in the book of Revelation by John are representations of one in the same thing with the exception of the ten horns, which I will be explaining later. To be clearer, the beast that John depicts is actually a consolidation of these four beasts all rolled into one beast. That is why his beast has the body of a leopard, the feet of a bear, the mouths of a lion, and ten horns.

But there are still more clues to be had from another dream that King Nebuchadnezzar had that Daniel came to tell both the dream and its interpretation to the king, so as to spare all the wise men of Babylon from execution, which comes from the second chapter of the book of Daniel. The following is that dream and its interpretation as Daniel tells it to King Nebuchadnezzar:

Facing the king, Daniel replied, 'None of the sages, soothsayers, magicians or exorcists has been able to tell the king the truth of the mystery which the king has propounded; but there is a God in heaven who reveals mysteries and who has shown King Nebuchadnezzar what is to take place in the final days. These then, are the dream and the visions that passed through your head as you lay in your bed:

Your Majesty, on your bed your thoughts turned to what would happen in the future, and the Revealer of Mysteries disclosed to you what is to take place. The mystery has been revealed to me, not that I am wiser than anyone else, but for

187

this sole purpose: that the king should learn what it means, and that you should understand your inmost thoughts.

You have had a vision, Your Majesty; this is what you saw: a statue, a great statue of extreme brightness, stood before you, terrible to see. The head of this statue was of fine gold, its chest and arms were of silver, its belly and thighs of bronze, its legs of iron, its feet part iron, part clay. While you were gazing, a stone broke away, untouched by any hand, and struck the statue, struck its feet of iron and clay and shattered them. Then, iron and clay, bronze, silver and gold, all broke into pieces as fine as chaff on the threshing-floor in summer. The wind blew them away, leaving not a trace behind. And the stone that had struck the statue had grown into a great mountain, filling the whole world. This was the dream; we shall now explain to the king what it means.

You, your Majesty, king of kings, to whom the God of heaven has given sovereignty, power, strength and honor—human beings, wild animals, birds of the air, wherever they live, he has entrusted to your rule, making you king of them all—you are the golden head. And, after you, another kingdom will arise, not as great as yours, and then a third, of bronze, which will rule the whole world. There will be a fourth kingdom, hard as iron, as iron that pulverizes and crushes all. Like iron that breaks everything to pieces, it will crush and break all the earlier kingdoms. The feet you saw, part earthenware, part iron, are a kingdom which will be split in two, but which will retain something of the strength of iron, just as you saw the iron and the clay of the earthenware mixed together. The feet were part iron, part potter's clay: the kingdom will be partly strong and partly brittle. And just as you saw the iron and the clay of the earthenware mixed together, so the two will be mixed together in human seed; but they will not hold together any more than iron will blend with clay. In the days of those kings, the God of heaven will set up a kingdom which will never be destroyed, and this kingdom will not pass into the hands of another race: it will shatter and absorb all the previous kingdoms and itself last forever—just as you saw a stone untouched by hand, break away from the mountain, and reduce iron, bronze, earthenware, silver and gold to powder. The Great God has shown the king what is to take place. The dream is true, the interpretation exact.

Daniel 2:27–45 (TNJB)

THE SEVEN HEADS OF THE BEAST

As we can see from these two dreams shown to Daniel, the beast with the seven heads, as depicted in the book of Revelation by the Apostle John, is symbolic of the four kingdoms that would eventually come to rule the world and the three divided kingdoms that would follow, of which the interpretation of the first five are given to us in this last dream that was given to Daniel and the last two divided kingdoms lie presently before us. They are as follows, as history, the Bible, and our present time bears witness to this record.

The first kingdom, as symbolized by *the first head of the beast,* is told to us by the interpreter of Daniel's second dream. It is the kingdom of Babylon as ruled by King Nebuchadnezzar and later by his son Belshazzar; which corresponds to the beast that appeared like a lion with two great eagle's wings and the head of gold as seen on the great image. For all three of these depictions, as described throughout the first part of this chapter, are symbolic of one in the same thing.

The second kingdom, as symbolized by *the second head of the beast,* is the dawning of the Persian Empire. Where it is written, "That same night, the Chaldaean king Belshazzar was murdered, and Darius the Mede received the kingdom, at age of sixty-two" (Daniel 5:30–31, TNJB). Six kings reigned over Persia shortly thereafter, and they are as follows: the first Persian king to rule after Darius the Mede, who was the son of Ahasuerus, was Cyrus the Great of Persia. He overthrew the Medes in 549 BC and is most known for being the king that freed the Jews from their captivity, where by royal decree and with a special commission from Cyrus himself, a great number of Jews were sent back to Jerusalem to rebuild the holy temple of God. He is also accredited for his great work in establishing the far reaching boundaries of the Persian Empire. He is killed in 529 BC; Cambyses, the son of Cyrus, takes the throne after his father and goes on to conquer Egypt in 525 BC but dies on his way back to Persia. Then Darius I, a relative of Cambyses, becomes king in 521 BC and does much to reorganize the government and establishes the absolute power of the King of kings. He also builds the palaces at Persepolis and Susa, the two capitals of the Persian Empire. Darius I dies in 486 BC while preparing for new attacks on Greece. His son, Xerxes I, also called Aartaxerxes, inherits the throne from his father in 485 BC and is the most powerful and wealthiest of all the other kings of Persia. He is also the one king remembered best for his starring role in the Biblical story of Esther, which was recently made into a full length motion picture entitled: "One Night with the King." But as history picks up from where the movie leaves off, his military quest that he sets off to fulfill after his marriage and troubles with Esther are resolved is beleaguered by crushing military defeats in Europe and in Greece which costs him his political popularity near the end of his reign where he is finally murdered in 424 BC. He is succeeded by his son Xerxes II but because his reign only lasts 45 days he is not recognized as an actual king of Persia. He too is murdered as was his father before him by political assassins. Then Darius II, whose reign marks the beginning of the decline of the Persian Empire, comes to the throne. He reigns from 424 to 404 BC. He is succeeded by Darius III, who is the last king of Persia. He rules from 336 to 331 BC, and his reign marks the end of a very weak and corrupt empire.

This empire corresponds to the beast that was like a bear, which had three ribs in its mouth and also the breast and arms of silver as seen on the great image. The three ribs are symbolic of the three kings that came to represent the Babylonian and short-lived Median Empire just before the Persian Empire

THE BOOK OF REVELATION AND THE BIBLE
AS NEVER EXPLAINED BEFORE

came to rule the world. The three kings are as follows: King Nebuchadnezzar, who was the first Babylonian king, his son Belshazzar, who was the second and last Babylonian king, and finally Darius the Mede, who was the only king of the short-lived Median Empire.

The third kingdom, as symbolized by *the third head of the beast,* is the Macedonian Empire of Alexander the Great. His kingdom comes in 331 BC, soon after a series of crushing defeats leveled against the Persian forces at Hellespont, Issus, Tyre, and Gaza. But the most decisive battle won was that of the Battle of Arbela, also called the Battle of Gaugamela, where the forces of Alexander the Great went on to defeat a huge Persian army led by Darius III, and it is after this battle that the Persian Empire, also called the Achaemenid Empire, comes to its end. Alexander the Great then goes on to conquer much of what was then known to be the civilized world. The empire of Alexander the Great stretched from Greece to northwestern India at the height of his career. He died abruptly on June 13, 323 BC from malaria at the age of thirty-three while in the midst of his plans to reorganize his government and start a new expedition into Arabia.

History acclaims him as being one of the greatest generals to ever live and command an army. After his death, his empire is held together for a little while by his four generals, but by 311 BC, the empire is divided up into successor states as his generals begin quarreling among themselves. General Ptolemy took Egypt and Israel while General Seleucus I took charge over Syria and Mesopotamia; General Lysimachus chose the rulership of Thrace and the Asia Minor, and finally General Cassander chose the dominion of Macedonia and Greece. Only General Ptolemy's dynasty in Egypt lasted until Cleopatra's death in 30 BC. She was the last Ptolemy to rule in Egypt before it was conquered by the Romans under Octavian in the same year.

This empire corresponds to the beast that appeared like a leopard with four heads and four birdlike wings and also the belly and thighs of bronze as seen on the great image. The body

191

of the leopard symbolizes the strength and speed at which Alexander the Great was able to conquer all the different nations of the world at that time. The four heads signify the four generals who would inherit the kingdom after Alexander's death in 323 BC, and the four birdlike wings signify their weakness to carry the weight of his kingdom afterward.

The fourth kingdom, as symbolized by *the fourth head of the beast*, is the dawning of the great Roman Empire. How fitting it is that this empire, which is represented by the fourth beast in Daniel's second dream and the two legs of iron on the great statue, is depicted as being dreadful and grisly, exceedingly strong, and having great iron teeth and bronze claws for which to crunch and devour and trample under foot all that was left. We have seen in history how this was just what the Roman legions did to all who came before them. But added to this beast are the ten horns and finally the last little one that had eyes like a man and a mouth that spoke proud words and who, because of these proud words, is killed and its carcass finally cast into the fire, which then consumes it.

You may well be wondering who these ten kings were that the interpreter to Daniel's dream said signified these ten horns of the Roman Empire and especially who this last king is who he said would also come from among their number. The following is the answer to this mystery.

The first thing that must be understood in this explanation, as I mentioned earlier, is that these ten horns as depicted on the fourth beast from the book of Daniel and the ten horns on the beast with the seven heads from the book of Revelation do not represent the same thing. In either case, they do both represent ten kings, along with their corresponding kingdoms, but that is as far as their similarities go. However, as the angel told Daniel, the ten horns on the fourth beast represent ten kings that would come to reign during this empire's time in power, and the ten horns on the beast with the seven heads from the book of Revelation represent ten kings that have not yet begun to reign but who, for one hour, are to share with the beast the exercise of royal authority, for they have but a single purpose among them and will confer their power and authority upon the beast. After doing this, they will then join together with him to destroy the great whore of Babylon, and soon after that they will go to wage war with the Lamb of God upon his return. But the Lamb will defeat them because he is the King of kings and the Lord of lords, and his followers will share in his victory, as they are the Called, the Faithful, and the Chosen. Reference Revelation 17:12–18 regarding the ten horns of the beast.

They are Called because out of all the inhabitants of the earth, these will be the only ones called out of it that will be taken up to heaven either secretly or at the last trumpet call. Both of these groups will be called the immortal priests of God who shall reside with Christ in the royal house for a thousand years. They are, once again, the hundred and forty-four thousand and the great multitude and they are the only ones from all of earth who shall attend the Lamb's great wedding feast, whereas the survivors of all Israel who will be saved later will not.

They are Faithful because they alone endured the pains and sufferings of this world to the end and were found waiting faithfully for Christ's return and who by the seal of the Holy Spirit shall be delivered up into heaven at the last trumpet call.

They are Chosen because they alone shall have the seal of God placed upon their foreheads, and because of their perfection in love they shall be the first fruits of humanity to be taken up into heaven just before the sixth trumpet.

The following is my determination of who the ten kings are, as depicted by the ten horns on the fourth beast from Daniel's first dream and also what these kings represent as viewed from within the monarchal reign of the Roman Empire as it has evolved throughout history. It should also be pointed out that in the history of the Roman Empire, as it was ruled by Romans, there have been seventy-six emperors, but it is interesting that only ten horns are depicted on the beast with iron teeth and bronze claws. It must then be concluded from this that the ten horns do not necessarily signify successive kings nor do they signify every king or emperor that came to rule over the empire. Rather, they would have to signify ten very significant time periods that have occurred during this empire's dominion on earth. These next five kings that I am about to name are in keeping with this idea and ruled the empire when Romans had their dominion over it, and they are as follows:

1. Emperor (Octavian) Augustus reigned from 27 BC to AD 14 and was the first emperor of Rome. He is remembered for having conquered Egypt in 30 BC and as the one who ordered the census that caused Joseph and Mary to have to travel to Bethlehem where the birth of Jesus the Messiah would occur, as was prophesied.

2. Emperor Tiberius reigned from AD 14 to AD 37 and was the emperor during the time when Jesus Christ would be crucified.

3. Emperor Nero reigned from AD 54 to AD 68 and was the cruelest emperor to reign over the Roman Empire. His reign marks the beginning of the time when Christians would be led like lambs to the slaughter. His persecution of the Christians can only be rivaled by the coming of the beast and his great reign of terror, as told to us by John in the book of Revelation. Nero bears significance here because he is actually the beast's forerunner but is himself not the beast that is to return from the abyss at the time of the end.

4. Emperor Constantine reigned from AD 306 to AD 337 and is the emperor that brought the great persecution of Christians to an end and went on to make Christianity the official religion of the Roman Empire. It was also from this time on that the Roman Catholic Church, or as it was otherwise called, the universal church of Rome, had its beginning.

5. Emperor Romulus Augustus reigned from AD 475 to AD 476 and was the last Roman emperor of the Western empire. His ousting by the German tribal chieftain Odoacer marks the end of Roman dominion over the Western empire.

These last five kings mark the time when German emperors reigned over the western half of the Roman Empire as it would eventually come to be called the Holy Roman Empire. But this was only after several hundred years of tribal conflict had come to divide the former empire into different territories.

6. Then in AD 800, Pope Leo III crowned Charlemagne the first German emperor of the Romans. He reigned from AD 800 until his death in AD 814. After his death, his empire was divided up among his three grandsons: Louis II, who received the land today known as Germany, Charles I received the land that would later be called France, and Lothair I received the middle kingdom, a narrow strip of land that stretched from the North Sea all the way down to Italy. Lothair also kept the title of emperor. Their dominion lasted until 911 when the last of the royal family died out. After this, the kingdom consisted of five very powerful territories, each ruled by a duke. The territories were called Bavaria, Lorraine, Franconia, Saxony, and Swabia. Ultimately, two kings were elected from two of these territories. The first, named Conrad I, from Franconia ruled until 919. Then Henry I from Saxony ruled until 962, but it was not until then that the next emperor was crowned in Rome.

7. Then in 962, Otto I (The Great), the son of Henry I, is crowned emperor in Rome by the German princes because of his great victories in battle. His reign marked the beginning of what would later be called the Holy Roman Empire. It was during this time that the Holy Roman Empire, under the Saxon emperors, became the most powerful entity in Europe. It also had the best organized government. But

under the Salian Dynasty, which lasted from 1024 to 1125, a long power struggle began that left the empire weak and disorganized. In 1075, Pope Gregory VII disputed the right of Emperor Henry IV to appoint bishops. Many German princes sided with the pope and fought a series of civil wars against the emperor. The princes grew stronger, and by the 1300s, the position of emperor had become almost powerless. Another dynasty followed, but it would not be until 1273 that the princes would elect another emperor of Rome.

8. Rudolph I of Hapsburg was crowned emperor of Rome in 1273 and is accredited for having seized Austria from another rival German prince and making it the main territory of his family's kingdom. After the death of Rudolf I, the other families of Hapsburg reigned almost continuously until 1806, when Napoleon finally brought the Holy Roman Empire to an end. His reign marked the beginning of the longest period of stability the empire would come to have under German dominion.

9. Then from 1740 to 1786, Frederick the Great united Prussia into a great empire, which set up the establishment of the North German Confederation in 1867. This confederation eventually became the German Empire after Germany defeated France in the Franco-Prussian War of 1871.

10. On January 18, 1870, Wilhelm I of Prussia was crowned the new Kaiser, or Caesar, of this newly revived German Empire, or as it was also called, the Second Reich, which literally means the second empire, or more clearly, the second rise of the former Holy Roman Empire, which was the First Reich. As his first act as emperor, Wilhelm appointed Otto Von Bismarck chancellor of the government. As the chancellor, Bismarck went on to do a lot of great things for the German people, which launched Germany well ahead of the rest of the world in the industrial revolution. His

THE BOOK OF REVELATION AND THE BIBLE
AS NEVER EXPLAINED BEFORE

foreign policy was aimed at securing the peace so as to allow Germany time to develop its new industries and also its power and military might. He also worked hard at securing Germany's borders through the formation of military alliances. In 1873, he tried unsuccessfully to create an alliance between Russia and Austria-Hungary but was finally successful in creating another military alliance between Austria-Hungary and Italy from 1879 to 1882, which was called the Triple Alliance. Then in 1890, Kaiser Wilhelm II came to power and dismissed Bismarck so as to allow Germany's foreign policy to become more ambitious. War eventually broke out between those in the Triple Alliance with Germany and the Triple Entente that was established between England, France, and Russia, with the United States joining in later. But in 1918, the Allies defeated Germany in World War I, and the German Empire, or Second Reich, ended. This war also marked the beginning of the final empire as depicted by the great image's ten toes of iron and clay, when the world from this point on would be ruled by leagues, alliances, and finally confederations of nations.

These then are the ten kings of the Roman Empire, which constitute the ten horns on the fourth beast and also the two legs of iron as seen on the great image.

The little horn that sprang up that was unlike all the rest and in whose coming had uprooted three of the first horns to make room for it is the man the book of Revelation depicts as the beast with the seven heads, ten horns, and ten diadems who shall rise up from the abyss to begin his final reign of terror upon all the inhabitants of the earth at the fifth trumpet. The reason why this man, who shall come to rule the world at the time of the end, is symbolized as a beast having seven heads, ten horns, and ten diadems is because the great red dragon, which is Satan, had conferred his own power and authority upon him, and these seven heads, ten horns, and ten diadems (or crowns)

197

are symbolic of that dominion, which was granted to Satan by God since the beginning of the world. This dominion basically gives Satan full power and authority over all the kingdoms of this world until such time as the Lamb of God, who is the true Messiah, shall make his triumphant return and take it all away from him and the beast. That is why Satan is first symbolized as a great red dragon, having these same seven heads, ten horns, but differing slightly in that he had only seven diadems instead of ten and the body and heads of a dragon instead of the multiple parts of the other beasts.

The difference of Satan's seven diadems as opposed to the beast's ten diadems signifies the time of the end when Satan will confer his own power and authority over to the beast, which will last for a period of three and a half years, but they also symbolize the ten kings who at the time of the end will also confer their own sovereignty upon the beast as well, hence the three extra diadems.

The first divided kingdom, which marks the dawning of the fifth empire, is symbolized by the fifth head of the beast and the ten toes of iron and clay as seen on the great image and was the creation of the first confederation of nations called the League of Nations. The League of Nations was an international association of countries created to maintain peace among the nations of the world by the victors of World War I. These victors included France, Great Britain, Italy, Japan, and the United States. The constitution for the league was drawn up in 1919 and was later established in January 1920 with its headquarters in Geneva, Switzerland. President Woodrow Wilson was the chief planner of the league but could not persuade the United States to join it.

Wilson and the other statesmen who helped designed the league hoped it would stop other nations from seeking protection through special alliances. Instead, they favored a system of collective security in which the security of each member would be guaranteed by the protection of all. For collective security to work, it was essential that all league members, especially the most powerful ones, come to the aid of any member attacked.

All of this sounded very good on paper, but in the actual application, it became a complete fiasco, as neither the council nor the assembly could force members to help an attacked nation. It became even worse when the most powerful nations were not even league members, and those that were did not agree that collective security was the main reason for the league. France saw the league mainly as an instrument to maintain the territorial settlement imposed on Germany after World War I. The Germans resented the league because it seemed to them that this was the league's real purpose as well and that it was being used to punish them. Britain's statesmen considered it a meeting place for the most powerful nations to consult in the event of a threat to peace. But they did not want to commit themselves in advance to do anything as a result of such talks. The Russians believed the league was an imperialist fraud because communism taught that war was inevitable among capitalist nations. Japan and Italy showed their disregard for collective security by attacking member nations.

Japan withdrew from the league in 1933 because the league refused to recognize its conquest of Manchuria. Germany was admitted to the league in 1926 but withdrew in 1933 because the league would not change the arms limitations imposed on Germany after World War I. Italy withdrew from the league in 1937 to join Japan and Germany in an alliance against the Soviet Union. The Soviet Union, which joined the League in 1934, was expelled in 1939 for attacking Finland. But it was when Italy attacked Ethiopia in 1935 that the league showed itself for what it really was: a paper tiger. The league was finally dissolved in 1946 at the end of World War II, and the United Nations took its place.

The League of Nations ultimately came to signify what the ten toes of iron and clay actually meant, as clay and iron can never be made to bond together or make a strong and lasting alliance either between the nations or between those who were inspired to become interracially married because of such alliances. But as the great image had only five sections and the beast has seven heads, we know that this also signifies that the last empire of the world, being composed of a confederation of strong and weak nations, would then have to be divided into three time periods, which then brings me to the last two confederations of this fifth empire.

The second divided kingdom of the fifth empire, as symbolized by *the* sixth head of the beast and the ten toes of iron and clay as seen on the great image, is the confederation of nations called the United Nations, and the reigning superpower of the world holding sway over it is the United States. It is within the United States that the great seaport city of New York may also be found, which has more commonly been referred to as the economical capital of the world. This is where the world stands right now, according to the book of Revelation, until such time as the beast shall come back in great pomp and triumph to finish what he first started with his vision for the new world order.

The third divided kingdom of the fifth empire, as symbolized by the seventh head of the beast and the ten toes of iron and clay as seen on the great image, will be the European Union, but this confederation of nations can only be brought to power by the beast and the false prophet upon the first one's return and the other one's arrival into the world's political arena. It will be through the European Union that this man the book of Revelation calls the beast shall rise to power and come to rule the world.

These then are the four empires and three divided kingdoms of the world as symbolized in part by the four beasts in Daniel's second dream, the great image in his interpretation of King Nebuchadnezzar's dream, and the incorporation of both of these by the beast with the seven heads, ten horns, and ten diadems as depicted by John in the book of Revelation, but this is not all that is said about the beast. In the seventeenth chapter of the book of Revelation, we are given even more clues as

THE BOOK OF REVELATION AND THE BIBLE
AS NEVER EXPLAINED BEFORE

to what the beast with the seven heads was further shown to mean and symbolize, as the angel of the Lord finally tells John the secret of the beast and the woman who rides him in a very mystifying way. Where it is written:

> The beast you have seen was once alive and is alive no longer, (and) it is yet to come up from the Abyss, but only to go to its destruction. And the people of the world, whose names have not been written since the beginning of the world in the book of life, will be astonished when they see how the beast was once alive and is alive no longer, and is still to come.
>
> This calls for shrewdness. The seven heads are the seven hills, on which the woman is sitting. The seven heads are also seven emperors, (or Kings). Five of them have already gone, one is here now, and one is yet to come; once here, he must stay for a short while. The beast, who was alive and is alive no longer, is at the same time the eighth and one of the seven, and he is going to his destruction. The ten horns which you saw are ten kings who have not yet been given their royal power but will have royal authority only for a single hour and in association with the beast.
>
> Revelation 17:8–12 (TNJB)

It is important to understand that the angel here under God's direction has purposefully made this chapter out of the book of Revelation an extremely challenging riddle to solve, and if it were not for the time that we are now living in, it would be impossible for anyone to solve it. For here is the first key to solving this riddle that only now has been made available to us: "for he once was alive, and is alive no longer, and has still to appear." In this one verse, the angel has told us the time period he was referencing for this riddle to be solved in, and that time is now. At no other time in history would this riddle have made any sense because the man who is symbolized by the beast had not yet been born, but now at this time we know this man to be dead, but no one believes that he will ever appear again. That is why the

201

angel has told us that when the beast does finally appear, we will all be astonished to see him. Why? Because we will not be able to believe that it is him and that he has returned from the dead, and everyone will recognize him and know him as the man the Bible calls "the destroyer" who once was alive, and for a time, we all knew him to be dead, but now he has appeared again, and at some point after this reappearance he will receive a mortal wound to the head from an assassin's bullet, but to the amazement of the world, that mortal wound will be healed.

Then, as the angel also points out to John, in this section of chapter seventeen, the seven heads also represent seven hills. It is no secret to most Bible scholars that these seven hills that the angel is referring to here are none other than the Seven Hills of ancient Rome. But to truly understand what the Seven Hills of Rome in this context signify is to have in your possession the second key that unlocks the mystery to the riddle of who and what all the woman represents that sits upon the beast holding reign over its seven heads with the ten horns. I will be speaking about this woman later in much greater detail when I get to that chapter of my book called "The Great Whore of Babylon."

But as you can see from all of this information that has been revealed to us through the book of Daniel, the historic record, and the book of Revelation, the beast with the seven heads and ten horns has multiple meanings, of which you cannot simply stop in any one place and then suppose that you have all you need to know about the beast as so many pastors, Bible scholars, and doctors of theology have done up to now. In retrospect, here are all the things that the seven heads have been shown to symbolize:

1. The seven heads of the beast symbolize the four empires and three divided kingdoms that God ordained since the beginning of creation to rule the world until the time of Christ's triumphant return. It will be then that Satan's dominion over all these kingdoms of the earth will be brought to an end.

THE BOOK OF REVELATION AND THE BIBLE
AS NEVER EXPLAINED BEFORE

2. The seven heads also symbolize the seven kings who have been designated to represent those four kingdoms and three confederations of nations which are as follows: (a) King Nebuchadnezzar, who was the first and greatest king of the Babylonian Empire; (b) King Cyrus the Great of Persia, who was the first Persian king to rule the Persian-Median Empire; (c) King Alexander the Great, who was the great king of the Macedonian Empire; (d) Emperor Augustus, who was the first emperor of the Roman Empire; (e) Kaiser Wilhelm I, who was the first emperor of the newly restored German Second Reich, which began the time of the first series of triple alliances, which later evolved into The League of Nations at the conclusion of World War I; (f) The great whore of Babylon, which is symbolic of the great seaport city—New York, that can only be found within the present reigning superpower of the world—the United States of America, whose combined economic and military might, are now reigning over all the symbolic or otherwise real kings of the earth from within the sixth confederation of nations called the United Nations; and finally (g) the beast, who shall come back to rule the world from where he had failed the first time with his last attempt to revive the old Holy Roman Empire with what was then called the Third Reich. But this time he will succeed to do through the European Union what he had so miserably failed to do during his very short time with the League of Nations. Yes, the beast is Adolf Hitler, and his new name shall be Apollyon, which means "the destroyer." He is also the man the world has come to call the antichrist, or son of Satan or else the seventh head of the beast; and yet he is also the beast itself, hence the eighth and final Roman king of the world, destined to be resurrected from the pit of hell.

3. Finally, the seven heads also symbolize the Seven Hills of Rome, which, as we can see from the seven kings' repre-

203

sentation, symbolizes the fourth beast's initial, and most importantly, its final reign upon the world through the relatively three short terms of Germany's First, Second and Third Reich, and finally with Hitler's return and rapid rise to power through the European Union, the Third Reich's finale. Then shall the great destroyer achieve what he was denied the first time he was here: full world power and divinity. That is why Daniel was only shown four beasts, of which the fourth beast had ten horns that didn't just signify ten kings but that also signified ten time periods that would come to divide the Roman Empire from era to era, or from Roman dominion to German dominion. Finally, we were shown how an eleventh horn sprang forth from this same beast that differed from all the rest, who mouthed bombast and blasphemy against the Most High, and how upon his arrival the angel told us that three kings would be brought low, which was signified by the uprooting of the three other horns. The eleventh horn is the last Roman king of the fourth beast and, as such, of the age of man as we know it before Christ comes to put an end to it. The three kings are symbolic of three nations that the eleventh horn shall bring low before the Third Reich can be brought to full world power through the European Union and they are: the United States, England, and Israel. Here, it is critical to see and understand that the eleventh king was an offshoot from Rome. It is also critical to see that Augustus was the first emperor of Rome and that Hitler, renamed Apollyon, shall be the last. Hitler was and remains to be the last man in history who tried to revive the old Holy Roman Empire, which was the First Reich that Napoleon brought to an end in 1806. That is why he allied himself with Italy, hence Rome, and why he used the Roman standard bearing the spread eagle as his standard and the Roman salute and why all the people shouted, "Hail Hitler," just as the Roman people shouted, "Hail Caesar" to the emperor. There is much more that can be said about Hitler and the occult history of the Third Reich, but I must save it for the next chapter, as there is still one last thing that I must mention about the seven heads of the beast that the angel of the Lord did not mention here to John, and that is this:

The seven heads of the beast also signify how the very power and authority granted to it by Satan himself comes under the divine power and authority of God! It is no secret to most Bible scholars that the number seven, as it is used in the Bible, denotes the holiness of God; even as it was in the beginning when God so created the earth and everything in it in six days, and on the seventh day he rested and called that day holy. But what they don't normally mention is that the number seven is also God's signature number for his divine authority. This is especially true as it is being used all throughout the book of Revelation. For example, the book of Revelation begins with the message of the seven churches, and from then on, every revelation that is given to John is given to him in sets of seven, showing to all who will come to read this book that the true author of this book is not John but God himself; most importantly, every dominion that is granted therein comes under God's divine power and authority.

THE SEVEN BLASPHEMOUS NAMES

After the description of the beast is given in the seventeenth chapter of the book of Revelation, we are then told that on each of the seven heads is written a blasphemous name. Here is another mystery that has troubled me well into the night as I have long pondered what these seven names could possibly be. I went so far as to draw up lists of the different possibilities. On one list, I tried to think of the seven great perversions that Satan has spewed across the face of the earth. I would begin by making a list having such things as satanic worship,

205

mythology, homosexuality, bestiality, pornography, abortion, and gay marriage written upon them. But these were not really names as much as they were grievous sins being committed against God, and there have been a lot more than seven of these kinds of sins—and how do you really know the order of their arrangement?

So I finally asked God to reveal this mystery to me, and he still made me wait another day before granting my request. Then the following day, as I was continuing to pester God for the answer, the Holy Spirit finally revealed them to me, as if to say, "All right, so you finally give up trying to figure it out on your own. Now then, here is the answer that has been before you all along. The seven blasphemous names that you are seeking are the same seven names as the seven kingdoms that you have just written about." When the Spirit told me this, I was beside myself. I can't believe I couldn't see that, and then I understood why he made me wait an extra day before revealing the answer to me. With this answer came the peace of the Spirit, and I knew that he had given me the right answer. The seven blasphemous names written upon each of the seven heads are as follows: Babylon, Persia, Macedonia, Rome, the League of Nations, the United Nations, and the European Union.

THE TEN HORNS OF THE BEAST WITH THE SEVEN HEADS

In this next section, I will be revealing for the first time what the ten horns on the beast with the seven heads actually signify, as John describes them to us in the book of Revelation. After this explanation and the next concerning the false prophet, I will then talk about the occult history of the Third Reich and why it is that Hitler is the eleventh horn that we are told would come being different from all his predecessors and worshipping an alien god never before known to his forefathers. I will then prove to a disbelieving world that it can only be Hitler who will

THE BOOK OF REVELATION AND THE BIBLE
AS NEVER EXPLAINED BEFORE

come back to rule the world, and as I have already stated, it will be by the supernatural power of God that he will be brought back from the abyss and allowed to fulfill his destiny as the great destroyer. I will also explain why it is that God has chosen to do such an unprecedented thing and how the beast will be allowed to take away from the Lamb of God the very power and authority that were given to him by his Father for a period of no more than three and a half years. That is why Daniel tells us that during this time even the Prince of the Covenant (which is Jesus Christ) will be broken (Daniel 11:21–23). What this truly means is that Jesus will be broken in spirit and in heart as he must, by a special command from his Father, submit all the power and authority granted to him in heaven before the beast's power and authority granted to him by Satan, on earth; whose authority also comes from the Father. At which time Jesus must then stand by and watch and listen as his chosen people are led like lambs to the slaughter by the beast and the false prophet. But when their appointed time has elapsed and everything that has been written by his Father is fulfilled, then shall the Lamb of God be given full dominion over both heaven and earth, and it shall be from then on that his kingdom and dominion upon the earth will be everlasting.

The following are the ten nations that are symbolized by the ten horns on the beast with the seven heads that will, at the time of the end, confer their power and authority upon the beast who, as we all now know, is Hitler. They, together with the beast, shall wage war on that nation whose great seaport city is symbolized by the great whore of Babylon and will in one day and in one hour burn this city to ashes through a combined and all-out nuclear attack. The ten nations are: Germany, Italy, Japan, China, North Korea, Iran, Afghanistan, Pakistan, Syria, and the former Soviet Union. Otherwise, as I mentioned earlier, I will be explaining who and what all the great whore of Babylon has been shown to symbolize a little later on. But first I need to clarify why it is that these ten nations are in fact

207

the ten horns of the beast as depicted by John in the book of Revelation.

First, let me say that when Hitler returns, he will be well received, and because of this, he will be able to pretty much pick things up from where he left them the last time he was here, as the false prophet will have done a masterful job of preparing the way for him. This means that the greater part of the Muslim world, joined together with the European Union, will have already been driven into a feeding frenzy over wanting the destruction of Israel and also its chief ally, the United States, who is more affectionately referred to as being "the great Satan" by Osama bin Laden. I would say that given the attacks on September 11, 2001, that we are very close to that place in Revelation now.

What still remains are the other signs that must be completed as written, along with the events that will follow the sounding of the first four trumpets of the seven archangels. Then shall the fifth archangel blow his trumpet and Satan be handed the key to the shaft of the abyss where he will unlock what has been sealed ever since the beginning of creation. Then as the whole world watches in disbelief through the thousands of satellite news networks, a porthole into another dimension in time and space will be opened up from beneath the depths of the sea from within the Bermuda Triangle. Out of it will come a sight that shall herald in what many will believe is the second coming of Christ, but it will not be Christ. At first, the meteorologists will believe that there has been a volcanic eruption from beneath the abyssal plain of the sea near Bermuda, but they will soon learn that it is not a volcanic eruption at all but something more hideous.

Suddenly, there shall be seen rising up out of the smoke from this newly opened shaft from beneath the sea thousands of locustlike hell's angels with the faces of humans having women's hair and the tails of scorpions with enough venom to plague mankind for five months. On their heads shall be crowns of gold, and they shall also have teeth like a lion. Their breast-

THE BOOK OF REVELATION AND THE BIBLE
AS NEVER EXPLAINED BEFORE

plates will be like iron, and the sound of their wings will be like horses and chariots rushing to battle. At the finale of their demonic entrance shall come the appearance of the man the book of Revelation calls the real scorpion king, who will be the last one to rise up out of the shaft of the Abyss. He will be called Apollyon, or "the destroyer," who will, in essence, be the resurrected son of Satan, as symbolized by the beast with the seven heads, ten horns, and ten diadems, but who will in actuality be Adolf Hitler returned from the dead. He will bring to the world what it truly wants to see in a new world order messiah. The lies and empty promises of a peace accord brokered between Israel and Palestine that will promise peace, but, in the end, will only lead the world into a war of such magnitude that if it is not cut short, no living thing will survive. There will be killing on a massive scale and all for the sake of the new world order, which Apollyon promises will come after the United States and England are destroyed and Israel is driven into the sea. Only then can there be peace in the world for what he promises will last for a thousand years. These will be the same lies as he told before, but only with a new twist toward Israel, England, and the United States. That is why the first three nations must be Germany, Italy, and Japan, as old alliances are hard to break. The three kings of the east must also be a part of this alliance, and that is another reason why Apollyon must have Japan, along with the addition of China and North Korea. Then there are those Muslim terrorist nations who are hostile to both Israel and the United States that either have nuclear weapons or soon will have them via the others that do, which are Iran and the terrorists elements found between the borders of both Pakistan and Afghanistan. Afghanistan, which closely borders Pakistan, is the home of the new terrorist front where Osama bin Laden, al-Qaeda, and the Taliban have made their stand against the United States and her allies; and they have already made it known that they will not rest until they have been the cause of their complete destruction. Syria espe-

209

cially had these weapons of mass destruction on its wish list until President Bush ended that dream by taking out Saddam Hussein. But I think the Soviet Union, as the wild card in this coalition, will be the one to remedy this country's situation as well as any others of those already mentioned, who do not now, but who may find themselves in quick need of nuclear weapons in the future, as they not only have a very large nuclear weapons arsenal, but they also still have a very formidable military force to back it up. I believe they will, if they are not already, be in the business of nuclear weapons supply for a good price.

It should also be pointed out that I do not believe this alliance will be formulated out of any love that any of these nations will have for one another; rather, it will really be a matter of them all wanting to see the end of the United States as the reigning superpower of the world, and after that England and Israel will be easy to finish off without their big brother there to help them. Japan, on the other hand, will find this opportunity offered to it by the beast the perfect payback for the nuclear attack once leveled against its country in 1945 by the United States, which effectively brought World War II to an end and Japan to its knees. Then with these three nations brought down, the United Nations will effectively be ended, and the European Union will rise to power.

Today one of the first things needed before this scenario can be completed is already beginning to take shape before our very eyes, as the liberal democrats' have now made their return to power, and in so doing have begun to make their advance toward the ultimate takeover of the government of the United States of America. As it will be through their failed leadership, disobedience, and outright hatred of God that this nation's reign will be brought to its end by the will of God. As it is written regarding the ten horns of the beast: "For God has put it into their heads to carry out his purpose, by making common cause and conferring their sovereignty upon the beast until all that God has spoken is fulfilled" (Revelation 17:17–18, TNEB).

THE BOOK OF REVELATION AND THE BIBLE
AS NEVER EXPLAINED BEFORE

Afterward, even though the beast has promised it, there will still not be peace in the world as the whole world will soon erupt into a state of all out war and utter chaos as nation will rise against nation and kingdom against kingdom just as it has been written. In the end it will become a time of unimaginable horror, death and destruction as the nations will at this time begin their struggle for dominance. All the strong nations will turn on the weaker ones and there will be those who will even challenge the beast for world dominion and more nuclear exchanges will follow. But the beast will maintain his Arab coalition which will eventually be joined by other European countries and even some from Asia where he will ultimately bring the whole world into submission to himself and to the brink of its total extinction through his indiscriminate use of the nuclear missile.

But there are still three things that must happen in the midst of all this horror and one thing that must happen that will set it all off. The first thing that must happen before all of the hostilities can begin is that the hundred and forty-four thousand must be removed from off the face of the earth and taken up into heaven, for they are not just holy unto God, but they are also untouchable to both Satan and the beast. Only with them out of the way will Hitler be allowed to make his transition from the minster of peace to the minister of death and destruction. He does this by making a surprise attack on Israel to capture Jerusalem and the newly restored holy temple of God just after its completion. This is where he comes to set up his throne in the holy of holies and declare himself to be the divine king of the world that it has been waiting for. This is also where he comes to do away with the regular offering and to set up the abomination of desolation in the holy sanctuary and proclaim it to be his god. Then, in a final act of defiance toward God, he will begin to worship this thing as his god and pay it tribute with gold and silver. It is only after this that the United States and England then come to the aid of Israel, and the beast's three-and-a-half-year reign of terror officially begins as set forth by God.

211

Of the three things that must happen within the midst of Hitler's great reign of terror before the end can come is first of all the thief in the night harvest, which is where God's faithful church is suddenly taken from off the face of the earth and up into heaven. The second thing that must take place will be the burning of the great whore of Babylon, which will follow close behind this harvest; and finally the preaching of the "eternal gospel" to the ends of the earth by the three archangels. And then shall the end come with the second coming of Christ. This great event marks the time when all the warring armies of the world will stop their individual wars and join together to wage war against the Lamb of God and his mighty heavenly host as they descend upon Mount Zion, which will suddenly come into view before all men by the supernatural power of God.

With regard to the abomination of desolation, which the beast will come to set up in the holy sanctuary, there has been much confusion about what this terminology actually means, and so I would like to take this time now to explain it. First of all, it should be pointed out that the term *the abomination of desolation* or also the *abomination that causes desolation,* as it has been used in different contexts within the book of Daniel, as well as in other places of the Bible, does not in each case mean the same thing. As is very often the case with God's symbolism, the meaning of one description or term, depending on the particular context that it is being used in, may have multiple meanings, as I have already shown by the various other explanations I have given in this book concerning God's symbolic depictions. With that being said, the term *the abomination of desolation* also has multiple meanings. The following are the three different meanings of this term as it has been used in different places within the Bible.

In the first sense, the sins of the nation of Israel brought to both houses the abomination of desolation as they were each taken by foreign powers into slavery and the land of Zion, and especially the holy city of Jerusalem, were each left in total des-

THE BOOK OF REVELATION AND THE BIBLE
AS NEVER EXPLAINED BEFORE

olation. We have seen this in the past with the nation of Israel, and we will continue to see this in the future as the abomination of desolation brought about by sin will ultimately bring total desolation to any nation that rebels against God and refuses to listen to its prophet's warnings to repent. Reference Daniel 9:15–19 regarding the sins of the nation of Israel and the desolation of Jerusalem that followed.

In the second sense, the beast, along with his impiety against God, but especially his holy sanctuary, will bring the complete and utter desolation of the world. In this context, the beast is another meaning of the term *the abomination that causes desolation* (Daniel 8:11–14).

In the third sense, the god of the beast, which is also called the god of the citadel and a god unknown to Hitler's ancestors, is the nuclear missile, and it is in this thing that he, the beast, puts his faith and trust and finally worships as his god. It is in this third sense that the abomination that causes desolation takes on the full meaning of the term as it is being used here in the eleventh chapter of the book of Daniel and also as it is being quoted from the book of Matthew in the next paragraph. Reference Daniel 11:31–39 regarding the god of the beast.

Matthew tells of the time in this way:

> Therefore when you see the abomination of desolation, spoken of by Daniel the prophet, standing in the holy place" (whoever reads, let him understands), "then let those who are in Judea flea to the mountains. Let him who is on the house top not go down to take anything out of his house. And let him who is in the field not go back to get his cloths. But woe to those who are pregnant and to those who are nursing babies in those days. And pray that your flight may not be in winter or on the Sabbath. For then there will be great tribulation, such as has not been since the beginning of the world until this time, no, nor ever shall be. And unless those days were shortened no flesh would be saved; but for the elect's sake those days will be shortened."
>
> Matthew 24:15–22 (NKJV)

213

For a greater understanding of these events as told to the prophet Daniel by one of the seven archangels of the Lord, read Daniel 11:21–45, also continued through Daniel 12:1–13.

BUT JUST WHO IS THE FALSE PROPHET?

The second beast that John saw in the book of Revelation, which came up out of the earth having two horns like a lamb but who spoke like a dragon, is the *false prophet*. From the symbolism offered here about the false prophet, we know that he must be here now and waiting for the beast's return, as he is shown to rise up out of the earth and not the sea. That he has two horns like a lamb but spoke like a dragon signifies that he will appear to be sent by God and a man of peace, but he will really be sent by Satan and a man of pure evil. Otherwise, he will be the man who shall come first to prepare the way for the beast as John the Baptist came first to prepare the way for Christ but will not make himself fully known to us until after the beast's return.

Before I reveal the identity of the false prophet, I need to first lay out a complete character analysis of the man. The first thing that we know about this man is that he will have a very commanding presence and charismatic effect on all who will come to see and hear him, even before the beast's return but most noticeably thereafter. With this charismatic appeal, coupled with his ability to perform great signs and wonders, he will quickly win over the Muslim world, but they will especially be drawn to him by his public exhortations leveled against the nation of Israel as well as its chief ally, the United States, which is now, and will be at that time, the reigning superpower of the world. Soon after the beast's arrival, the false prophet will proclaim him to be the long-awaited Messiah who has come back, as promised by God, to usher in the new world order, an order that promised once before to bring a thousand years of peace to the world after the Jews had been exterminated and the other inferior races of the world were either conquered or enslaved.

THE BOOK OF REVELATION AND THE BIBLE
AS NEVER EXPLAINED BEFORE

And now this same promise will be made again, but only this time they will both vow together that the great Satan must first be destroyed before the Jews can then be driven into the sea.

Then, in keeping with this renewed vow of the false prophet, they will set about the task of carrying out the planned execution of the great Satan by first destroying New York City, which is also called the great whore of Babylon in the book of Revelation. Other cities will also be attacked until the United States finally submits. Then, in keeping with the doctrines of the Third Reich, all the other inferior races of the world will also be conquered as the Aryans become the master race whose destiny it was prophesied by Madame Helena Vablatzki would come to rule the world. But God will not allow the beast's dominion to last beyond the three and a half years he has granted it, and then shall his and the false prophet's end come.

As a special note: For those who do not know, Madame Vablatzki is the author of "The Secret Doctrine" a book, published in 1888, that would come to change the world. It was through her mystical writings that she became credited for having introduced the German people to the doctrines of the Aryan man along with all the other ideas about them achieving world dominion by right of their racial supremacy. There is a lot more to be learned about her from within the three DVD set entitled, "The Occult History of the Third Reich." For more information on how to obtain a copy of this DVD set, reference the "sources used for research" pages at the end of this book.

It is worth mentioning all this as a prelude to the identity that I am about to give next because this is perhaps the best character analysis that can be made of the false prophet, which is based upon the two descriptions that are given about him in the book of Revelation and as it has also been revealed to me by the power of the Holy Spirit. The other little tidbit that is mentioned about him, aside from that section that I have already quoted from chapter 13, comes from chapter 19 of the book of Revelation, where it is written:

215

> And I saw the beast, the kings of the earth, and their armies gathered together to make war against Him who sat on the horse and against His army. Then the beast was captured, and with him the false prophet who worked signs in his presence, by which he deceived those who received the mark of the beast and those who worshiped his image. These two were cast alive into the lake of fire burning with brimstone.
>
> Revelation 19:19–20 (NKJV)

It is important to understand that all of this comes to pass under God's divine power and authority because of Israel's rejection of his son, Jesus Christ, and the message that he sent to them through him. It is also important to understand that the United States and England have come to represent to some extent the ten lost tribes of Israel, which is also called the house of Israel. Having said that, it must also be pointed out that there are still those who will remain scattered throughout all the other nations and islands of the world until Christ comes back to gather them back to Zion.

The nation of Israel, on the other hand, has come to represent the house of Judah, whose people are more commonly referred to as the Jews, which is short for Judeans. But their reconciliation will come in the end by way of the everlasting covenant that God made between himself and Abraham in Genesis 17:7–8. That is why all three of these nations must be brought low by the beast and the false prophet, as it is, in essence, the final judgment that shall be brought against all Israel by God before her reconciliation and ultimate restoration can come later in the land of Zion. It is, in fact, the land of Zion that shall constitute the inner kingdom of God, and it shall be by the fleshly seal of circumcision that all the lost Israelites will be found and gathered back unto Zion.

So with all that being said, there is still the one question that remains: who then is the false prophet?

Given all the criteria that the book of Revelation has to offer about this man and the explanation that has come forth

THE BOOK OF REVELATION AND THE BIBLE
AS NEVER EXPLAINED BEFORE

by the power of the Holy Spirit, there is only one man that it can be, and that man is Osama bin Laden. The scripture that describes the false prophet as the beast that rose up out of the earth, as I said before, tells us about a man who will come before the beast to prepare the way for his return. That man, once again, can only be Osama bin Laden. The scripture that describes him as having two horns like a lamb but who spoke like a dragon suggests that he will look and dress very much like a prophet of God, appearing almost Christlike in his humble attire, featuring his long robes, long hair and even a long beard. All of these are the unmistakable traits of this seemingly true spiritual leader that Osama bin Laden has come to portray. Especially inspiring to the people are his soft spoken messages of bold defiance brought against the great Satan, or else the United States, after his not too distant attacks of September 11, 2001, that still remain unanswered. Because of this, he has already won for himself the undying love and adoration of the people in that region of the world. Osama bin Laden has not just become the great spiritual leader of the Taliban in Afghanistan, but he has also become the most charismatic of all the spiritual leaders found anywhere within the other terrorist nations of Islam as well, and, as such, he remains a great threat to the peace and security of the United States. It is this same charismatic appeal and love from the people of Islam that has protected him up to now and provides him with this very thin disguise for who he really is, as the gospel that he has been preaching is, and remains to be, all about war. He still lacks the power to perform miracles because his time for these things has not yet come. Only God the Father can decide when that time is to be, and only then will those special powers be given to him by the supernatural power of God.

The scripture that tells how he made them erect an image in honor of the beast and how later he was allowed to give breath to that image speaks of modern-day technology as the great flat screens featuring high-definition video and television imaging

217

are already being erected all over the world in sports arenas and public venues of every kind and type. With this technology, it is not so hard to imagine how the false prophet will cause everyone to worship the beast and its image twice a day as he substitutes the praise and worship of Allah for the praise and worship of Apollyon, the beast.

For his part, Osama bin Laden is all about the art of war, as he has already vowed in the name of Allah that he will not rest until he has destroyed the United States, whose government it is that trained him in this art and in which nation he now calls the great Satan. He has even provided us with a preview of just how he will go about doing this thing that he has vowed to do with his last attack on New York City and the Pentagon, which occurred on September 11, 2001. He and that part of the world that is currently following after him already believe in this gospel that he follows, which teaches them all about the art of war, where murdering and killing on a grand scale as only the nuclear missile can do will soon become the accepted morality.

All of this they shall do in the name of the Father, whom they call Allah, and the last false prophet, whom they called Mohammed. But Allah is none other than Satan, the father of all lies, and Mohammed, his so called last prophet and apostle, was in the final analysis only another one of the many false prophets who he had sent out to deceive the world with yet another placated message of peace whose ultimate end has and will only lead the world into war. Only in Mohammed's case, he had been sent by Satan with the special mission of stealing the glory away from our heavenly Father's true Son, Jesus Christ, who, by his resurrection, had become both our everlasting high priest in heaven and our one true living prophet on earth as I had explained earlier in chapter one. It was also by his Father's gospel, which was and is the gospel of peace, that Jesus preached the complete and final word for what all men must do to be saved and perfected in his love so as to be ready and able to enter his kingdom when it is finally brought down to earth.

THE BOOK OF REVELATION AND THE BIBLE
AS NEVER EXPLAINED BEFORE

By his very words, "It is finished," Jesus made it clear that there shall be no other gospel or attachment to it and no other name by which men shall be saved.

The name Allah appears to be derived from the two Arabic words, *al* (the) and *ilah* (god). Allah in Arabic is also understood to mean the Supreme Being, or else *the One God*, as written in the Koran. But it has long been written in the Bible that Jehovah, or Yahweh, depending on which pronunciation you choose, is the everlasting name of God, which shall endure for all generations. This is the same God who appeared to Moses in the burning bush and proclaimed himself to be the great "I Am," which Jesus later told the Jews and some of the Pharisees in the Gospel of John that, in essence, it was he who spoke these words to Moses in behalf of his Father, as he and his Father are one. In revealing this truth to the Jews, Jesus did not mean that he and his Father are one in the same person, but rather that they are in appearance seemingly identical, sharing the same name and being of the same mind and spirit as the other, as we shall also be with them as we become perfected in their love. This same God went on to say that he was also the God of Abraham, Isaac, and Jacob. Reference Exodus 3:13–16, John 8:56–58 and then also read John 10:30. It was also this same God that the Muslims now have the audacity to say is Allah, who decreed that there shall be only one name under heaven by which all men shall be saved, and that name was and still is Jesus Christ, who is the Son of God the Father, Jehovah.

219

THE OCCULT HISTORY
OF THE THIRD REICH

For all those who still refuse to believe that Adolf Hitler is the beast who shall return from the abyss to be the last king to rule the world through the final rise of the Roman Empire, I now recommend that you purchase over the Internet and view this relatively new three-DVD collection called *The Occult History of the Third Reich*. This very remarkable three-DVD collection explores the phenomenon that so mesmerized Germany in the 1930s and 1940s, but it also adds another very interesting and yet conclusive perspective to the account that I have already given. It was put together by Madacy Entertainment Group, LTD out of Canada and was copyrighted in 1998. The account itself features newly discovered archive film footage that has been used to validate an eye-opening documentary of "Adolf Hitler" on DVD one, "The Enigma of the Swastika" on DVD two, and

"The S.S. Blood and Soil" on DVD three, all of which will help prove to a disbelieving world that there has never before in the history of the world been a more purely evil man than Hitler. Not even Emperor Nero could hold a candle to the cold-hearted, bloodless, beastly nature of Hitler.

For those who wish to follow all my research I would also recommend that you purchase or obtain a copy of the book: "The Rise and Fall of the Third Reich" and read chapter four. It is entitled: *The Mind of Hitler and the Roots of the Third Reich.* This reading will further help to expose the actual philosophers and others who inspired him whose occult and mystical teachings helped to shape his very mind as he perfected himself in those teachings. With this, Hitler then ultimately became the very messiah that the German people had been waiting for. Through it all, and in a total mockery of God, Hitler caused himself to perversely silhouette the very life of Christ with the preaching of his gospel of war and the one-thousand-year Reich, which threatened to bring the whole world to the brink of total destruction had he not been stopped. His mockery went on as he was ultimately betrayed by his closest and most trusted general, Heinrich Himmler, just as Jesus was by Judas Iscariot, and finally by his self-sacrificing death, and yet, just before his death and fiery end, he did recite his last will and testament to his secretary, Miss Traudl Junge (as recorded in the 2008 DVD movie release *Downfall*). In that testament he did say that all those who had betrayed him, especially the Jews, would ultimately pay for that betrayal at some future date. Earlier in this documentary movie, he also prophesies that he and his empire would one day rise again out of the ashes of the fire that he so willingly had consigned himself and his nation.

Hitler had made this statement in a reference to the mythical firebird, the phoenix, which had also renewed itself from the flames of its own self-sacrificing death, where in the end it too rose again out of the ashes, thus suggesting that he believed one day he too would be returning from the dead, just like the phoe-

THE BOOK OF REVELATION AND THE BIBLE
AS NEVER EXPLAINED BEFORE

nix, in a final mockery to the resurrection and second coming of Jesus Christ, as the book of Revelation had also prophesied he would nearly two thousand years ago. Thereby fulfilling the one purpose granted to him by God the Father, that the beast, alias Apollyon the Destroyer, as spoken of in the ninth chapter of Revelation, also known as the antichrist by most Christians, would precede the second coming of Christ to deceive and punish the inhabitants of the earth for rejecting the Lamb's gospel of peace and love over their greater love for the beast's gospel of war and hate.

THE SEVEN PLAGUES
OF THE SEVEN BOWLS
(REVELATION CHAPTER FIFTEEN)

And I saw in heaven another sign, great and wonderful: seven angels were bringing the seven plagues that are the last of all, because they exhaust the anger of God. I seemed to be looking at a sea of crystal suffused with fire, and standing by the lake of glass, those who had fought against the beast and won, and against his statue (or his image) and the number which is his name. They all had harps from God, and they were singing the hymn (or song) of Moses, the servant of God, and the hymn of the Lamb:

How great and wonderful are all your works, Lord God Almighty; upright and true are all your ways, King of nations. Who does not revere and glorify your name O Lord? For you alone are holy, and all nations will come and adore you for the many acts of saving justice you have shown.

After this, in my vision, the sanctuary, the tent of the Testimony, opened in heaven, and out came the seven angels with the seven plagues, wearing pure white linen, fastened round their waists, with belts of gold. One of the four living creatures gave the seven angels seven golden bowls filled with the anger of God who lives forever and ever. The smoke from the glory and the power of God filled the temple so that no one could go into it until the seven plagues of the seven angels was completed.

Revelation 15:1–8 (TNJB)

THE SEVEN PLAGUES OF THE SEVEN BOWLS CONTINUED (REVELATION CHAPTER SIXTEEN)

Then I heard a loud voice from the sanctuary calling to the seven angels, 'Go, and empty the seven bowls of God's anger over the earth.'

The first angel went and emptied his bowl over the earth; at once, on all the people who had been branded with the mark of the beast and had worshipped its statue (or its image), there came disgusting and virulent soars.

The second angel emptied his bowl over the sea, and it turned to blood, like the blood of a corpse; and every living creature in the sea died.

The third angel emptied his bowl into the rivers and springs of water and they turned into blood. Then I heard the angel of water say, 'You are the Upright One, He who is, He who was, the Holy One, for giving this verdict: they spilt the blood of the saints and the prophets, and blood is what you have given them to drink; it is what they deserve.' And I heard the altar itself say, 'Truly, Lord God Almighty, the punishments you gave are true and just.'

THE BOOK OF REVELATION AND THE BIBLE
AS NEVER EXPLAINED BEFORE

The fourth angel emptied his bowl over the sun and it was made to scorch people with its flames; but though people were scorched by the fierce heat of it, they cursed the name of God who had the power to cause such plagues, and they would not repent and glorify him.

The fifth angel emptied his bowl over the throne of the beast and its whole empire was plunged in darkness. People were biting their tongues for pain, but instead of repenting for what they had done, they cursed the God of heaven because of their pains and sores.

The sixth angel emptied his bowl over the great river Euphrates; all the water dried up so that a way was made for the kings from the East to come in. Then from the jaws of dragon, and beast and false prophet I saw three foul spirits come; they looked like frogs and in fact were demon spirits, able to work miracles, going out to all the kings of the world to call them together for the war of the Great Day of God the Almighty— Look I shall come like a thief. Blessed is anyone who has kept watch, and has kept his clothes on, so that he does not go out naked and expose his shame.—They called the kings together at the place called, in Hebrew, Armageddon.

Then the seventh angel emptied his bowl into the air; and a great voice boomed out from the sanctuary, 'The end has come.' Then there were flashes of lightning and peals of thunder and a violent earthquake, unparalleled since humanity first came into existence. The Great City was split into three parts and the cities of the world collapsed; Babylon the great was not forgotten: God made her drink the full wine-cup of his retribution. Every island vanished and the mountains disappeared; and hail, with great hailstones weighing a talent each (or a hundred weight) fell from the sky on the people. They cursed God for sending a plague of hail; it was the most terrible plague.

Revelation 16:1–21 (TNJB)

As we can see from this account given to us through John by Jesus Christ, the seven bowls full of the last seven plagues are very much self-explanatory, but still there are a few things worth mentioning here that might help the reader gain a more comprehensive understanding of all that is being said or not said within these seven bowls full of the last seven plagues.

First of all, it is important to understand the time frame that has been given to us already by God with regard to the beast leading up to this time. As I mentioned earlier, the beast, will be resurrected from the abyss at the time of the fifth trumpet, and for the first three and a half years of that time, he will spend it deceiving the world into believing he is the Stark von Oben, the strong one from above, as prophesied by Madame Helena Vablatzki, who has been sent back from the dead to usher in the new world order and God's millennial reign of peace. To make this deception appear real in the eyes of the world, he will do what no other world leader has been able to do up until then. He will broker a peace accord between Israel and the Palestinians that will finally allow Israel to rebuild God's holy temple. All this happens while the beast is still posing as the messianic minister of peace to the world while all along planning the destruction of Israel and her two chief allies, the United States and Britain. It will be shortly after the time that the temple is completed, but not before the hundred and forty-four thousand are first taken up into heaven, that the beast will suddenly and in a style similar to his former blitzkriegs, launch a surprise attack upon Israel as he incorporates the use of the combined Islamic militant forces and the other surrounding Arab nations that are hostile to Israel. With them he will very quickly overrun the unsuspecting Israeli Army and capture Jerusalem and the holy temple of God. Here is also where the beast will finally reveal to the world his true nature and ultimate gospel of war. It is at this exact time that the beast's three-and-a-half year reign of terror begins and ends at the seventh bowl with the very words from God saying, "It is over!"

THE BOOK OF REVELATION AND THE BIBLE
AS NEVER EXPLAINED BEFORE

This is also the time when the Lord sends his two prophets, Moses and Elijah, to prophesy all throughout the beast's remaining time on earth, and even allows them to be killed by him at the conclusion of that time, in much the same way as when he lifted the pillars of cloud and fire that stood between pharaoh's advancing armies and his chosen people then. Which in the latter case will allow the beast to think that he had suddenly developed a power greater than God's that will enable him to kill his two prophets just as the pharaoh thought he had it then over the Lord's chosen people. But after three-and-a-half days, his two prophets, who had been left lying in the street where they fell, will come to life again and be summoned back up to heaven by a loud voice from above. Then there will be a violent earthquake that will cause a tenth of the city to fall killing seven thousand of its inhabitants. This then concludes the sixth trumpet.

It will be just after the beast's sudden attack upon Israel is complete, that the United States and Britain will come to the aid of Israel as they join with her to launch a massive counteroffensive against the beast, but though in the beginning they will have some major successes against the beast, in the end their best efforts will fail against him. He will further go on to desecrate all that is holy and mouth bombast and blasphemies against the Almighty God who has granted him this time and last dominion on earth so as to punish the wicked inhabitants of the earth with his gospel of war but also to test the faithful people of God even unto death. This is in accordance with everything that is told to us in Mathew chapter 24, especially within verses 9 through 22. It will be a time of unimaginable horror, death, and destruction, and if God did not cut this time short, no living thing would survive.

It will be during the last days of the beast's great reign of terror that these seven bowls full of the seven last plagues will be poured. Notice how some of these plagues are very similar to those delivered to the people of pharaoh in the days of Moses, and I suspect that these will probably be poured out upon the wicked inhabitants of the earth in a similar time frame, perhaps in as little as a day apart, or until God declares their end. It will be during the sixth bowl that Christ shall come like a thief in the night for all his surviving faithful left behind after the second harvest of the hundred and forty-four thousand. These are all those that constitute the great multitude and who are also sealed with the seal of the Holy Spirit, as I described earlier. These are also all those who were described just before the seven bowls were poured that were singing the song of Moses beside the sea of glass shot with fire in heaven in verse two of chapter 15. Here also is where the final trumpet is blown and the great whore of Babylon meets her doom.

Otherwise, it is here in this chapter, which speaks about the seven bowls full of the seven plagues, that you will either take God at his word for all that he has promised to do during this time on earth or else you are going to be among those who suffer through this very terrifying time along with the beast and the false prophet and all the rest of those who join forces with them.

THE GREAT WHORE OF BABYLON
(REVELATION CHAPTER 17–18)

Then one of the seven angels who had the seven bowls came and talked with me, saying to me, "Come, I will show you the judgment on the great harlot, who sits on many waters (*or who is enthroned above the ocean*), with whom the kings of the earth committed fornication, and the inhabitants of the earth were made drunk with the wine of her fornication."

So he carried me away in the Spirit into the wilderness. And I saw a woman sitting on a scarlet beast which was full of names of blasphemy, having seven heads and ten horns. The woman was arrayed in purple and scarlet and adorned with gold and precious stones and pearls, having in her hand a golden cup full of abominations and the filthiness of her fornication. And on her forehead a name was written: "Mystery Babylon the Great, the Mother of all Harlots and of the Abominations of Earth." *I saw the woman, drunk with the blood of the saints and with the blood of the martyrs of Jesus.* And when I saw her I marveled with great amazement.

But the angel said to me, "Why do you marvel? I will tell you the mystery of the woman and of the beast that carries her, which has the seven heads and the ten horns. The beast you saw was, and is not, and will ascend out of the bottomless pit and go to perdition. And those who dwell on the earth will marvel, whose names are not written the Book of Life from the foundation of the world, when they see the beast that was, and is not, and yet is.

"Here is the mind which has wisdom: The seven heads are seven mountains (or hills) on which the woman sits. There (They) are also seven kings, five have fallen, one is, and the other has not yet come. And when he comes, he must continue a short time. The beast that was, and is not, he is himself also the eighth, and is of the seven, and is going to perdition. The ten horns which you saw are ten kings who have received no kingdom as yet, but they receive authority for one hour as kings with the beast. These are of one mind, and they will give their power and authority to the beast. These will make war with the Lamb, and the Lamb will overcome them, for he is the Lord of lords and King of kings; and those who are with Him are called, chosen, and faithful."

Then he said to me, "*The waters (The ocean) which you saw, where the harlot sits,* are people, multitudes, nations, and tongues (languages). And the ten horns which you saw on the beast, these will hate the harlot; make her desolate and naked, eat her flesh and burn her with fire. *For God has put into their hearts to fulfill His purpose, to be of one mind and to give their kingdom to the beast until the words of God are fulfilled.* And the *woman* you saw is that *great city* that reigns over the kings of the earth."

Revelation 17:1–18 (NKJV)

THE BOOK OF REVELATION AND THE BIBLE
AS NEVER EXPLAINED BEFORE

After these things I saw another angel coming down from heaven, having great authority, and the earth was illuminated with his glory. And he cried mightily with a loud voice, saying, "Babylon the great is fallen, is fallen, and has become a dwelling place of demons, a prison for every foul spirit, and a cage for every unclean and hated bird! *For all nations have drunk of the wine of the wrath of her fornication, (or of the fierce wine of her fornication) the kings of the earth have committed fornication with her,* and the merchants of the world have become rich through the abundance of her luxury."

And I heard another voice from heaven saying, "*Come out of her, my people, lest you share in her sins, and lest you receive of her plagues. For her sins have reached to heaven,* and God has remembered her iniquities. Render to her just as she rendered to you, and repay her double according to her works; in the cup which she has mixed, mix double for her. In the measure that she glorified herself and lived luxuriously, in the same measure give her torment and sorrow; for she says in her heart, 'I sit as queen, and am no widow, and I will not see sorrow.' Therefore her plagues will come in one day—death and mourning and famine. And she will be utterly burned with fire, *for strong is the Lord God who judges her.*

The kings of the earth who committed fornication and lived luxuriously with her will weep and lament for her, when they see the smoke of her burning, standing at a distance for fear of her torment, saying, 'Alas, alas, that great city Babylon, that mighty city! For in one hour your judgment has come.'

And the merchants of the earth will weep and mourn for her, for no one buys their merchandise anymore: merchandise of gold and silver, precious stones and pearls, fine linen and purple (or purple linen), silk and scarlet, every kind of citron wood, every kind of object of ivory, every kind of object of most precious wood, bronze, iron, and marble; and cinnamon and incense, fragrant oil and frankincense, wine and oil, fine flour and wheat, cattle and sheep, horses and chariots, and

233

bodies and souls of men. The fruit that your soul longed for has gone from you, and all things which are rich and splendid have gone from you, and you shall find them no more at all. The merchants of these things, who became rich by her, will stand at a distance for fear of her torment, weeping and wailing, and saying, 'Alas, alas, that *great city* that was clothed in fine linen, purple and scarlet, and adorned with gold and precious stones and pearls! For in one hour such great riches came to nothing.' Every ship master, all who travel by ship, sailors, and as many as trade on the sea, stood at a distance and cried out when they saw the smoke of her burning, saying, 'What is like this *great city?*'

They through dust on their heads and cried out weeping and wailing, and saying, 'Alas, alas, that *great city,* in which all who had ships on the sea became rich by her wealth! For in one hour she is made desolate.' Rejoice over her, O heaven, and you holy apostles and prophets, for God has avenged you on her!"

Then a mighty angel took up a stone like a great millstone and threw it into the sea, saying, "Thus with violence *the great city Babylon* shall be thrown down, and shall not be found anymore. The sound of harpists, musicians, flutists, and trumpeters shall not be heard in you anymore. No craftsmen of any craft shall be found in you anymore, and the sound a millstone shall not be heard in you anymore. The light of a lamp shall not shine in you anymore, and the voice of bridegroom and bride will not be heard in you anymore. For your merchants were the great men of the earth, for by your sorcery all the nations were deceived. *And in her was found the blood of the prophets and saints, and of all who were slain on earth.*

Revelation 18:1–24 (NKJV)

Regarding the great whore of Babylon, which, by the way, is not the Roman Catholic Church, as the Mormon Church and so many of the other Protestant Christian churches teach and would very much like everyone to believe, nor is it all the rest of Christendom who are not Jehovah's Witnesses, but rather it is exactly as the book of Revelation states: a great city, which is also, a great seaport city, who has this one great mystery attached to her: *that within her may be found the blood of all who had been done to death on earth.* She is further described to us by John as having great economic power and might, as she reigns over all the kings and nations of the world as the symbolic sixth head of the beast, hence the ocean upon which her throne sits. She is further shown to be a city of great wealth having an over abundance of every kind of merchant's wares, gifts, talents, and fineries known to man. It is also to be noted that her dominion is full of corruption, along with every kind of evil and abomination that is also known to God. The book of Revelation also makes it clear that this is a modern-day city that at the time John wrote about her was nonexistent but who was still destined by God to rule the world at the time of the end, just as the first Babylon ruled at the beginning. But instead of another kingdom of man coming to remove this head of the beast from power it will be by the supernatural power of God that the beast comes to do so.

At this point, it is important to understand that the nation that encompasses this modern-day city is synonymous to the ancient kingdom and city of Babylon. In other words, this city's great economic power and military might comes to a greater extent from the superpower status of the very nation that encompasses her, just as the first kingdom of Babylon was to its capital city, which was also called Babylon. As I pointed out earlier with regard to the seven heads of the beast, they are symbolic of multiple things, namely, the seven preordained kingdoms of the world, the seven kings who would come to reign from within those kingdoms, the Seven Hills of Rome, and finally the very signature of God himself. However, the seven heads, with regard to the Seven Hills of Rome symbolism, in no way designates the physical location of the city itself as the Mormons and the Protestant Christians of the world have come to mistakenly believe. The beast and the great whore who sits upon it represent two completely different things, as I have in part already explained with regard to the beast and will be explaining here shortly with regard to this *great city*, also called the great whore of Babylon.

Regarding the great whore of Babylon: based upon all the criteria that has been given about her in the book of Revelation, there is only one city that this could be and one nation whose superpower standing that presently encompasses her can also be. That great seaport city, as I mentioned earlier, is none other than New York; and the nation that encompasses her is the United States of America, which is the reigning superpower of the world today. It rules through a combination of both the United Nations and NATO.

With regard to the relationship between New York City and the United Nations, this is how God sees it when he describes her as having committed fornication with all the kings of the earth where these same kings were also shown to have become drunk on the fierce wine of her fornication. In a faithful relationship bound in marriage, there is only one husband with whom a wife, or in this case, a nation of God, may be bound to and likewise owe her fidelity, and that husband is God himself. The United States was made great in her humble beginnings by the blood covenant she made with the one true God; in return God blessed this nation of ours above all other nations, and they became bound in marriage. But by the very freedoms that brought our forefathers to America, where once they were used to trust in and worship their God with all their hearts, soul, mind, and strength, they have now become the fierce wine of her fornication, as she has turned those very freedoms into the vile abominations that have come to test the very patience of God.

Today, the acceptance of homosexuality, gay marriage, partial birth abortion, and the murdering of the unborn have since become the freedom to choose. I ask how will any of these who work such evil in the eyes of the Lord ever escape damnation? As if these things were not bad enough, many of her children

THE BOOK OF REVELATION AND THE BIBLE
AS NEVER EXPLAINED BEFORE

have now turned to the worship of Satan himself while so many others run the streets in violent gangs, owing their love and allegiance to none but the gang. Murdering and killing, thieving and lying, adultery, fornication, drunkenness, and drug abuse are all running out of control throughout the inner cities of this nation either because of the gangs or not, and on and on the list goes, hence the meaning of the scripture, "For her sins have reached to heaven, and God has remembered her iniquities" (Revelation 18:5, NKJV). Where once America put her faith, hope, and trust in the one true God, Jehovah, the husband of her blood covenant marriage, now she has left her husband and decided to play the harlot by chasing after all the other man-made gods and lusts of the world. She, in her arrogance, has gone on to set herself up as the queen of the earth where she now trusts only in her military might and her alliances, where, in the end, ten of those very nations will destroy her. And so she has committed fornication with all the kings of the earth as they have come to believe and trust in one another rather than the one true God who has the power to bless or curse all who live upon the face of the earth. And so, like her, the very nations or kings of the earth have become drunk on the fierce wine of her fornication as they too have become corrupted by those very freedoms that in the beginning were meant for good but now have come to serve only the vile disguise of this new satanic world order.

The North Atlantic Treaty Organization was formed in 1959 and was the world confederation of nations answer to the Cold War threat of the Soviet Union, North Korea, and China and was also contingent upon the use of the United States' Strategic Air Command for its defense of any member nation being attacked or invaded by any one of these three. Basically, an attack upon any one of the member nations is considered by NATO to be an attack upon all, or more specifically, upon the United States. Today, the purpose and scope of NATO has changed with the advent of the terrorist nations and their desire to acquire weapons of mass destruction.

It is interesting to note how in the beginning NATO and the United Nations catapulted the United States into its super-power status because of its nuclear weapons technology. Now these very weapons have set the stage for its total destruction as the terrorist nations one by one have begun to acquire their own nuclear weapons. In conjunction with this, the European Union, the seventh head of the beast, looms on the horizon, taunting the United States as the American economy with its once great and mighty dollar weakens to the ever-rising power of the euro. But the book of Revelation puts its emphasis on the great city of New York rather than the nation of the United States because it was from Babylon, the first great city of the first kingdom of the world that all power flowed from the throne of King Nebuchadnezzar. God chose to use this same scenario to create the mystery and the puzzle of how in the end this mys-tery Babylon could be determined but only by those qualified and chosen to solve this puzzle.

With regard to the mysteries that surround the understand-ing of who the great whore of Babylon is, the first great mystery to unlock lies in the understanding of how any city in the his-tory of the world can have found within it the blood of all who have been done to death on earth. On its face, this clue is an impossible piece to match to the puzzle. For Jerusalem herself is described by God as having murdered all its prophets. But we know that Jerusalem is destined to be restored to her former glory and, as such, cannot be this mystery city that is destined for total and irrevocable destruction. Geologically speaking, Jerusalem is also not a great seaport city and neither is she the economic capital of the world. On the other hand, Rome mur-dered a lot of the early Christians under the Emperor Nero but still cannot hold a candle to the murders committed by the city of Jerusalem of all her prophets sent to her by God. The ques-tion is how can any city be held accountable for the murders of

238

THE BOOK OF REVELATION AND THE BIBLE
AS NEVER EXPLAINED BEFORE

all who have been done to death on earth since the beginning
of creation? The answer to this question is once again very profound and requires special insight into the ways and especially
the thinking of God on this matter. The following is the answer
given to me by the power of the Holy Spirit.

To begin this explanation, one might just as easily ask how
could God offer his own Son up as an innocent lamb to be
sacrificed for the sins of the world since creation until the end
of Satan's dominion on earth? Or too, how could he hold that
generation of Jews who had his most beloved Son crucified
accountable for the blood of every prophet murdered from Abel
to Zachariah? Both of these questions seem impossible to justify as well, but it was God who justified them to himself. And
so to understand how it is that God is going to use New York
City as the city to pay the price for every city that has ever
committed murder on earth seems, at least from this perspective, a little less of an impossibility to imagine. But there is still
something missing from this analogy. Which brings me to the
next mystery verse: For the blood of all God's saints was found
within her and she was drunk on their blood.

It is from here, as I just stated, that the explanation becomes
very profound. To begin with, you should remember earlier in
chapter 1 how I spoke of the holy city of God being then Jerusalem and how the unholy city of Satan was Rome. Here it is
critical to understand that for every thing that God holds sacred
and true, Satan has his perverse opposite. And so where there
is God's holy city, there is also Satan's unholy city. Jerusalem
was God's holy city up until the Jews cast his people out of it,
and then it became cut off from God and a cursed thing thereafter to the world as it remains so to this day. So God sent his
servants Peter and Paul to Rome to make that which was once
unholy holy and to make that which was once holy desolate
as a punishment for the murdering of his Son, who God the
Father sent to the Jews first for their salvation. It should also be
understood that at that time, the Jews were his chosen people,

239

but when Pilate washed his hands of the crucifixion of Jesus and the Jews said, "Let his death be upon our own heads and on our children's," God the Father took note. So in 70 AD, the Roman General Hadrian destroyed Jerusalem and the holy temple, and in 313, the Emperor Constantine converted all Rome to Christianity, and Satan was there and then made to go off in search of a new unholy city to call his own.

On the other side of this equation, it is sad to note how upon her official debut in 1886, the Statue of Liberty became a symbol for America's basic freedoms of which religion was one of the first to be recognized. How ironic it is that in the end she will only be remembered as having become the symbol of Revelation's mystery Babylon, the mother of all whores and of every obscenity on earth. For just as Rome became destined to become the new holy city of God after Jerusalem's fall from grace, so now has New York City been chosen during our time to become the new unholy city, the mystery Babylon, the city where Satan has now set up his perch and dominion over all the earth as he did in the first Babylon. All the kingdoms of the earth each had a capital city that symbolized the center of its authority, and each of these during their reign upon the earth, as designated by the seven heads of the beast, were under the dominion of Satan as it was granted to him by God. Just as God had in the beginning the holy city of Jerusalem and now has Rome, Satan had each of these: as Babylon was to the Babylonian Empire, as Suza was to the Persian-Median Empire, as Alexandria was to the Macedonian Empire, as Rome was to the Roman Empire, as Berlin was to the German Empire, and now as New York City is to the United States of America's world empire. All have been the unholy cities of Satan, just as New York City is today. There will be no seventh unholy city of Satan even though the beast shall come to trample Jerusalem underfoot and set up the nuclear missile as the god of the citadel in the holy of holies and mouth bombast and blasphemies against God from within her. Jerusalem, the once holy city of God, shall be rescued from her torment and her disgrace during that time and reclaimed by God. Then shall she be made holy again and then shall none but the righteous be found within her gates.

But now having said all that, there is still one last very critical point that must be made to finish this explanation: Because New York City has been designated by God to be the last unholy city of Satan, Satan must therefore be found within her, and within Satan is found the blood of all who have been done to death on earth and in no other. Also, by her rejection of God, and especially by our nation's rejection of God by a popular vote, a new covenant will be made between the great whore and Satan. It will be a symbolic blood covenant just like the one the eleven disciples made with Jesus. It happened during the Last Supper and is now regarded as the rite of Holy Communion by the Catholics and the taking of the sacraments by most other Christian faiths. This is where we as Christians take and eat the Eucharist or the bread of Christ, which symbolizes our eating the flesh of Christ who was the ultimate manna from God, which came down from heaven to give us everlasting life, and the drinking of the wine, which symbolizes the blood of Christ that was shed for us, and by drinking it we are reminded that it was by his blood that we have become cleansed from our sins. And so by engaging in this holy rite of communion with God, we are joined together with his body and blood and also absolved from our sins and thereby made ready for the kingdom of God that is to come, but most importantly by partaking of this rite of Holy Communion we as Christians then have the body and blood of Christ found within us.

In a perversion of this holy rite instituted by God, Satan has his own rite of unholy communion, where with the exception of the body being excluded because he is without a body, all those who worship him must also drink his blood in a similar substitution of either wine or animal blood and in so doing will also have the symbolic blood of Satan found within them. The problem comes, as I stated earlier, as Satan is the only one on earth to have found within him the blood of all who have been done to death on earth, that by participating in this unholy rite of communion with him, either knowingly or unknowingly, all those who do so will consequently take upon themselves the blood of all who have been done to death on earth. With this comes total damnation, as all these will then have an equal share in Satan's condemnation and eternal punishment.

In conjunction with this, all these inhabitants of New York City, except for those who keep faith with God, will also take upon their right hands and foreheads the mark of the beast during the time of his return and his ensuing great reign of terror. Such shall be the case for all those who hate God and who have literally chosen to pledge their allegiance to Satan and his gospel of war and hate. All of this, along with all the other great sins and perversions of Satan as outlined within the Democratic Party's liberal agenda and the fierce willingness of her people to put their complete faith and trust in it through the popular vote, constitutes the fierce wine of her fornication.

With regard to the unholy communion, I do not know if this great and unholy event has taken place yet on a grand party scale, but I do know that the church of Satan is alive and doing very well within the borders of the United States. Given all the murdering and killing that is going on within most of our inner cities because of the out of control state of gang violence, the ever rising popularity of gangster rap and its close counterpart, death metal music, and given all the gay marriage enactment laws that are beginning to sweep across the different states of this nation, I would say we are getting pretty close to that time. As I said before, it begins with the popular vote to accept the satanic liberal agenda and ends up with a major part of our nation's population rejecting God and making this new blood covenant with Satan.

But there is still one last all-telling event that must take place first before God's final judgment will fall upon the great city of New York and this nation of ours that encompasses

THE BOOK OF REVELATION AND THE BIBLE
AS NEVER EXPLAINED BEFORE

her, which is contained within this verse: "Come out of her, my people, lest you share in her sins and lest you receive of her plagues. For her sins have reached to heaven" (Revelation 18:4–5, NKJV). And this verse: "For mighty is the Lord God who has pronounced her doom" (Revelation 18:8, TNEB). Yes, as long as there are at least ten faithful people of God left on earth and as many may be found within her, God will stay his mighty hand of this final judgment that is to be passed upon her and the nation that encompasses her. But once all the righteous men and women have been removed from the face of the earth, and especially from within her, then shall all these prophecies about her be fulfilled.

With regard to New York City being symbolized as a blasphemous whore, or more particularly, the mother of all whores: out of all the other kingdoms and dominions of the beast's seven heads, the United States, along with its great seaport city of New York, is in the first instance the only one that does not have at its head a reigning king. Instead it rules the world through a democratic system of government that incorporates, among other things, a political president; it uses New York City's great economic capital and prowess as a means to control the monetary systems of the world. New York City also hosts and headquarters the gathering of the United Nations, which is the sixth head of the beast, hence her fornication with all the kings of the earth. The beast, on the other hand, is a separate entity from the whore who sits on its back; it symbolizes all of Satan's power and dominion over all the kingdoms of the world that have been since the first kingdom of Babylon came into full world power under King Nebuchadnezzar until the last kingdom of the world shall come at the time of the end, which is the European Union, that shall be ruled over by the beast. That is why John called her the mystery Babylon, because she had not yet come into existence, and he could only liken her to the first Babylon in spite of the fact that Rome was also being regarded by some of the apostles as the Babylon of their time, (reference

243

1 Peter 5:13–14). In the second instance, New York City is considered to be "the mother of all whores" because out of all the other unholy cities that have reigned upon the earth, none have come to be as greatly blessed by God and then out that greatness turned to embrace all the evils of the world with the same unrepentant boldness as her adultery is to God. But even more so than this, none have ever had the medical marvels, the war technology, the electronic technology, the Internet capabilities, the movies, the DVDs, the CDs, the magazines, the books, and all the other industries that she has that are now being used to either blaspheme or commit some of the most horrendous sins ever imagined before God. And so it is only fitting that this great city should be called the mother of all whores because she has earned that title.

This then is the last mystery that God had for me to explain to all those of you who are considered his people and who have long marveled at the meaning of all these things as they are contained within the book of Revelation and also the Bible itself. It is important to remember that I have not come to take anything away from or, in the other case, to add anything to the book of Revelation. It remains as it was written by the Apostle John under the divine inspiration of Jesus Christ, the Son of God. My mission was, in part, to explain these mysteries of the Bible to you as they have been given to me, for they have been misunderstood long enough and also to reveal those things that have been hidden or else deeply layered in various levels of understanding. For we are now living in the time of the book of Revelation and soon for all those who can attain to the perfection of God's love and receive either the seal of God, or the seal of the Holy Spirit, or the fleshly seal of circumcision, our time of deliverance will be at hand in the sequence that has been revealed. Peace be with all you who take these words to heart, and may the Holy Spirit guide and comfort you during the days of our testing that are so close at hand. I look forward to meeting you all in the kingdom of God.

THE BOOK OF REVELATION AND THE BIBLE
AS NEVER EXPLAINED BEFORE

So to the faithful, I can only say hold on to your faith and be of good cheer no matter what happens around you, for the Day of the Lord is close at hand. Remember also not to store up your treasures on earth. For where your treasure is, there also is your heart, and the destruction of war and the wrath of God's all-consuming fire await all those who will turn to wage war against him here. Rather, it is very pleasing to God that we who are called his children give generously to the poor and strive toward humility and holiness so that our treasures will be in heaven waiting for us when at the appointed time the kingdom of heaven shall be brought down to earth to reign in peace and love for a thousand years. May the grace of God be with all of you who are the Called, the Faithful, and the Chosen.

THE RECORD OF THE KINGS OF ISRAEL

King Saul is the first king of Israel anointed by the prophet Samuel. He does what is wrong in the eyes of the Lord and is the only king to lose his anointing because of it.

THE KINGS FROM THE HOUSE OF JUDAH

1. King David is anointed the new king of Israel by the prophet Samuel and is considered by God to be the most righteous man to ever live, except for his sin in killing Uriah the Hitite for his wife, Bathsheba.

2. King Solomon: The son of King David by Bathsheba reigns for forty years. Though he is considered to be the wisest man to ever live, he does what is wrong in the eyes of the Lord and worships other gods. At the end of his reign, the ten tribes from the house of Israel are torn away from him, and his son Rehoboam is left with only the one tribe of Judah where later the tribe of Benjamin also joins them. It was from that time on that Israel became a house divided where the northern kingdom of Israel would establish the city of Samaria for its capital and the southern kingdom of Judah would keep Jerusalem. They remain divided and torn apart to this day as God's judgment continues until such time as he shall come to reconcile himself back to them in the land of Zion. The following is the record of kings from the house of Judah from that time until God finally brings the last king's reign to an end.

3. King Rehoboam: The son of Solomon succeeds his father and reigns as king for sixteen years over the southern kingdom of the house of Judah and does what is wrong in the eyes of the Lord.

4. King Abijam: The son of Rehoboam succeeds his father and reigns for three years after him and does what is wrong in the eyes of the Lord as his father had done.

5. King Asa: The son of Abijam succeeds his father and reigns for forty-one years and does what is right in the eyes of the Lord.

6. King Jehoshaphat: The son of Asa reigns for twenty-five years and does what is right in the eyes of the Lord.

7. King Joram: The son of Jehoshaphat reigns for eight years and does what is wrong in the eyes of the Lord.

8. King Ahaziah: The son of Joram reigns for one year and does what is wrong in the eyes of the Lord by following the practices of the house of Ahab, the king of Israel, during his reign. He is killed by Jehu from the house of Israel for all the evil that he had worked in the eyes of the Lord.

9. Queen Athaliah reigns for six years after her son, Ahaziah, is killed by Jehu. She was very evil in the eyes of the Lord and would be put to death by Jehoiada, the priest of the Lord who anoints Joash, son of Ahaziah, who was then in hiding, king of Judah.

10. King Joash: The son of Ahaziah reigns for forty years and does what is right in the eyes of the Lord.

11. King Amaziah: The son of Joash reigns for twenty-nine years and does what is right as his father before him. He is murdered by a conspiracy, and his son Azariah succeeds him.

12. King Azariah: The son of Amaziah reigns for fifty-two years and did right in the eyes of the Lord, just as his father did before him.

THE BOOK OF REVELATION AND THE BIBLE
AS NEVER EXPLAINED BEFORE

13. King Uzziah: The son of Azariah, though there is no record of his reign in the book of 2 Kings, the record may be found in 2 Chronicles in chapter 26. There in chapter 26 it states that he reigns for fifty-two years. He does what is right in the eyes of the Lord for much of his life, except for the one offense in his later years where he entered the sanctuary of the temple of the Lord to burn incense to him on the altar of incense, overstepping his boundaries with the holy priests whose place it was to do such a thing. Because of his indignation at their reproof of his actions, the Lord struck him with leprosy, and he would finish the last days of his life stricken with this disease. He reigns during the beginning of the time of the great prophet Isaiah and would come to the throne at the age of sixteen.

14. King Jotham: The son of Uzziah reigns for sixteen years. He is remembered for the construction of the upper gate to the house of the Lord. He does what is right in the eyes of the Lord just as his father, Uzziah, had done before him, but the hill shrines are allowed to remain, and the people continue to burn sacrifices to them.

15. King Ahaz: The son of Jotham reigns for sixteen years and did what was wrong in the eyes of the Lord.

16. King Hezekiah: The son of Ahaz reigns for twenty-nine years and does more right in the eyes of the Lord than any other king in all Israel, except for King David. It was he who suppressed the hill shrines, smashed the sacred pillars, cut down every sacred pole, and broke up the bronze serpent that Moses had made because the people had come to burn sacrifices to it. He is the last king to have the council of the great prophet Isaiah.

17. King Manasseh: The son of Hezekiah reigns for fifty-five years and does great wrong in the eyes of the Lord.

18. King Amon: The son of Manasseh reigns for only two years and did what was wrong in the eyes of the Lord by following in the footsteps of his father before him. He is murdered by his courtiers, but the people kill them soon after and put Josiah, Amon's son, on the throne.

19. King Josiah: The son of Amon reigns for thirty-one years and does much right in the eyes of the Lord by following in his forefather's, King David's, footsteps.

20. King Jehoahaz: The son of Josiah reigns for only three months and does what is wrong in the eyes of the Lord. The Pharoah Necho removes him and puts his other brother, Eliakim, whose name is then changed to Jehoiakim, on the throne.

21. King Jehoiakim: The son of Josiah then reigns for eleven years. During his reign, King Nebuchadnezzar comes to take him as a vassal, but three years later, he revolts. Because of this revolt, the Lord sends raiding parties of Chaldeans, Aramaeans, Moabites, and Ammonites against them for the remainder of his reign, as was foretold by the prophet Jeremiah. He is succeeded by his son Jehoiachin. He does what is wrong in the eyes of the Lord by not listening to the prophet Jeremiah.

22. King Jehoiachin: The son of Jehoiakim reigns for three months and also refuses to listen to the prophet Jeremiah. So the Lord sends King Nebuchadnezzar to take over the southern kingdom of Judah, as was foretold by the prophet, carrying off all the treasures from the house of the Lord and the royal palace. After his surrender, Jehoiachin, along with his entire family, his courtiers, his officers and fighting men, his craftsmen and smiths, ten thousand in all, are taken into exile. Only the weakest classes of people are left. They are all taken back to Babylon as prisoners and slaves of his empire. King Nebuchadnezzar then sets Mattaniah, Jehoiachin's uncle, up as king in his place. Mattaniah's name is later changed to Zedekiah.

THE BOOK OF REVELATION AND THE BIBLE
AS NEVER EXPLAINED BEFORE

23. King Zedekiah: The third son of Josiah is the last king of Judah and of all Israel and reigns for eleven years before King Nebuchadnezzar finally comes one last time to completely destroy the southern kingdom of Judah. This final act by King Nebuchadnezzar is actually a punishment decreed by God against Judah for all her abominations and sins committed against him. After Zedekiah's sons are killed, he is then blinded and the rest of house of Judah is then taken away as slaves to the kingdom of Babylon. They will remain there for the next seventy years. It is during this time that the prophet Daniel comes into God's service.

Otherwise, it is interesting to note that the entire line of descendants from Joseph, the husband of Mary who gave birth to Jesus, is not traced back through Zedekiah, the last king of Judah to David, nor is it traced through the other two sons of King Josiah—Jehoahaz and Jehoiakim—neither is it traced through Jehoiachin, the son of Jehoiakim. This is primarily because of the fact that aside from all Zedekiah's sons being slain before his eyes as I just mentioned, the other two sons, and one nephew of King Josiah would also see their lineage ended in bondage as they were each changed into eunuchs because of all the evil that they had also worked in the eyes of the Lord. So the Lord takes another son from King Josiah's stock, whose name is Jeconiah, and traces his Son's, Jesus Christ's, lineage back to David through him instead. Reference Matthew 1:1–17 for the complete lineage from Jesus all the way back to Abraham. Also notice that Queen Athaliah's short term after usurping the throne is not recognized by God and that, according to Matthew's account, there are fourteen generations between each subgroup from Abraham to David, from David to the deportation to Babylon, and from the deportation to Babylon to Jesus Christ, who is called son of David. However, according to the record of 1st and 2nd Kings, the house of Judah clearly has eighteen kings from David to Josiah, excluding his other three sons and one nephew, Jehoiachin.

251

THE KINGS FROM THE HOUSE OF ISRAEL

1. King Jeroboam: The son of Nebat reigns for forty-one years and does what is wrong in the eyes of the Lord by building the two golden calves in Bethel and Dan for the people to worship in place of God.

2. King Nadab: The son of Jeroboam reigns for two years, and because he continues on in the sins of his father and refuses to obey the commandments of Lord, his throne is taken away from him and given to another.

3. King Baasha: The son of Ahijab, who is the prophet of the Lord, usurps the throne as he is commanded to do by God. He then anoints his son Baasha as king, and he reigns for twenty-four years. As soon as Baasha becomes king, he strikes down the entire family of Jeroboam, leaving not one survivor. All this is done to fulfill the word of the Lord because Jeroboam had led the people of Israel into committing grievous sins against the Lord and also because he had so greatly provoked the anger of the Lord the God of Israel. However, Baasha goes on to do as Jeroboam had done, leading Israel into the same grievous sins as Jeroboam had done, and so he too, along with his entire family, would meet a similar fate as foretold by the prophet Jehu.

4. King Elah: The son of Baasha then comes to the throne but only reigns for two years before the word of the Lord is fulfilled. Then while in Tirzah, drinking himself drunk at the house of Arza, he is attacked and assassinated by Zimri, who was in the service of commanding half the king's chariotry. Zimri, after murdering Baasha, then makes himself king.

5. King Zimri: As soon as he had become king and was enthroned, he went on to destroy the entire family of Baasha, as was foretold by the prophet Jehu, and thus fulfilled

THE BOOK OF REVELATION AND THE BIBLE
AS NEVER EXPLAINED BEFORE

the word of the Lord. Seven days later, because of the great outcry of the people, he is overthrown by Omri, the commander of the Israelite Army, who himself, by the common consent of his soldiers, is made the new king of Israel. Zimri's reign is soon ended as he retreats inside the royal palace to escape the siege of Omri's army and once there, sets it on fire, sealing his own fate.

6. King Omri: He is ultimately made king by the common consent of the people and reigns for twelve years. He was very wicked in the eyes of the Lord as he outdoes all those who come before him in leading the nation to sin.

7. King Ahab: The son of Omri surpasses even his father's wickedness by taking for a wife Jezebel, the daughter of Ethbaal, king of Sidon, and worshipping their god, Baal. He, under the direct influence of his wife, Jezebel, would be responsible for the murder of several hundred of God's prophets and ultimately does more to provoke the anger of the Lord, the God of Israel, than all the other kings of Israel combined. He reigns for twenty-two years and has for his unwilling council the prophet Elijah.

8. King Ahaziah: The son of Ahab reigned for two years. He did what was wrong in the eyes of the Lord by following in the footsteps of his father and mother and those of Jeroboam, son of Nebat, by leading Israel into sin by the service and worship of Baal and, as such, provoking the anger of the Lord the God of Israel, as his father had done. He also received unwilling council from the prophet Elijah.

9. King Jehoram: The brother of Ahaziah then comes to the throne because Ahaziah had no sons to succeed him. He reigned for twelve years and was not as bad as his father and mother, but Jehu picks up a bow and shoots him through the heart. Soon after, he also kills Ahaziah, the king of Judah. It is during his reign that the prophet Elijah is taken up into

253

heaven by chariots and horses of fire while walking with the prophet's successor, Elisha.

10. King Jehu: The son of Jehoshaphat, son of Nimshi, is anointed king of Israel by a prophet under Elisha and commanded to strike down the entire house of Ahab his master and also to take vengeance on Jezebel for the blood of all the Lord's servants and prophets killed by her. As such, the word of the Lord would then be fulfilled through Jehu, and this was very pleasing to the Lord, the God of Israel. Jehu reigned for twenty-eight years, but after ridding the house of Ahab from Israel, he went on to maintain the worship of the two golden calves at Bethel and Dan, and in doing this one thing he once again brought the disfavor of God upon the house of Israel.

11. King Jehoahaz: The son of Jehu reigns for seventeen years and does what is wrong in the eyes of the Lord by continuing the sinful practices of Jeroboam, son of Nebat, the first to lead the separated house of Israel into sin.

12. King Jehoash: The son of Jehoahaz reigns for sixteen years and does what is wrong in the eyes of the Lord by continuing on in the sinful practices of Jeroboam son of Nebat, just as his father had before him.

13. King Jeroboam: The son of Jehoash reigns for forty-one years and does what is wrong in the eyes of the Lord.

14. King Zechariah: The son of Jeroboam reigns for six months. He is murdered by a conspiracy led by Shallum, who then usurps the throne from Zechariah.

15. King Shallum: The son of Jabesh reigns for one month and does what is wrong in the eyes of the Lord. He is then attacked and killed by Menahem, who comes up from Tirzah to Samaria and usurps the throne away from Shallum.

THE BOOK OF REVELATION AND THE BIBLE
AS NEVER EXPLAINED BEFORE

16. King Menahem: The son of Gadi reigned for ten years and does what is wrong in the eyes of the Lord. He exacted a terrible vengeance on the territory of Tappuah for not opening its gates to him, and he continued the sinful practices of Jeroboam that first led Israel into sin.

17. King Pekahiah: The son of Menahem reigns for two years and does what is wrong in the eyes of the Lord. Then Pekah, his lieutenant, formed a conspiracy against him and, with the help of fifty of his Gileadites, attacked him in the citadel of his royal palace, killed him, and usurped the throne.

18. King Pekah: The son of Remaliah reigns for twenty years and does what is wrong in the eyes of the Lord.

19. King Hoshea: The son of Elah kills Pekah and usurps the throne in the twentieth year of Jotham, son of Uzziah, king of Judah. Hoshea reigns for nine years before the king of Assyria, Shalmaneser, finally takes the northern kingdom into captivity in 721 BC. Then in 612 BC, after Nineveh, the capital city of the Assyrian empire, is completely destroyed by the Babylonians under King Nebuchadnezzar, they simply disappear according to the historic account.

THE RECORD OF BIBLE QUOTES

THE HISTORIC RECORD OF THE SEVEN CHURCHES

1. Quote: page 20, 18 words: (Romans 9:27, TNJB).

2. Quote: page 26, 18 words: (John 14:2, NKJV).

3. Quote: page 26, 30 words: (Hebrews 3:6, NKJV).

4. Quote: page 26, 7 words: (Proverbs 7:27, NKJV).

5. Quote: page 26, 17 words: (Acts 16:31, NKJV).

6. Quote: page 26, 11 words: (Joshua 24:15, NKJV).

7. Combined quote: page 28, 44 words NKJV combined with 42 words taken from the KJV: (Matthew 16:18–19, NKJV—KJV).

8. Quote: pages 30-31, 37 words: (Matthew 16:19, KJV, page interrupt).

9. Quote: page 31, 15 words: (Acts 9:34, NKJV).

10. Quote: page 32, 118 words: (John 21:15–17, NKJV).

11. Quote: page 39, 52 words: (Matthew 5:17–19, TNJB).

12. Quote: page 39, 20 words: (Matthew 7:12, NKJV).

13. Quote: page 39, 64 words: (Matthew 22:36–40, TNJB).

14. Quote: page 47, 61 words: (John 6:67–70, NKJV).

15. Quote: page 50, 65 words: (1 Corinthians 13:4–7, TNJB).

16. Quote: page 51, 26 words: (Matthew 23:11–12, NKJV).

257

17. Quote: page 51, 24 words: (Matthew 18:1–4, NKJV).

18. Quote: page 51, 35 words: (John 14:21, NKJV)

19. Quote: page 52, 13 words: (Romans 10:17, NKJV).

20. Quote: page 52, 6 words: (James 2:20–21, KJV).

21. Quote: page 52, 16 words: (Hebrews 11:1, KJV).

22. Quote: page 53, 15 words: (John 4:24–25, NKJV).

23. Quote: pages 53-54, 35 words: (Matthew 15:8–9, NKJV page interrupt).

24. Quote: page 55, 16 words: (John 15:13, NKJV).

25. Quote: page 56, 10 words: (Luke 23:34, KJV).

26. Quote: page 56, 14 words: (Psalm 118:1, TNEB).

27. Quote: page 59, 24 words: (Psalm 51:2–3, KJV).

28. Quote: page 59, 15 words: (Psalm 51:10, KJV).

THE HIDDEN MESSAGE OF THE SEVEN CHURCHES

29. Quote: page 68, 17 words: (Revelation 1:19, NKJV).

30. Quote: page 69, 57 words: (1 Corinthians 13:1–3, NKJV).

31. Quote: page 76, 36 words: (Ephesians 4:11–13, NKJV).

32. Quote: pages 81-82, 227 words: (Revelation 3:14–22, NKJV, page interrupt).

33. Quote: page 83, 73 words: (John 21:18–19, TNJB).

34. Quote: pages 83-84, 15 words: (John 8:17–19, NKJV, page interrupt).

35. Quote: page 86, 5 words: (Revelation 15:4, NKJV).

36. Quote: page 87, 19 words: (Ephesians 4:30–31, NKJV).

37. Quote: page 94, 12 words: (Mark 10:31, NKJV).

THE BOOK OF REVELATION AND THE BIBLE
AS NEVER EXPLAINED BEFORE

38. Quote: page 97, 32 words: (Luke 21:16–17, NKJV).

39. Quote: page 98, 23 words: (Revelation 19:9–10, NKJV).

THE SCROLL WITH THE SEVEN SEALS

40. Quote: pages 99-100, 328 words: (Revelation 4:1–11, NKJV, page interrupt).

41. Quote: pages 100-101, 426 words: (Revelation 5:1–14, NKJV, page interrupt).

42. Quote: page 102, 28 words: (Revelation 4:4, NKJV).

43. Quote: page 103, 165 words: (Revelation 21:9–14, NKJV).

44. Quote: page 104, 9 words: (Revelation 4:5, NKJV).

45. Quote: pages 104-105, 23 words: (Revelation 4:6, NKJV, page interrupt).

46. Quote: page 105, 191 words: (Isaiah 6:1–7, NKJV).

47. Quote: pages 106-108, 820 words: (Ezekiel 1:1–28, NKJV, page interrupt).

48. Quote: page 109, 14 words: (Revelation 4:8, NKJV).

49. Quote: page 109, 74 words: (Revelation 17:8, TNJB.

50. Quote: page 110, 36 words: (Revelation 5:6–7, NKJV).

51. Quote: page 110, 52 words: (Revelation 5:10, TNEB).

52. Quote: page 111, 135 words: (Revelation 20:4–6, TNJB.

53. Quote: page 111, 68 words: (Matthew 19:27–29, NKJV).

54. Quote: page 112, 27 words: (Revelation 3:21–22, NKJV).

55. Quote: page 113, 188 words: (Revelation 3:8–13, NKJV).

56. Quote: page 116, 33 words: (Revelation 5:11–12, NKJV).

259

THE KINGDOM OF GOD

57. Quote: page 123, 59 words: (Mark 10:29–30, NKJV).

58. Quote: page 125, 169 words: (Zechariah 12:9–14, NKJV).

59. Quote: page 126, 175 words: (Zechariah 13:1–5, NKJV).

60. Quote: pages 126-127, 534 words: (Zechariah 14:6–21, NKJV, page interrupt).

61. Quote: pages 127-128, 238 words: (Micah 4:1–7, NKJV, page interrupt).

62. Quote: page 128, 137 words: (Joel 2:28- 32, NKJV).

63. Quote: page 129, 91 words: (Joel 3:1–3).

64. Quote: pages 129-130, 327 words: (Joel 3:9–21, NKJV, page interrupt).

65. Quote: page 130, 337 words: (Revelation 19:11–21, NKJV).

66. Quote: pages 131-134, 1,255 words: (2 Esdras 13:1–56, TNEB, page interrupt).

67. Quote: page 136, 114 words: (Revelation 20:7–10, NKJV).

68. Quote: page 136, 13 words: (Romans 10:13, NKJV).

69. Quote: page 138, 11 words: (Revelation 19:15, NKJV).

THE SEVEN SEALS

70. Quote: page 139, 56 words: (Revelation 6:1–2, TNEB).

71. Quote: page 144, 47 words: (Revelation 6:3–4, TNEB).

72. Quote: page 145, 78 words: (Revelation 6:5–6, TNEB).

73. Quote: page 145, 63 words: (Revelation 6:7–8, TNEB).

74. Quote: page 147, 96 words: (Revelation 6:9–11, TNEB).

75. Quote: page 147, 32 words: (Revelation 14:13, TNEB).

76. Quote: page 148, 157 words: (Revelation 6:12–17, NKJV).

THE BOOK OF REVELATION AND THE BIBLE
AS NEVER EXPLAINED BEFORE

77. Quote: pages 148-150, 480 words: (Revelation 7:1–17, NKJV page interrupt).

78. Quote: pages 151-152, 141 words: (Revelation 8:1–5, TNJB, page interrupt).

THE SEVEN TRUMPETS

79. Quote: page 153, 41 words: (Revelation 8:7, TNEB).

80. Quote: page 154, 49 words: (Revelation 8:8–9, TNJB).

81. Quote: page 154, 61 words: (Revelation 8:10–11, TNJB).

82. Quote: page 155, 86 words: (Revelation 8:12–13, TNEB).

83. Quote: pages 155-156, 269 words: (Revelation 9:1–12, TNJB, page interrupt).

84. Quote: pages 156-157, 96 words: (Revelation 9:13–16, TNJB, page interrupt).

85. Quote: page 157, 85 words: (Revelation 9:17–19, TNJB).

86. Quote: page 159, 55 words: (Revelation 13:7–8, TNJB).

87. Quote: pages 159-160, 307 words: (Revelation 11:1–14, TNJB, page interrupt).

88. Quote: pages 160-161, 178 words: (Revelation 11:15–19, TNJB, page interrupt).

89. Quote: page 162, 52 words: (Matthew 5:17–20, TNJB).

THE SEVEN THUNDERS

90. Quote: page 166, 99 words: (Revelation 14:3–5, TNJB).

91. Quote: page 169, 22 words: (Revelation 19:9, TNJB).

92. Quote: page 170, 26 words: (Zechariah 14:12, TNJB).

93. Quote: page 173, 40 words: (Ezekiel 36:22–23, NKJV).

THE GREAT RED DRAGON

94. Quote: pages 175-176, 510 words: (Revelation 12:1–17, NKJV, page interrupt).

95. Quote: page 178, 33 words: (Revelation 12:12, TNEB).

THE BEAST AND THE FALSE PROPHET

96. Quote: pages 181-182, 274 words: (Revelation 13:1–10, NKJV, page interrupt).

97. Quote: pages 182-183, 238 words: (Revelation 13:11–18, NKJV, page interrupt).

98. Quote: pages 185-187, 826 words: (Daniel 7:2–27, TNJB), page interrupt.

99. Quote: pages 187-189, 573 words: (Daniel 2:27–45, TNJB, page interrupt).

100. Quote: page 189, 22 words: (Daniel 5:30–31, TNJB).

101. Quote: page 201, 188 words: (Revelation 17:8–12, TNJB).

102. Quote: page 210, 32 words: (Revelation 17:17–18, TNEB).

103. Quote: page 213, 146 words: (Matthew 24:15–22, NKJV.)

104. Quote: page 216, 77 words: (Revelation 19:19–20, NKJV).

THE OCCULT HISTORY OF THE THIRD REICH

No quotes taken in this chapter.

THE BOOK OF REVELATION AND THE BIBLE
AS NEVER EXPLAINED BEFORE

THE SEVEN PLAGUES OF
THE SEVEN BOWLS

105. Quote: pages 225-226, 244 words: (Revelation 15:1–8, TNJB, page interrupt).

106. Quote: pages 226-227, 528 words: (Revelation 16:1–21, TNJB, page interrupt).

THE GREAT WHORE OF BABYLON

107. Quote: pages 231-232, 530 words: (Revelation 17:1–18, NKJV, page interrupt).

108. Quote: pages 233-234, 705 words: (Revelation 18:1–24, NKJV, page interrupt).

109. Quote: page 237, 13 words: (Revelation 18:5, NKJV).

110. Quote: page 243, 26 words: (Revelation 18:4–5, NKJV).

111. Quote: page 243, 11 words: (Revelation 18:8, TNEB).

Seven quotes totaling 178 words were taken from the KJV.

Fourteen quotes totaling 1,896 words were taken from TNEB. Twenty-seven quotes totaling 4,324 words were taken from the TNJB. And sixty-six quotes totaling 8,705 words were taken from the NKJV.

All together there were a total of 111 quotes taken from the four different Bible translations and a total of 15,081 words used within those quotes.

263

BIBLICAL REFERENCES AND SOURCES NOTED

- Originally I had planned to use The New English Bible translation for the greater part of those quotes that have been written in this book, but because of copyrights and permission fee issues I was forced to consider the use of other translations. The reason why I had chosen this Bible over all the others is because I believed it to be the best written English translation of all the others out there and because of this it provides the reader with what I can only describe as a very enjoyable read. Now unless noted, only 14 scripture quotations have been retained from The New English Bible translation which is also one of the very few translations that has all 15 books of the Apocrypha included in it. With this personal bias in mind I strongly urge every reader, and all who are able to do so, to seek out a copy of this translation and keep it for their personal enlightenment and reference.

The following facts are the reasons why this Bible has been translated and written as well as it has:

- In the first instance it was translated from the original tongues of the traditional Hebrew or (Massorectic Text) known as the Biblia Hebraic (3rd Edition 1937). Otherwise to further aid in the translation of this ancient text into modern day English many other translations of this same text were used. Of these translations there were in part, the Dead Sea Scrolls, the Samaritan Pentateuch (or the "Seventy" elders from the twelve tribes of Israel) also known as the Greek version, the new Latin version known as the Vulgate, the Aramaic Targums which language later came to supplement the Hebrew language, the Syriac translation known as the Peshitte or "simple" version, and finally cognate languages were also used to help in the understanding of the limited Hebrew vocabulary as studied through other translations from the Ethiopic, Babylonian, Assyrian, as well as other kindred dialects of those recovered by Archaeologists. This New English Bible translation was Copyrighted in 1961, 1970, by the delegates of the Oxford University Press and the Syndics of the Cambridge University Press. The New Testament first edition was published in 1961 and the second edition was published in 1970. The Old Testament and the Apocrypha were also published in 1970.

- The New English Bible translation itself was planned and directed by representatives of the following: The Baptist Union of Great Britain and Ireland, The Church of England, The Church of Scotland, The Congregational Church in England and Wales, The Irish Council of Churches, The London Yearly Meeting of The Society of Friends, The Methodist Church of Great Britain, The Presbyterian Church of England, The British and Foreign Bible Society, and finally The National Bible Society of Scotland. At a much later stage, representatives from the Roman Catholic Church in England and Scotland were also invited and came to attend the translation conferences as observers.

- All scripture quotations noted: *reference,* are especially intended to cause the reader to reference at least four different Bible translations to see how often times the same thing may be said using different words, while on other occasions using different words has caused a very slight loss of some of the originally intended scriptural meaning of those verses quoted.

- As a special note: Whenever a loss of scriptural meaning of any kind was found to be the case by a comparison of

THE BOOK OF REVELATION AND THE BIBLE
AS NEVER EXPLAINED BEFORE

these different translations the lost wordage was super-imposed back into the quoted translation by a three to one comparison using (brackets).

The following are the five different Bible translations that were used either as a reference or in the writing of this book:

- In the final book, fourteen scriptural quotations were retained from The New English Bible with the Apocrypha. All copyrights are already noted above. This translation is also the base translation, or more clearly, the one from which all the other translations noted were later compared. The New English Bible translation is one of any number of different translations used by the Roman Catholic Church as well as the other Protestant churches of England who participated in the translation of this Bible.

- All scriptures noted *reference,* were compared first, using this base translation, to the King James Version, copyright © 1984, 1977 by Thomas Nelson Inc. Publishers out of Nashville. This translation is very popular among many Protestant as well as Mormon faiths.

- All scriptures noted *reference* were compared second to the New King James Version, copyright © 1979, 1982, and 1980 by Thomas Nelson Inc. This is one of any number of different alternative translations used by the Protestant faiths as well.

- All scriptures noted *reference* were compared third to the New World Translation of the Holy Scriptures, or otherwise known as the Bible of the Jehovah's Witnesses, copyright © 1961 and 1981, by the Watch Tower Bible and Tract Society of Pennsylvania. Publishers: Watchtower Bible and Tract Society of New York, Inc.

- All scriptures noted *reference* were compared fourth to The New Jerusalem Bible, copyright © 1999 by Dou-

267

PETER J. DAVIS

bleday, a division of Random House, Inc., and Darton, Longman & Todd Ltd.

- Biblical text copyright © 1985 by Darton, Longman & Todd Ltd. and Doubleday, a division of Random House, Inc.

- The New Jerusalem Bible was printed in the United States of America in March 1999. It is a First Doubleday Standard Edition Bible.

HISTORICAL REFERENCES AND RESEARCH SOURCES NOTED

- The World Book Encyclopedia, Copyright 1971, USA, by Field Enterprises Educational Corporation. Subjects researched: The Roman Catholic Church, Popes, The Apostle Peter, The Apostle Paul, The Apostle John, The Saint Peter's Basilica, The Lateran Basilica, Jerusalem, Israel, the Franciscans, the Jesuits, The Babylonian Empire, The Persian Empire, The Macedonian Empire, Alexander the Great, Rome and the history of the Roman Empire, Adolf Hitler, the history of Germany, The League of Nations, The United Nations, NATO, France, and The Emperor Constantine I, and Richard Wagner just to name a few.

- "The Rise and Fall of the Third Reich" Copyright 1959, 1960 by William L. Shire. Published by Simon and Schuster Inc. All rights reserved.

- "The Occult history of the Third Reich" A three DVD collection made in Canada, Copyright Madacy Entertainment Group, Ltd. 1998. These three transcripts, although originally intended to be used as a historic reference within this book, have now, because of a variety of permissions and copyright's issues, been struck from this book. This information remains only as a resource for those who wish to purchase a copy of this remarkable DVD collection for their personal viewing.

- The American Heritage College Dictionary Copyright 1997, 1993 by Houghton Mifflin Company. All rights reserved.

Internet sources noted:

- Google search: "Mein Kampf" the complete book written by Adolf Hitler.
- Google search: "The Bermuda Triangle" analyzed different takes on this subject.
- Google search: The Jesuits, the Franciscans, the Eastern Orthodox Church, the Jehovah's Witnesses, Jerusalem the holy city, Israel the land of Zion, and Mount Zion.
- Google search: Circumcision in the Catholic Church and circumcision in general.
- Google search: WHO, The World Health Organization. Subjects concerning the great diseases of the world: Malaria, The Asian Flu, The Bird Flu, the Swine Flu from Mexico, Influenza in general, AIDS/HIV and the EBOLA virus some of which to this day have no cure.
- Google search: The destructive cults of the world, or (doomsday) destructive religious cults such as: the Family; Charles Manson, The Branch Dividians, Heaven's Gate, Aum Shinri Kyo, the Movement for the restoration of the Ten Commandments of God (Uganda), The People's Temples (Jim Jones), and the Solar Temple to name only a few.
- Google search: Animal attacks on mankind: The Hippopotamus, the Nile crocodile, the water buffalo, the African elephant, the Bengal Tiger, lions, bears of all species on all continents, the mountain lions of North America, and finally the great white shark and the bull sharks. All are known to attack mankind without provocation.